WOMEN *of* CHARACTER

Profiles of 100 Prominent
LDS *Women*

Cover images: *Still Life of Ranunculus Flowers in a Jar* © Rosanne Olson courtesy Getty Images.

Cover design © 2011 by Covenant Communications, Inc.

Published by Covenant Communications, Inc.
American Fork, Utah

Printed in the United States

First Printing: March 2011

21 20 19 18 17 16 15   10 9 8 7 6 5 4 3 2

ISBN: 978-1-68047-018-5

WOMEN *of* CHARACTER

Profiles of 100 Prominent LDS *Women*

SUSAN EASTON BLACK *and* MARY JANE WOODGER

INTRODUCTION

For generations latter-day prophets have extolled the noble role of womanhood. When speaking of a daughter, wife, or mother, they often express heartfelt admiration for the women who have influenced their lives. In addition to the prophets, other LDS leaders often tell of the wonderful contributions women in their lives have made both in and outside of the home. From rearing a faithful posterity to defending choice in the halls of Congress, Latter-day Saint women are recognized by the great men of this dispensation for being a positive influence for good and for shaping the destiny of future generations.

It is the noble women in The Church of Jesus Christ of Latter-day Saints whose impressive accomplishments and quiet acts of kindness we wish to applaud. In so doing, we recognize that there are thousands, if not millions, of Latter-day Saint women whose lives and characters witness that Jesus is the Christ. Choosing just a hundred women to feature has been difficult; after all, each woman makes a contribution and each is worthy of recognition. In an effort to limit our choice, however, we looked for women who accomplished something extraordinary and left an indelible mark on history that cannot be obscured. The women we have remembered create a type of legacy—a unique story. They stood out in a crowd. Whether that crowd was at beauty pageant or a political debate, they made a difference.

For example, Lucy Mack Smith, the mother of the Prophet Joseph Smith, and Mary Whitmer, the mother or mother-in-law of eight of the Eleven Witnesses of the Book of Mormon, left a mark on history that will be remembered throughout time and eternity. Emma Ray McKay's devotion to President David O. McKay will long be spoken of as the epitome of an ideal wife. Susa Young Gates, daughter of Brigham Young, lived her life in such a manner as to bring honor to her father. Other women magnified their Church callings; for instance, Eliza R.

Snow, Aurelia Rogers, and Ardeth Kapp made an incredible difference as auxiliary leaders in their respective generations.

Most of the featured women in this book, however, excelled in a particular talent. Minerva Teichert painted stories from the Book of Mormon. Looking through binoculars turned upside down, she created murals in her small front room. Ettie Lee, a school teacher, advocated that every boy deserves a good home and did something about it. She went to a library and checked out a book on how to become a millionaire by investing in real estate. By carefully investing half of her paycheck each month—$100—she was able to purchase ten homes and over decades help thousands of young boys find a secure place to live. Then there was Patty Sessions. Acting as a midwife, she delivered more than 3,000 babies in the pioneer West. The beauty of Colleen Hutchins captivated a nation while the courtroom persona of Christine Durham helped define the laws of the land. The philanthropic outreach of Karen Ashton brightens the lives of millions each year as they stroll through the beautiful gardens at Thanksgiving Point.

Each of these women and more have a story to tell. Their stories are about life, love, and an unusual determination to succeed. Within these pages you will find biographical vignettes that will make a difference in how you live your life. Learn why some LDS women made history in the professional world while others reached out to strengthen government, education, the arts, and families. Discover why many women chose to hone their talents through long hours of patient practice while others were simply thrust onto center stage. For many of these prominent LDS women, balancing family life and prominence came easily. For others, juggling family life and fame was not an easy balancing act. And in the midst of it all, most of them shared the message of the restored gospel at home and abroad.

For the authors, there has been much to learn in writing about the lives of these famous women. We resonate to their stories and empathize with their tears and defeats. To stand back and view another is to learn volumes about yourself. The messages of these women, both loud and soft, reveals that true happiness or greatness is never found in compromising self. It is found in reaching beyond self to a higher source. By reaching up, these women reached out to make a difference. Some learned the hard way that keeping the commandments of God brings inner peace and happiness; others found that neglecting God-given roles or talents for a time led to sorrow and disappointment. For others, the path through life was smooth. For each of their lives, we give thanks. By knowing something of their story, our lives are more complete.

Why a book featuring LDS women? Through the years, "his story" has dominated LDS literature. Our purpose is to tell the largely untold "her story." It is our hope that *Women of Character* will help readers realize that they, too, can develop talents, serve within their families, and leave a lasting legacy for future generations to emulate.

TABLE *of* CONTENTS

ACKNOWLEDGMENTS

We express appreciation to Richard E. Bennett and the Religious Studies Center at Brigham Young University for research support. We are particularly grateful to several student writers, editors, and research assistants: Wendy V. White, Melissa Rehon, Jessica Wainwright Christensen, Rachel Davison, Diana Dzubak, Michelle V. Brodrick, Diana Venagas, Charlotte Carol Searle, Miguel Venegas, Clinton Brimhall, Chanel Arts, Rebecca Allen, and Sarah Allen for sharing their scholastic talents. We are also grateful to library and archival personnel for their kindness and expertise. We are also indebted to Kathryn Jenkins of Covenant Communications, Inc., for her encouragement and confidence that a book about the lives of famous LDS women would inspire generations of readers.

MAUDE ADAMS

Kindness

Theater actress Annie Kiskadden often brought her baby, Maude, backstage for her performances. When she was starring in *The Lost Baby* at the Brigham Young Theatre, the plot called for an infant to be brought on stage atop a silver platter. When the two-month-old baby who played the part threw a tantrum, the manager grabbed seven-month-old Maude as a stand-in to play a sleeping baby. Maude sat up on the platter to the delight of a surprised audience. Baby Maude, upon hearing the laughter, cooed and blinked at the crowd—and with that a star was born. Maude subsequently became one of America's greatest actresses of the late nineteenth and early twentieth centuries.[1]

Daughter of James Henry Kiskadden and Asaneth Ann Adams, Maude was born November 11, 1872, the product of Mormon pioneers on her mother's side and, as Maude put it, "gentiles" on her father's side.[2] Although she spent little time in Salt Lake City, whenever she was complimented for a kindness she would say, "It was not kindness. It was Salt Lakeness."[3] Maude viewed herself as an ambassador for the Rockies. She wrote of the Swiss Alps, "They are inspiring but not friendly like the mountains that protect the lovely Valley of Salt Lake. . . . a lovely valley protected by friendly mountains is always 'home.' The people of the valley have gentle manners, as if their spirits moved with dignity. . . . The memory of them, the thought of them, and their lovely valley is an anchor in a changing, roving life."[4]

When Maude was four, she moved with her mother to San Francisco. There Maude—who became known by the stage name of Little Maudie Adams—was cast in child parts that had a "strong tendency toward realism," while her mother was cast in a variety of roles. By age six, Maude "was involved in every aspect of her career, including business arrangements" and refusing roles that "paid too little." When Maude was nine, she was sent to live with her grandmother in the Salt Lake Valley to begin her formal education. Longing for the stage, at age eleven Maude left school and joined her mother again in San Francisco. [5]

While performing on stage in San Francisco, Maude met Charles Frohman, an up-and-coming New York producer. At sixteen she joined the Charles Frohman Traveling Stock Company and performed on stage for two years with them. In early Frohman productions, Maude was ignored by critics but never by the public. "There's a charming little girl in Hoyt's new play," audiences would say. "I think her name is Adams or something like that."[6] On September 28, 1897, Maude made her debut as the leading actress in *The Little Minister* at the Empire Theatre in New York—and became an overnight star. For the next thirty years Maude was the highest-paid actress on the American stage, earning $40,000 her first year.[7]

Maude is best remembered for her starring role in *Peter Pan*, playing the role of Peter 223 times.[8] *Peter Pan* author James Barrie said to Maude, "I want you to know that it was you that inspired the writing of the play."[9] When Barrie sent the play to her, she was intrigued with the quaint character of Peter Pan. She "could feel the presence of the Fairies and the Indians and the Pirates and the lost boys of Never-Never-Never Land, and in their midst the dashing winsome 'Peter Pan.'" Maude performed the play *Peter Pan* before crowded houses

in all the major U.S. cities.[10] Her audience included such notables as President Theodore Roosevelt, who came backstage to compliment her, and Mark Twain, who said, "It is my belief that Peter Pan is a great and refining and uplifting benefaction to this sordid and money-mad age; and that the next best play on the boards is a long way behind it as long as you play Peter." But it was to the children and those who sat in the balcony that Maude showed her characteristic kindness. "She insisted upon having a good number of seats selling at 50 cents available" at every performance. When an unscrupulous house manager charged more, she "demanded that there be a refund of fifty cents to every person who had paid a dollar to get into the gallery that evening."[11]

When Maude retired from the stage, she was not finished thrilling audiences. She worked with General Electric to develop improved and more powerful stage lighting.[12] From 1937 to 1950 she led the Drama Department at Stephens College in Missouri. Remarkably, even her passing did not erase her ability to charm and thrill audiences. The 1975 character of Elise McKenna in Richard Matheson's novel *Bid Time Return* and the 1980 film adaptation *Somewhere in Time* were "inspired by a photo [of Maude] that Matheson saw hanging in the Virginia City Opera House."[13]

1   Ada Patterson, Maude Adams: A Biography (New York: Meyer Bros. & Co, 1907), 12–13; Rachelle Pace Castor, "Maude Adams: No Other Actress Can Take Her Place," in Worth Their Salt: Notable but Often Unnoted Women of Utah, ed. Colleen Whitley (Logan, Utah: Utah State University Press, 1996), 191.

2   Maude Adams was billed as the "Mormon Actress." To date, a baptismal record has not been found. Patterson, Maude Adams; Castor, "Maude Adams," 189–190; Phyllis Robbins, The Young Maude Adams (Francestown, New Hampshire: Marshall Jones, 1959), 30.

3   Patterson, 27.

4   "Actress found her career—on a tray," News Centennial Utah, Deseret News, January 30, 1996; Castor, 191.

5   Patterson, 19, 28–30; Castor, 190–194.

6   Patterson, 39; Castor, 195.

7   Patterson, 53, 76.

8   "Actress found her career—on a tray."

9   Patterson, 67.

10 Patterson, 66; Robbins, 89–109.

11 Robbins, 90, 92; Patterson, 71–72.

12 "Maude Adams as an Inventor: Famous Actress Perfects New Device for Showing Picture in Lighted Auditorium," The Bee Va, October 16, 1922.

13 Castor, 200–201.

LINDSEY ANDERSON

Determination

Courtesy of Weber State Athletics.

"I used to be really nervous but now I get excited to race," says 5'3" steeplechase Olympian Lindsey Anderson. "I get excited to go out there and see what I can do." Although she is usually the shortest in any race, she says, "I think I can go faster if I have some competition."[1]

Lindsey Olson, an identical twin and daughter of Scott and Sherillee Olson, was born May 23, 1985, in Payson, Utah. From the time she was young she loved to run; in junior high school her goal was to beat the boys in the gym classes. It was not long until *their* goal was to beat *her.* At Morgan High School in Morgan, Utah, she ran the 800 meter, the mile, and the 3200 meter.

Although she was an accomplished Utah state cross-country and track champion in level-3A schools, she remembers that "in high school I would get so nervous I would be too scared to race and then not do what I wanted to."[2] Nevertheless, by the time Lindsey graduated in the class of 2003 she had earned four letters in track, four in soccer, three in cross-country, and two in basketball. She was recognized as a five-time state champion in both track and cross-country.

With such an outstanding athletic record in high school, Lindsey was surprised that only two Utah colleges offered her athletic scholarships. Of the two, she chose Weber State University. As a freshman she was introduced to the steeplechase and liked it. "I loved it from the beginning and thought it was a lot of fun," she said. "It was so different than all the other races with the hurdles and the barrier/water jump . . . After I raced it that first time as a freshman, I knew I wanted to keep doing it. It is definitely something that you love or you don't."[3]

While working toward her degree in teaching mathematics at Weber, she coached the cross-country team at Morgan High School and did a lot of running herself—each week she ran between eighty and eighty-five miles. It was Coach Paul Pilkington at Weber who recognized Lindsey's amazing running talent and who entered her in competitive college races, where he soon found that Lindsey was leaving competitors far behind. Continual victories on the track led to her being honored with the Weber State Female Career Achievement Award in 2007 and being named the Weber State Female Athlete of the Year for the 2007–2008 season. She was also honored as a Big Sky Scholar Athlete during her senior year.

As a result of her outstanding performance, Lindsey holds school records at Weber in four track events. One is the collegiate 3000-meter steeplechase record of 9:39.95 set at the Cardinal Invitational Games, a time that qualified her for the 2008 U.S. Olympic trials in the steeplechase. She was surprised to qualify—she'd never before considered being an Olympian. "Before this year I didn't have these things going through my head," said Lindsey. "Now it is exciting to have these things to look forward to. . . . All of a sudden I have this whole new set of goals. It is fun to think about the future."[4]

How did she become a world-class athlete? Lindsey credits both her coach and her marriage to Mark Anderson—a fellow runner who is her biggest fan. Lindsey and Mark live in Morgan, where Mark works full-time as a manager while still working on a degree in business administration at Weber. He takes time away from his work and studies to come to all of Lindsey's races. "He gets so nervous, even more than I am," says Lindsey.[5] He was with Lindsey when she received All-American honors in the steeplechase at the 2007 NCAA Outdoor Championships, an event in which she set NCAA records.

Another reason for her success is her strong determination to win. Although she has been an NCAA All-American twice, she believes there are still records to beat. Nike believes that Lindsey can beat those records and put her under contract. In 2009 she qualified to run in the world championships at Berlin, Germany.

Lindsey is the first former Weber State University track and field athlete to compete in a summer Olympics. She hoped to beat all contenders at the Beijing Olympics in the steeplechase, a new Olympic event. Though she finished second in the Olympic trials of the first women's 3000-meter steeplechase with 9:36.81, beating her personal best score by nine seconds, she did not become a medal contender.

As to her future, Lindsey says, "I am excited to start teaching and coaching at a high school."[6] She is employed as an assistant coach of track and field at Weber State and works with the men's and women's middle- and long-distance runners. Can she help the runners beat their best times? Of course, but only if they have her determination. As for Lindsey, she still races competitively and continues to win.

1   Pat Goodwin, "Interview with Lindsey Anderson," on May 4, 2010, posted on May 10, 2007, http://www.fast-women.com/athletes/interviews/2007/lindseyanderson051107.html.
2   Ibid.
3   Ibid.
4   Ibid.
5   Ibid.
6   Goodwin, "Interview with Lindsey Anderson," *Fast-Women,* May 4, 2007.

KAREN ASHTON

Generosity

Photo by Doti and Ralph Photography.

Generosity is a hallmark that describes Karen Ashton. Through the generosity of Karen and her husband, Alan, Thanksgiving Point in Lehi, Utah, was created and funded; it includes a fifty-two-acre garden, the largest dinosaur museum in the world, a working farm, shops, restaurants, fifteen theme areas, nearly five miles of walking trails, a championship-caliber golf course, and a multi-screen movie theater. Her generosity and leadership are also responsible for the Timpanogos Storytelling Festival, which has grown into one of the largest storytelling festivals in the West.[1] And Little Wonders, a nonprofit family construction company organized under her direction, restores dilapidated homes for cost-only to new owners in Utah County.

Daughter of Carl E. Jackman and Edna Christiansen, Karen was born in the 1940s in Salt Lake City and was raised in Murray, Utah. She attended Brigham Young University, where in 1966 she met Alan C. Ashton on a blind date. At the time Alan was a mathematics graduate of the University of Utah who was pursuing a graduate degree in computer science. They were married in 1968 in the Salt Lake Temple.

While working on his PhD, Alan submitted two proposals for computer research projects to his thesis committee—one proposal pertained to music (he had played the trumpet in the 23rd Army Band in the Utah National Guard) and the other to word processing. He completed the music project and graduated with a PhD. Two years later he accepted employment in the computer science department at BYU, where he pursued his interest in a word-processing program. Together with a BYU graduate student, Alan created what at that time was the world's premiere word-processing software—WordPerfect. In 1987 Alan left BYU to devote more time to his position as president and CEO of the WordPerfect Corporation.

As Alan was changing the world of word processing, Karen was enjoying her role as homemaker and mother of eleven children. During these busy family years, she often found herself looking for places of respite for her children. A local library proved to be a resource of both education and entertainment, as did outdoor activities in beautiful parklike gardens. Believing other families wanted the same type of enjoyment, she and Alan purchased the historic Fox dairy farm in Lehi in 1995 with the idea that they would create an education center in a garden-like setting called Thanksgiving Point.

"During the early days [of the Thanksgiving Point project] new and better ideas surfaced every week," says Karen. "I wanted incredible gardens with lots of roses, pansies, geraniums and tulips."[2] Alan wanted vegetable gardens. There was much discussion and many changes to the master plan, but some subjects were not negotiable—the importance of children, education, and gardens. Through the efforts of Karen and Alan, today Thanksgiving Point has amenities at every turn. Nearly 1.5 million people visit Thanksgiving Point each year.

Another civic project Karen spearheaded is the Timpanogos Storytelling Festival. In 1989, while serving as a member of the Orem City Library Board, Karen looked for projects to raise funds for a much-needed children's library. In that process, she attended the National

Storytelling Festival in Tennessee, where she found thousands of adults crowded into tents listening to dynamic storytellers. At the festival she saw storytelling bring people of all ages together as they listened to narrative spiced with fiddles, harmonicas, banjos, and spoons.

Wanting stories to come alive in Orem, in 1989 Karen launched the Timpanogos Storytelling Festival as well as raised funds for the new children's wing of the library. From modest beginnings, this festival has become a national storytelling venue. The festival features the best storytellers in the nation as well as local amateurs. "If just one family leaves the Festival and begins to share stories with each other, it will be worth it," says Karen.[3] In 1999 the National Storytelling Network honored Karen with its leadership award, and today approximately 30,000 people attend one or more festival events each year.

Karen is not through making a difference in Utah County. She is now giving of her means to Little Wonders, a nonprofit family construction company that restores old, dilapidated homes for new owners. "The spiffed-up homes then not only bless the lives of those who are able to purchase their American dream, but bless the neighborhoods that no longer have an eyesore house in their area," Karen says. "It makes me happy. It makes the couples who buy them happy. It makes the neighbors happy. I think it even makes the house happy. It's just a happy thing."

As for Karen, Little Wonders has proven a creative outlet. She says, "I love the building process. It's very creative and it gives me a chance to decorate. . . . If I were to design a sign for Little Wonders, I would design a little house with a great big smile on it!"[4]

A "big smile" is descriptive of the lives of Karen and Alan Ashton. Throughout their lives they have actively looked for ways to lead and make others happy. From 2004 to 2007 Alan served as president of the Canada Toronto West Mission.[5] Karen's leadership talents have also been called upon by LDS Church leaders. She has been a member of the Primary General Board, a ward Relief Society president, a ward

Young Women president, and a member of the Young Women General Board.

Karen is a model Latter-day Saint woman on every front. As a wife and mother, she has been selfless in giving of her time and talents to her family. As a neighbor, she and her husband have given back to their community in meaningful ways that have blessed the lives of millions of people on a yearly basis. It is unusually rare to find someone as richly blessed as Karen who so selflessly shares her happiness with others.

1   "New Board Members," *LDS Church News,* August 15, 1992; Ben Fulton, "Timpanogas Storytelling Festival: Utah's Big Tale-all," *Salt Lake Tribune,* September 7, 2010.

2   "Thanksgiving Point Gardens: History," thanksgivingpoint.com/visit/gardens/about/history.html (accessed on September 11, 2010).

3   "Timpanogos Storytelling Festival: History," http://timpfest.org/background/history (accessed November 2, 2010).

4   Sharon Haddock, "Karen Ashton and Son Building American Dream," *Mormon Times,* January 1, 2010.

5   "New Mission Presidents Begin Service," *Ensign,* July 24, 2004, 74–75.

MAUD MAY BABCOCK

Determination

In 1892 when Susa Young Gates persuaded her twenty-four-year-old Harvard elocution and acting teacher, Maud May Babcock, to come to Utah, Maud never dreamed she would soon become a Mormon.[1] Having been raised an Episcopalian, she had been "piqued and even troubled by religious questions" but hadn't looked further for answers.[2] Upon investigation of Mormonism, however, she was surprised that the answers to her questions were found in Latter-day Saint theology.

Four months after becoming an instructor at the University of Utah, Maud joined the LDS Church. "Her family was so livid over her religious conversion that her mother said she would rather Maud May had had a child out of wedlock."[3] Her mother wrote, "I pray daily to God, [that] if you open your lips to defend that cause in publick [*sic*] your tongue may be paralyzed."[4] For the next four decades Maud's tongue was anything but paralyzed as she defended Mormonism and advanced education in Utah. Her forcefulness and "vigorous, at times militant, determination to make a name for herself and for the cause of physical culture and elocution in her new home" left a mark on education in Utah that affected generations to come.[5]

Daughter of William Wayne and Sara Jean Babcock, Maud May was born May 2, 1867, in East Worchester, New York. Her opportunities in life were not typical for a woman of her era. She graduated from the National School of Oratory in Philadelphia and the Lyceum School of Acting. She studied at Chicago University and for two additional years in London and Paris. After receiving a bachelor of arts degree from Wells College in New York, she taught at Harvard; the Engleside School for Girls in Berkshire, Massachusetts; Rutgers College; and public schools in New York before coming to Utah.[6]

University of Utah administrators had no idea of the force behind her petite 5'3" frame when they hired "Miss B." on a $500 annual salary.[7] Biographer David G. Pace wrote, "Though she was not considered beautiful, she was striking and had forcefulness, rectitude, even a defensiveness that would calcify during the next 47 years into one of the most eccentric characters on campus."[8] Miss B. spoke her mind without exception. Student Bob Wilson liked to tell of smoking on a street corner when "he was unexpectedly beaned on the head" by Miss B.'s umbrella. "Get that filthy weed out of your mouth!" she screamed.[9] Such disciplinary tactics are not tolerated today, but that was her way. It was said of Maud, "She was a taskmaster with high expectations."[10]

When Maud began teaching physical culture, her subject matter was not highly regarded by other faculty members. The "fledgling, slightly lurid 'fad' of physical culture" that Maud taught evolved from "introducing women to bloomer pants into a spectrum of contemporary industries from weight loss programs and beauty pageants to sports medicine and professional bodybuilding." Maud embraced the education of the whole individual: "Good health, good sense, and good manners—the civic being—were all fused together in Maud May's mind, and her students reaped—some said, suffered— from her zeal to that end."[11]

She started a private physical fitness school and was a founder of the Deseret Gymnasium and the University Dramatics Club, "the most

consistent and arguably the most prolific of its kind in the nation."[12] Her students performed what was to become the first play produced by a university in the United States. Former students remembered that at "rehearsals she was ruthless; her verbal criticism to her students was withering, punctuated as it was by a pointed finger. And yet dozens of her students credited Maud May with their accomplishments." One such student was Utah Governor Herbert Maw, who credited Miss B. with helping him develop confidence to speak in public settings. Miss B. cast him—then a shy freshman—in the role of King Theseus in *A Midsummer Night's Dream.* By the end of what he described as eight weeks "of torture [rehearsals]," where she demanded that he walk through the lines acting and speaking like a king, Maw's confidence grew.[13]

During her career, Maud directed more than eight hundred plays and taught speech and drama to thousands of students. She founded the Theatre and Communication departments as well as the College of Health, Physical Education, and Recreation at the University of Utah. Retiring at age seventy-one, Maud looked back on her career and felt pleased that she had influenced four decades of college students.

When Maud died in 1954, she was referred to as the "grande dame" of Utah theater.[14] Joseph Fielding Smith said of her, "[She was] dedicated to the proposition that the only true and unfailing practicality is unswerving rectitude."[15] Though she was a "woman [that] could frighten you to pieces; she was also a woman of great dignity [who] could also be the sweetest," said Professor Wanda Clayton Thomas.[16] Carl G. Markworth said, "In her forceful way, she offered the people of Utah an opportunity for personal growth through speech, arts, and physical culture. . . . the people of Utah rallied round this new future through the forceful insistence of Maud May Babcock."[17]

1   R. Scott Lloyd, "Remembering, recording: 4 women profiled in history lecture," *LDS Church News,* August 21, 2010, 11. See also Janet Peterson, "Leading Ladies: Four Grande Dames of Early Utah Theatre," *Pioneer* (Winter 2003), 18.

2   David G. Pace, "Maud May Babcock: Speak Clearly and Carry a Big Umbrella," in Worth Their Salt: Notable but Often Unnoted Women of Utah, ed. Colleen Whitley (Logan, Utah: Utah State University Press, 1996), 150.

3   Peterson, 18.

4   Pace, 150.

5   Ibid., 149–150.

6   Pace, 149.

7   Howard R. Lamar, "The Theater in Mormon Life and Culture," *The Arlington Lecture Series* (Utah State University, Logan, Utah: Logan State University Press, 1 December 1998), 15–18; Pace, 149.

8   Pace, 150–151.

9   Ibid., 157.

10   Lloyd, 11.

11   Pace, 153.

12   Ibid., 152.

13   Lamar, 15–18.

14   Peterson, 18.

15   Joseph F. Smith, "Maud May Babcock," *Quarterly Journal of Speech* 41 (April 1955), 211.

16   Lamar, 15–18.

17   Carl G. Markworth Jr., "Prominent Teachers of the Speech Arts in Utah before 1920, Their Significant Theories and the Effect of the Teachings upon Their Contemporaries," Master's Thesis, Brigham Young University, 1958, 67–98.

JENNY OAKS BAKER

Testimony

Photo by Russ Dixon. Courtesy of Shadow Mountain Records.

Jenny Oaks Baker does not live what one would call an ordinary life. She has been a featured violin soloist at Carnegie Hall, Strathmore Hall, the Library of Congress, and Lincoln Center. She has also soloed with the National Symphony Orchestra at the Kennedy Center and has been a guest soloist with the Jerusalem Symphony, the Concerto Soloists Chamber Orchestra of Philadelphia, the San Diego Symphony, the Utah Symphony, the Orchestra at Temple Square, and the Mormon Tabernacle Choir. She has performed for audiences in Europe, Asia, and throughout the United States as well as on many radio and television broadcasts. As a popular Classical Crossover artist, in 2010 she even opened for Carrie Underwood in front of an audience of 48,000 at the "Stadium of Fire" in Provo, Utah. But this accomplished wife and mother of four young children has been able to reach the world through her music while fulfilling the everyday demands of womanhood—because, she says, "I do all I can and Heavenly Father makes up the difference."[1]

Jenny June, the youngest daughter of Elder Dallin H. Oaks and June Oaks, was born in 1975 in Provo while her father was president of

Brigham Young University. Her mother, a musician in her own right, recognized in Jenny a fascination with music and enrolled her in Suzuki violin lessons at age four. By age eight, Jenny had become so proficient with the violin that she was invited to be a guest soloist with the Utah Valley Symphony. Although there was school, play, and family time, the violin filled her life.

Jenny excelled at East High School in Salt Lake City, graduating in 1993. But even though she yearned to attend BYU like the rest of her friends and family, Jenny decided to pursue her passion and enrolled in the prestigious Curtis Institute of Music in Philadelphia. There she earned a bachelor's degree before entering The Juilliard School in New York City to complete her master's degree.

During Christmas vacation from school, while Jenny was performing in the pit orchestra for Ballet West's *Nutcracker,* she began talking to percussionist Kenny Hodges. He mentioned that he was a music producer for Deseret Book, whereupon Jenny flippantly proclaimed, "Well, **I** want to make a CD!" Kenny invited her to make a demo, but Jenny asked him instead to just watch her performance the next morning as a soloist with the Mormon Tabernacle Choir on their broadcast of *Music and the Spoken Word.* Kenny watched, and Deseret Book immediately made Jenny a Shadow Mountain Records Label artist. Her first album, *On Wings of Song,* was released in 1998 and established her as a powerful force in the faith-based music industry.

In August 1997 she met Matthew Baker at a singles ward in New York—a meeting she considers near miraculous. Matt had come to the Big Apple to interview for a job. About the same time, Jenny learned that her mother had been diagnosed with pancreatic cancer. One of her mother's hopes was that Jenny would be taken care of when she was gone. "Matt and I met on the day our family was having a special fast for my mom," she said. "It's touching to think that although our prayers weren't answered, hers were."[2] Jenny and Matt were married in the Salt Lake Temple in March 1998.

Matt is a great support for Jenny, encouraging her musical talents at every turn. Their move to the northern Virginia suburbs of Washington, DC, proved a great help in advancing both Jenny's talents and Matt's business career. For seven years, Jenny performed as a first violinist in the prestigious National Symphony Orchestra in Washington, affording her tremendous opportunities to perform alongside world-class conductors and musicians.

Although Jenny enjoyed performing in the National Symphony Orchestra, in 2007—at age thirty-two—she felt prompted to retire from the symphony to be a full-time mother to her four young children. This has also afforded her the opportunity to help her children develop their musical talents. Laura June plays the violin; Hannah Jean, the piano; Sarah Noelle, the cello; and Matthew Dallin, the violin.[3] The children practice their instruments daily—even on family vacations. Jenny packs instruments and sheet music just like other mothers pack books and toys. If necessary, Jenny even arranges to use a piano at Church meetinghouses so that her children can practice. Five hours a day of practicing is the norm in her household, and the hours of practice are paying off. Jenny now enjoys performing with her children at various firesides and concerts, including performing annually at the Washington DC Temple Visitors Center's "Festival of Lights."

Still in her thirties, Jenny keeps active as a concert violinist and her passionate delivery is acclaimed. "I love performing! It is such a thrill to connect with each audience and share the talents that Heavenly Father has given me. I also love recording! It gives me a way to perform for people all over the world, while I am at home taking care of my children," she says. Her nine albums have sold more than 150,000 copies and feature the arrangements of such composers as Kurt Bestor and Sam Cardon. As to the composers she works with, Jenny says, "I have been blessed to work with the best of the best."[4]

In her recordings, Jenny delights listeners with stunning arrangements of classical music, hymns, and popular favorites. Her passionate playing and soul-stirring renditions have gained her a broad and loyal fan base. Some of her most popular albums are *Silver Screen Serenade, O Holy Night, The Best of Jenny Oaks Baker,* and *Then Sings My Soul,* which hit No. 1 on the National Billboard Classical Charts. Her fans eagerly await the release of her upcoming Disney album, which is also expected to be a chart-topper.

She has been named Artist of the Year by the Faith-Centered Music Association and in 2008 was awarded the Governor's Mansion Artist Award for excellence in artistic impression by Utah Governor Jon M. Huntsman, Jr. Although Jenny can play anything from hoedown to Tchaikovsky, she prefers to play sacred music that touches hearts and brings people closer to the Lord.

What of her future? The world can expect more music from Jenny Oaks Baker. She will continue to record albums and tour the country as a popular performer and speaker, but her first priority is her family. Music and motherhood . . .

1   Laurie Williams Sowby, "Jenny Oaks Baker: Mormon, Mom, Musician," *Mormon Times,* August 14, 2009; Laurie Williams Sowby, "Musician Mom Making More Time for Her Family," *Deseret News,* August 27, 2007.
2   Sowby, "Musician Mom Making More Time for Her Family."
3   Sowby, "Jenny Oaks Baker: Mormon, Mom, Musician."
4   Sowby, "Musician Mom Making More Time for Her Family."

ALGIE EGGERTSEN BALLIF

Learning

In 1914, Algie Eggertsen wrote in her journal, "I had a right good cry this morning. So did Mama." It wasn't a quarrel between the two. Instead, "I decided to drop American Literature," she wrote, explaining, "It is too hard on Mama to have to do all the work."[1] At eighteen, Algie fully understood the importance of learning and reacted with sincere, tearful regret when an opportunity for education was lost.

Daughter of Lars Echart Eggertsen and Ane (Annie) Grethe Nielson, Algie was born May 3, 1896, in Provo, Utah. Although Algie was reared in an era when educational opportunities for women were not equal to those of men, her mother was determined to see that her daughters had the same opportunities as her sons. Algie's sister remarked that while growing up, "We were certainly all education-oriented. . . . As I look back on it now, I think how wonderful it was that there was never a question but that the girls would get the same education as the boys."[2]

Art and culture were emphasized in the Eggertsen household. There Algie developed a love for intellectual quests from her parents. They taught her two guiding principles: "Consider all sides and think seriously about any issue raised." Sundays were particularly an intellectual delight for the Eggertsen family as they hosted dinner guests that included artists, lecturers, school administrators, and local politicians who "provided a lively and informative discussion around the dining room table."[3]

Algie was taught to have an open mind at an early age and quickly learned that some cultural experiences were superior to others. For example, in 1915 a friend took her to a vaudeville show. After the show she lamented in her diary, "I can't imagine what will become of our civilization. . . . People enjoy amusement where they don't have to think." Mindless entertainment was outside of Algie's realm. She expressed gratitude for "parents who have inspired me in nobler lines."[4]

When Algie enrolled in Brigham Young High School, she was interested in drama and literature. Before she graduated Algie had an intense interest in dance. "At this time, I was beginning to be aware through the reading I did and pictures in magazines that there were in the United States great people who were expressing themselves in the dance," she said. "I read all I could about these interesting activities."[5]

At nineteen Algie's dedication to her educational pursuits was confirmed in a journal description of her schedule during the last weeks of 1915. She got up at 5 A.M. to study before attending a biology class followed by a biology lab. She supervised classes at the high school, made rolls for Thanksgiving, ran cross-country, did the family laundry while she read *The Tempest* and two or three love stories, started teaching private elocution lessons, attended a lecture, organized a literary society, taught a gym class, rehearsed for a play performance, and conducted a board of control meeting. As one biographer pointed out, "Going to dances and plays two or three times a week and staying up until 2 A.M. was not at all unusual." Although Algie's dedication to cultural interests and book learning made for a demanding schedule, her genuine interest in scholarship was later rewarded when she was

offered a position at Brigham Young University to teach "speech, English, physical education, and Book of Mormon."[6]

After teaching at BYU from 1919 to 1920, Algie decided to further her education. She spent twelve weeks of her summer break in Berkeley, California, taking graduate studies with an emphasis in dance.[7] When she returned to BYU, she shared what she had learned about modern dance with her students at Berkeley.

Following her marriage to George Ballif in December 1920 and two more years of teaching physical education classes, Algie became a mother. As one biographer noted, "[Algie] didn't let things like child care, housework, and home management slow down her other interests." In 1932 she became the membership chair of the American Legion Auxiliary. As such, she presented a paper at a national convention. Although some criticized Algie for leaving her four children—one of them only six weeks old—with a nurse for a few days, Algie insisted, "I couldn't have given up some of these experiences without losing some of my education."[8] Algie firmly believed that lifelong learning required sacrifice.

In 1935 Algie was elected to the Provo School Board—very unusual for her era. Algie served from 1935 to 1958. In reflecting on her experience on the board, she said, "[It] gave me insight, far more than I had ever had into the problems of public education and I hope that I did some good."[9]

From 1959 to 1960 she served in the Utah House of Representatives with a focus on educational issues. At the request of Eleanor Roosevelt, she served on the National Education Subcommittee based in Washington, DC, and later as chair of the Education Committee. Service on the national committee required Algie to travel to the nation's capital at least once a month to contribute to discussions on women's education in America. Algie's daughters claimed that their mother always felt inferior at the national meetings, never realizing how smart and talented she really was. "Sometimes I probably was over-awed with [other participants'] brilliance and their knowledge," she admitted, "but I did the best I could and I think what I did was appreciated."[10]

Algie's pursuit of a broad traditional and cultural education from formal and informal sources was a blessing to her family, students, and community. At Algie's death in July 1984, three members of the Quorum of the Twelve Apostles spoke at her funeral.[11] Eloise Bell, writing for *Network Magazine,* reported, "Algie . . . [was] part of a tradition of noblesse oblige. Like the Roosevelts and the Kennedys, the Eggertsens, and in turn the Ballifs, were brought up to believe that if you had advantages in life—brains, talents, education, means—you therefore owed something to the world, especially to the less fortunate members of the human race. It's a tradition that deserves to be passed on."[12]

1   Georganne B. Arrington and Marion McCardell, "Algie Eggertsen Ballif (1896-1984): No Subject Was Taboo," in *Worth Their Salt, Too,* ed. Colleen Whitley (Logan, Utah: Utah State University Press, 2000), 89.
2   Arrington and McCardell, 85–86.
3   Ibid., 84–85, 87.
4   Ibid., 84–85, 87.
5   Ibid., 90.
6   Ibid., 92, 98.
7   Ibid., 99.
8   Ibid., 104–105.
9   Ibid., 105–106.
10   Ibid., 108–109.
11   Ibid., 113.
12   Elouise Bell, "In Memoriam: Algie Ballif," *Network Magazine,* August 1984, as cited in Whitley, 102.

FLORA AMUSSEN BENSON

Devotion to Family

Photo by Busath Photography.

As the wife of a prominent political figure and Church leader and the mother of two sons and four daughters, Flora Amussen Benson had many demands on her time. Reflecting on her life shortly after her husband, Ezra Taft Benson, was ordained the thirteenth president of The Church of Jesus Christ of Latter-day Saints, she said, "If I'd have gone to work I would have missed so much."[1] Flora's strong convictions about the importance of her role as wife and mother helped her prioritize her time. By focusing time and talents on family, she blessed her life and the lives of her husband and children.

As a young adult Flora attended Utah Agricultural College (now Utah State University), where she participated in many campus activities. It was there that she met Ezra Taft Benson. Among the many qualities that attracted Ezra to her was a "reverent kindness to and deep love for her mother"—affectionate qualities she would later show in her own role as wife and mother.[2] After the two had both served LDS missions, they were married September 10, 1926, in the Salt Lake Temple.

Following more schooling for Ezra in Iowa, the young couple settled in southern Idaho and later northern California. Not long after their move to California, Ezra's scholastic talents and abilities in the field of agriculture propelled him to the national stage. Flora "cheerfully moved her family to the nation's capital, focusing her time and energies on her family while shunning much of the Washington social scene."[3] That same cheer was expressed when Ezra was called to be an Apostle and was appointed Secretary of Agriculture in the cabinet of President Dwight D. Eisenhower.

Flora's daughter Bonnie Madsen recalled that Flora neglected the whirlwind of social events in Washington to be with her: "Mother turned down a White House invitation so she could attend my high school choir program. . . . Do you know what kind of security and confidence it gives a child to know she is that important to her parents? That she is loved that much?"[4] Flora's journal entries also reveal support of her children: "Today I missed three parties I was invited to. The children's health and keeping the home in order are far more important than parties."[5]

She was just as caring about and attentive to the needs of her husband. When Ezra was in Europe on an assignment from President Eisenhower, Flora mailed him various food items, including tuna fish, pears, nuts, fruitcake, figs, and chocolate bars. In a letter, she asked, "Do you need sugar or anything in particular? Please let me know, and I'll send what you need. I am never too busy to do it."[6] President Benson remarked, "Flora was always there for the children and for me. . . . I can't remember a time when I came home and didn't find her there. She would meet me at the door with a smile and an embrace. It was that love and support that sustained me during my years in Washington."[7]

During these same years, she also found time to entertain President Eisenhower and other prominent dignitaries in her home. The most remembered event was a luncheon for Mrs. Mamie Eisenhower and the wives of cabinet members. Her daughter recalls that she spent several weeks preparing the home, planning the menu, and arranging

for entertainment. She "did not worry that her guests would miss the coffee, cigarettes, and card playing which normally was part of such affairs. The cocktails made from ginger ale and home-bottled apricot juice were a great success, as was the entertainment provided by the Benson children and the thirty-five madrigal singers from Brigham Young University who were touring the east coast." To Flora, the "most exciting part [of the luncheon] was the beautiful letters we received afterward from the women, telling us what a thrill it was to experience a touch of 'Mormonism' and family cooperation and what wonderful youth the BYU singers were."[8]

The legacy of Flora Amussen Benson lies in her commitment to family. Her dedication to family was appreciated not only by her mother and her children, but by her husband: Ezra Taft Benson referred to his wife as "a most devoted mother" and "the perfect lady."[9]

1   Sheri Dew, *Ezra Taft Benson: A Biography* (Salt Lake City: Deseret Book, 1987), 130.
2   Derin Head Rodriquez, "Flora Amussen Benson: Handmaiden of the Lord, Helpmeet of a Prophet, Mother in Zion," *Ensign,* March 1987, 14.
3   Rodriquez, 14.
4   Ibid.
5   Ezra Taft Benson and Flora Amussen Benson, *A Labor of Love: The 1946 European Mission of Ezra Taft Benson* (Salt Lake City: Deseret Book, 1989), 21.
6   Ibid.
7   Rodriquez, 14
8   Ibid.
9   Ibid.

JANE JOHNSTON BLACK

Service

"I was informed that on the first night of the encampment nine children were born into the world," wrote Eliza R. Snow of an Iowa encampment. "Mothers gave birth to offspring under almost every variety of circumstances imaginable, except those to which they had been accustomed; some in tents, others in wagons—in rainstorms and in snowstorms."[1] Jane Johnston Black assisted these young mothers with their babies. According to family records, Jane was called by the Prophet Joseph Smith to give medical aid and comfort to those in need. Whether comfort was needed in Nauvoo or that night on the banks of the Mississippi River, Jane stepped forward and offered her services. For her capable and unselfish medical service, generations of Latter-day Saints honor her name.

Jane was born June 11, 1801, in Antrum, Ireland; both she and her father were members of the Wesleyan Methodist movement. When her father died, sixteen-year-old Jane took his place as a preacher and spent the next four years visiting congregations and households in Ireland, spreading the good news of Jesus Christ.

At age twenty-one, Jane gave up the ministry to marry William Black, Jr., on July 31, 1822. The Blacks made their home in Lisburn, Ireland, where Jane became the mother of one daughter and three sons. In 1835 she and her family moved to Manchester, England, where they listened to LDS missionaries William Clayton and Joseph Fielding. Of their preaching, Jane penned, "Tidings of Great Joy."[2] In January 1839, she and her husband were baptized by William Clayton. Soon after, William Black was called to be a missionary in the British Isles. Jane and the children felt called to gather with the Saints in Nauvoo, Illinois.

In 1840 Jane and her children boarded a ship in Liverpool in hopes of reaching America within a few weeks. Soon after the ship left harbor, however, it encountered a terrible storm. As her son Joseph recalled, "One ship sank nearby us, and all were lost. Our ship narrowly escaped destruction. In the middle of the fearful storm Mother got the boys into berth, and after prayer William spoke in tongues, which was interpreted by Mother. We were exhorted to be of good cheer, for we would not be destroyed."[3] By the next day, Jane and her children were again safe in Liverpool. They waited out the storm before boarding the ship again. This time, there were no mishaps at sea.[4]

Jane and her family were welcomed into Mormon society in Nauvoo and in Augusta, Iowa. According to her son Joseph, "Through industry and economy Mother sustained the family until Father arrived" in 1843.[5] Of being reunited with his family, William Black wrote, "[I] found them safe and well, praise the Lord."[6] One reason for their good health was Jane's knowledge and practice of medicine.

Both Joseph Smith and John Taylor recognized Jane's medical abilities. When Elder Taylor was wounded at Carthage Jail on that fateful June 27, 1844, Jane was called to attend him. When she asked Elder Taylor why he had sent for her instead of another, he responded with, "Because I knew there was none better at such a job, and wanted you to stand at the morning of the resurrection and testify to the Lord against the assassins who murdered the Prophet and his brother Hyrum."[7]

When the Saints left Nauvoo to escape persecution, Jane and her children remained in town, hoping that William, who had gone to Canada to draw a military pension, would soon return so that they could join the Mormon exodus. By September 1846, the battle of Nauvoo was fought on William's property. During the battle, Jane was in the middle of the fray, insisting on ministering to the injured men. When a mob surrounded her wagon and demanded that she give up her firearms, Jane said, "Here is my pistol, but I will use it before I give it up." They did not take the pistol, but threatened to throw Jane into the Mississippi River that night.[8]

When it became too difficult to wait any longer for William to return, Jane crossed the Mississippi with her children and lived in a temporary encampment. "There were a great many sick among us and nothing to comfort and nourish them but corn meal, until the Lord sent quails among us," wrote Jane, "which supplied our wants." She concluded her words with, "Blessed be the name of the Lord."[9]

William returned soon after, and they journeyed together to Winter Quarters. "I, being a doctor and also a nurse, President [Brigham] Young set me apart to deliver all expecting mothers and care for the sick," recalled Jane of her stay in Winter Quarters.[10] On the trek west in 1850 and in early settlements in Utah, she faithfully fulfilled that calling. She delivered more than three thousand babies, and on one occasion successfully amputated a man's leg using a butcher knife and a carpenter's saw.

Jane and her family accepted a prophetic call to settle in San Pete Valley, about 140 miles south of Salt Lake City. From there, they were called to relocate in Spring City. They remained in that settlement until 1861, when they were called to St. George. They later moved up the Virgin River to Rockville in answer to yet another call. "I lived there until my husband died," Jane said.

Jane remained in Rockville for many years after all her children had moved away, giving medical assistance to those in need. Yet she wrote,

"I felt very lonely."[11] It was not until 1878, when feeling lonely for her children who lived in Deseret, that she was "persuaded to leave her home to live with them."[12]

In her eighty-seventh year, Jane wrote a brief history of her life. "My memory has failed me in many things, so that I have not been able to give a complete account," she confessed.[13] She could not remember the names or places of her service. Yet she knew that she had fulfilled the medical calling given her years before by prophets of God and was grateful for the lives that she had been able to touch. Jane died at age eighty-nine and was buried next to William Black in the Rockville cemetery.[14]

1   Eliza R. Snow as quoted in Edward W. Tullidge, *The Women of Mormondom* (New York: Tullidge and Crandall, 1877), 307–308.

2   "Jane Johnston Black," in *Our Pioneer Heritage,* comp. Kate B. Carter (Salt Lake City: Daughters of Utah Pioneers, 1963), 6:427.

3   See "Diary of Joseph Smith Black (1836–1910): Principal Residence Deseret," n. p., 1948, L. Tom Perry Special Collections, Harold B. Lee Library, Brigham Young University, Provo, Utah.

4   "Diary of Joseph Smith Black (1836–1910), Principal Residence Deseret."

5   "Diary of Joseph Smith Black," in *Our Pioneer Heritage,* 10:261.

6   Ibid., 10:259.

7   "Jane Johnston Black," 6:428.

8   Ibid., 6:427.

9   Ibid., 6:427–428.

10   Ibid., 6:428.

11   Ibid.

12   "The Diary of Joseph Smith Black," 6:428.

13   Ibid., 10:261.

14   Ibid.

EDWINA BOOTH

Family

Edwina Booth—the stage name of Josephine Constance Woodruff—was a leading actress of the early "talkie" period. In 1931 she was dubbed the "White Goddess of Classic Film" for her starring role in *Trader Horn*.[1] Yet for all her beauty and talent, her greatest strength was a supportive family. Her family—father, mother, brother, sister, nieces, and nephews—stood by her long after the glitter of Hollywood stardom faded.

As a child, Edwina never finished a full year of school due to poor health. When her physician father, Dr. James Lloyd Woodruff, contracted influenza, the family moved to Venice, California, hoping that both father and daughter could recuperate in the southern California climate. At the time, wrote a *Salt Lake Tribune* columnist, "She was really beautiful in a fragile sort of way."[2]

One day when Edwina was sunbathing in a red swimming suit at Santa Monica Beach, she caught the attention of film director E. J. Babille. He asked if she would like to be in movies and handed her a business card. A few days later, Edwina presented the card at the Metropolitan Studio and took her first screen test. (By coincidence,

it was the very same day that movie great Clark Gable took his test.) Critics agreed that Edwina had freshness, talent, and beauty. She was photogenic, exciting, and had a stage presence.

In 1926 Edwina got her first bit part in a silent movie; other roles followed. By 1930 Hollywood had opened its doors to Edwina, but not all was to her liking. She did not "subscribe to [Hollywood's] easy standards and soft morals." When a movie producer asked her to spend the weekend with him at a mountain cabin, she replied, "I would love to come. I'll bring my mother and you bring your wife." When another producer asked her to sign a seven-year contract with the stipulation that her body went with the contract, she refused.[3] She became known as "that Mormon girl" who would not bend standards to get ahead in Hollywood. Yet she succeeded.

Edwina is most remembered for her leading role in *Trader Horn*. A melodrama about a "white Goddess" in an African tribe, the film called for what the director described as "a milk-white blonde with a brunette's temper, or better yet a redhead's" to be cast as Nina Treet, the white goddess. More than two hundred young starlets tried out for the part. The role was given to Edwina when the director said that she had "a temper like a spanked cat."[4]

Although the part was hers, she was reluctant to accept it. Africa scared her. Her fears heightened when Trader Horn, the man on whom the film was based, predicted, "Some of [the cast] will never come back alive." But based on the assumption that she "would likely be one of the most highly publicized women of the year, and the role would likely lead to stardom," Edwina accepted. After all, "It would be a chance in a million."[5]

Before departing for Africa, she was inoculated against typhoid fever and other rare diseases. She left the United States with a fever of 104 degrees. When the first scenes were filmed, Edwina wore clothing made of monkey fur and lion's teeth. Between elephant grass that cut her bare feet and legs, African insects, and unbearable heat, fragile Edwina was in trouble. She contracted malaria and dysentery before suffering from sunstroke and falling out of a tree. In the Belgian Congo, she was bitten by a tse tse fly, a transmitter of African sleeping sickness.[6]

In spite of these problems, she finished filming, returned to the states, and attended the premier of *Trader Horn* at Grauman's Chinese Theater. The movie was a box office success, garnering an Academy Award nomination for best picture. She acted in three more films for independent producers before she collapsed in 1932. "I had driven myself as far as I could go," she said. "I had to lie down and rest."[7] She put a veil over her face and confined herself to bed.

Edwina sued MGM for a million dollars, claiming the studio failed to safeguard her health in Africa. To remedy her health problems, she demanded treatment at the School of Hygiene and Tropical Medicine in London.[8] The case of Edwina Booth vs. MGM was settled out of court for an undisclosed amount with the stipulation that Edwina be taken to Europe for treatment.

In April 1935, Edwina and her father went to Europe seeking a solution to health problems. They consulted doctors in England, Switzerland, Germany, and Austria. One of the doctors said, "I believe it is safe to say her picture career is ruined, even if her health is not."[9]

Edwina returned to the states and confined herself to a dark room, and her family devoted their lives to caring for her. During these years, a persistent Hollywood myth suggested that she had finally died of jungle fever.[10]

Edwina had short bouts of health, but never vigor. During these brief periods, she studied the Book of Mormon and accepted calls as a stake missionary and as an ordinance worker in the Los Angeles Temple. She married twice and died of old age on May 18, 1991, in Long Beach, California, at the age of eighty-six. At the time of her death, she was still receiving fan mail.[11]

Edwina's determination to go to Africa "was a decision against her better judgment that she was to regret for the rest of her life."[12] It

resulted in bed rest and dependency, but provided the opportunity for more than sixty years of unselfish service by her family.

1   Myrna Oliver, "Edwina Booth: White Goddess of Classic Film 'Trader Horn,'" *Los Angeles Times,* May 22, 1991, 20.

2   Hal Schindler, as quoted in D. Robert Carter, "Edwina Booth's Fast and Fateful Rise to Stardom," Provo *Daily Herald,* January 7, 2006.

3   Carter.

4   "Trader Horn's Goddess," *Time,* May 18, 1934.

5   Carter.

6   Ibid.

7   D. Robert Carter, "The Sun Sets on a Fallen Star," Provo *Daily Herald,* March 30, 2008.

8   "Trader Horn's Goddess."

9   Carter, "The Sun Sets on a Fallen Star."

10   See James Robert Parish, *The Hollywood Book of Death: The Bizarre, Often Sordid, Passings of More than 125 American Movie and TV Idols* (New York: Contemporary, 2002), 96–97.

11   Oliver, 20.

12   Carter.

TORAH BRIGHT

Perseverance

Courtesy of the Church History Library, The Church
of Jesus Christ of Latter-day Saints.

Few people are lucky enough to know what their future career will be before they even hit the teen years, but at age eleven, Australian Torah Bright tried snowboarding for the first time and announced that she would be a snowboarder. Three years later she was a professional snowboarder, and by age twenty-three, she was one of the top female snowboarders in the world.[1] Torah's sheer determination to be the best has brought her success in her chosen profession and her personal life.

Born December 27, 1986, Torah competed in the winter Olympics in Italy and Vancouver, in the World Snowboarding Championships, and in the X Games—widely recognized as one of the most important winter sports competitions. She has also won dozens of top awards for her performances.

Her success is due in large part to thousands of hours of practice combined with a great deal of self-discipline. Torah often trains as many as eight hours a day—a very physically exhausting schedule. While preparing for the winter Olympics in 2006, she was asked by an interviewer if she felt pressure to perform well. Torah replied, "The

only pressure I feel is the pressure on myself to see the sport progress and female snowboarders progress."[2]

Though Torah strives to be her best in competing situations, she is less concerned about winning than people might think. "I'm not naturally competitive," she told a British interviewer. Though her focus may not be to beat everyone else, Torah holds herself to a high performance standard to ensure that she will always try her hardest. "When I came in fifth in the [2006] Winter Olympics it was disappointing because I expected to win," she said, "but I was riding with a dislocated shoulder and thought I'd snowboarded pretty well. . . . It's a contest. It doesn't define who you are."[3]

Before her participation in the 2006 Winter Olympics, reporters asked her what defines her. "Religion is my life," she said.[4] One sports writer noted, "In a sport renowned for anti-social behavior, drug-taking, grungy clothing, and unkempt appearances, Bright is a breath of fresh mountain air."[5] It has not been easy for Torah to attend LDS services each Sunday with her demanding schedule, but she tries to compensate: "I always have my scriptures handy and I read a lot."[6]

Torah has won the respect of her peers for maintaining high standards in both her personal and professional life. Because of hard work and self-discipline, she is capable of performing extremely difficult snowboard moves. In 2006 Shaun White, the Olympic gold medalist in the men's halfpipe, said, "Torah Bright [does] tricks I can't do."[7] Torah is constantly pushing herself and her competitors to improve, and she doesn't shy away from difficult or even blind moves. Torah says, "We have not seen the best of this sport yet."[8] She explains, "I have always been taught to expect great things. I go through life waiting for beautiful things to happen. . . . I know I have been given a special talent."[9]

Torah demonstrated that talent again in the 2010 Winter Olympics at Vancouver when she came out nearly three full points ahead of her closest competitor in the women's halfpipe snowboard competition. She won a gold medal for Australia.[10]

Torah's name, meaning "bearer of great message," comes from the Old Testament. Her message that hard work and self-discipline equals success in personal and professional life is not lost on the rising generation.

1   Tom Lowrey, "Crunch Time for Bright: 'I just eat, sleep – and ride,'" *The Sydney Morning Herald*, January 15, 2010.
2   "Questions for Torah Bright," *The Sydney Morning Herald*, May 22, 2005.
3   Piers Hernu, "'I've never drunk or smoked,' says Champion Snowboarder Torah Bright," *United Kingdom Mail Online*, April 11, 2009, http://dailymail.co.uk/home/moslive/article-1168440/ive-drunk-smoked-says-champion-snowborder-Torah-Bright.html.
4   Australian Associated Press, "Religion Gives Olympian Bright a Boost," *The Age*, February 3, 2006.
5   Arthur Stanley, "Why Torah Bright is Destined for Olympic Gold," *The* [Sydney] *Daily Telegraph*, September 4, 2009.
6   Australian Associated Press.
7   Matt Higgins, "Few Fresh Challengers for Top Women in the Halfpipe," *The New York Times*, March 22, 2009.
8   Lynn Zinser, "A Look at the Medal Contenders: Snowboarder Torah Bright," *The New York Times*, November 25, 2009.
9   Stanley.
10 Lowrey.

JUANITA BROOKS
Disputatious Temperament

One of the foremost western historians of her day, Juanita Brooks was born in southern Utah, smack in the middle of the "richest supplies of pioneer diaries ever produced on the American frontier"—and she found and preserved the diaries that defined early LDS settlements in the West.[1] Using a typewriter on her kitchen table, she wrote dozens of award-winning articles and a number of books about the problems of establishing a society in the West. But because so few women wanted to write, "before answering a knock at the door, [Juanita] covered her typewriter with a cloth," hiding the fact that she was a writer.[2]

Daughter of Henry and Mary Ann Hafen Leavitt, Juanita was born January 15, 1898, in Bunkerville, Nevada. She attended one year of normal school before launching her career as a teacher.

She married Leonard Ernest Pulsipher at age twenty-one. Sixteen months after their marriage, Leonard died of lymphatic cancer. One son was born to their union. "I am sure that the sick have been restored through administration and the Spirit of the Lord. I have seen it many times," recalled Juanita of this most difficult time. "But I also learned, as I watched my young husband die of cancer at the age of 27, that no number of blessings—Patriarchal or otherwise—gave more than temporary relief, although they did promise without qualification that he should be restored, should live to be a father in Israel and to perform a great work. It really shook me at the time" and the experience was not readily forgotten through the years.[3]

To support herself and her infant son, Juanita turned to education; she attended Dixie Junior College in St. George and earned a bachelor's degree from Brigham Young University. She then left her son in the care of her parents and pursued a master's degree at Columbia in New York City. While thousands of miles away from home, she wrote of finding comfort in the hymn, "Lead, Kindly Light."[4]

Juanita returned to southern Utah, rejoined her son, and accepted employment as an English teacher and dean of women at her alma mater, Dixie Junior College.

In 1933 she resigned her positions at Dixie to marry widower William Brooks, sheriff of Washington County, in the St. George Temple.

While a busy mother and homemaker, Juanita always kept her hands in the professional world. She collected pioneer diaries and wrote her first biography using the journals of her grandfather.

Her interest in the Mountain Meadow Massacre led to a Rockefeller Foundation grant that allowed Juanita to spend the next fifteen years studying before she began to write. Her subsequent writings show that she could tell a gripping story of monstrous proportions.

Why did she spend so much of her life researching such a controversial topic? Why did she want to rekindle the worst tragedy in the Territory of Utah? Was it to break new ground by being the first to write a comprehensive account of the massacre? Perhaps. However, Juanita felt that as a "Latter-day Saint 'in good standing' and one who always cherished her faith [that] she was the best person to tell what had been untold or silenced."[5] Juanita eventually published three major works on the tragedy.

During these same years, she served in "every organization of the Church where women work, from organist in Primary to Stake President of Relief Society."[6] In addition, she belonged to a literary club and taught Sunday School classes. She was constantly involved in community affairs and in family matters—an "affectionate mother, a loyal wife, a respected schoolteacher, an energetic organizer of church and civic affairs."[7]

Yet there was another side to Juanita that manifested itself at the death of her first husband and was challenged when her writings on the massacre were placed on bookshelves—a "disputatious temperament."[8] When the issue called for a reserved reply, Juanita gave a loud and public response, and Church leaders weighed in on the matter. Juanita feared that she might lose her membership in the LDS Church. "I do not want to be excommunicated from my church for many reasons," she wrote. "But if that is the price that I must pay for intellectual honesty, I shall pay it—I hope without bitterness."[9] She penned, "The church was everything to us. It was for the church that we were all here; it was the church that had drawn our parents from all the far countries. Even the building of the ditch and the dam, the graveling of the sidewalks, the planting of cotton or cane had its inception in the church, for ours was a temporal gospel as well as a spiritual one."[10]

Juanita was never disfellowshipped or excommunicated, but she felt blacklisted. Former friends viewed her as the foremost symbol of dissent, a view she did not relish. Philanthropist Obert C. Tanner described her as "one of the Lord's lie detectors, carefully separating the bogus from the genuine, and may I add, courageously writing what you find—that's so very, very, very important."[11]

Although Juanita felt alone at times, she continued to plow through frontier diaries, editing *On the Mormon Frontier: The Diary of Hosea Stout,* authoring a biography on her husband, and serving as a member of the Utah Board of State History. For her efforts to preserve an "honest" history of the American frontier, she received the Distinguished Service Award from the Utah Academy of Sciences, Arts, and Letters and honorary degrees from Utah State University and the University of Utah.

In 1988, due to advanced age and poor health, Juanita was placed in a nursing home. She died on August 26, 1989. Unfortunately, Juanita did not live long enough to learn that Church Historian Richard E. Turley, Jr., and other key historians, with the encouragement of Church leaders, were asked to build on her efforts and write another documented book on the Mountain Meadow Massacre. Their much-touted work, published by Oxford University Press, would not have been possible without Juanita's tireless writing and determined efforts.

1   Levi S. Peterson, *Juanita Books: Mormon Woman Historian* (Salt Lake City: University of Utah Press, 1988), 2.

2   Levi S. Peterson, *Juanita Brooks Lecture Series* (St. George, Utah: Department of Printing Services at Dixie College, 1989), 18.

3   Peterson, *Juanita Books: Mormon Woman Historian,* 57.

4   Laura L. Bush, *Faithful Transgressions in the American West: Six Twentieth-Century Mormon Women's Autobiographical Acts* (Logan, Utah: Utah State University Press, 2004), 85.

5   Bush, 102.

6   Peterson, *Juanita Brooks Lecture Series,* 12.

7   Peterson, *Juanita Books: Mormon Woman Historian,* 2. See also Levi S. Peterson, "Juanita Brooks: Historian as Tragedian," *Journal of Mormon History* 3 (1976), 47–54.

8   Peterson, *Juanita Brooks Lecture Series,* 5.

9   Ibid., 9.

10 Bush, 87.

11 Peterson, *Juanita Brooks Lecture Series,* 5.

ANGELA "BAY" BUCHANAN

Standing for Something

The seventh of nine children, Angela "Bay" Buchanan's nickname came from a brother just a year older who couldn't say *Baby*. Her family taught her important ideals from the time she was young, including the need to stand up for her beliefs. Of her family, Bay says:

> I come from a loving, humble family with strong beliefs. We were taught to hold them close and always defend them. Every night my father sat at one end of the dinner table and engaged my brothers in healthy debate over a variety of topics, which generally turned into highly charged arguments. That was an environment in which I was raised—loud, boisterous men all around me, who held strong opinions and beliefs and were ready and willing to stand their ground and make their case.[1]

The love of debate and commitment to her beliefs has sustained Bay in the national political arena and in her own home.

The daughter of William and Catherine Buchanan, Bay was born December 20, 1948, and grew up in a devout Catholic family. She attended Catholic schools in the Washington, DC, area; she earned a bachelor's degree at Rosemont College in 1971 and a master's degree in mathematics from McGill University in 1973.[2] While a graduate student, Bay worked in the accounting department of President Richard M. Nixon's presidential campaign, where the Watergate investigation began just a week into her internship; her brother Pat was also working in the Nixon White House at the time. During the Watergate hearings, Bay finished her internship, returned to school, completed her degree, and taught mathematics at her high school alma mater in Washington, DC. She taught all four years of high school math and coached every team she could get her hands on.[3]

During the heat of the Watergate investigation, Bay immigrated to Australia out of a desire to know what it was really like to be an American—something she felt required living outside the country.[4] Bay lived in Sidney for eighteen months and learned much more than an appreciation for America: in Australia she was introduced to the gospel of Jesus Christ. She said of her conversion to Mormonism:

> I was not going to convert unless I had absolute testimony, and knew it, and was certain that this was what the Lord wanted me to do. . . . I received that absolute confirmation in Australia, and my testimony has never wavered from that moment.[5]

When she returned to the states, Bay went to work on former California Governor Ronald Reagan's presidential campaign. After he lost that race, she moved to California and worked with him until he ran again in 1980, when she was named his national campaign treasurer. When Reagan won, Bay was determined to be appointed Treasurer of the United States—after all, she had been with Reagan for five years. After learning that Vice-president-elect George Bush had someone else in mind for the job, Bay met with Ed Meese, a respected appointee in the Reagan administration, to get his support for her appointment.

"This can't happen" Bay told Meese. "After years of working to elect Reagan, I'm not losing to a Bush person. Ed, I want to see the president."[6] It wasn't going to be necessary. Ed told her the President was appointing her. At age thirty-two, Bay was named U.S. Treasurer in 1981—the youngest treasurer to serve in the history of the United States.[7] Under her leadership the Treasury Department was restructured to include the Department of the Mint and the Department of Engraving and Printing.

While serving as U.S. Treasurer, Bay met California attorney William R. Jackson. They were married in 1982. A year later Bay's first son, Billy, was born. By the time Bay had two more sons, Tommy and Stuart, her marriage with Jackson was over.[8]

As a single mother, Bay's political career took a backseat. Her son Tommy said, "She had a sense of urgency to make sure that we were well taken care of."[9] Bay put her family first and made sure that her children understood the importance of being a family and the blessings that come from living the gospel. "I raised those kids in the Church. The Church was the backbone of our family," she says. "[Church members] gave me guidance and support."[10] Bay also taught her children the importance of being aware of current events. Reminiscent of her own upbringing, Bay gave her children "challenges" or "games" at the dinner table to test their knowledge. Tommy remembers, "She encouraged us to read the news. I think she wanted us to pick our own path and make our own choices."[11]

Bay managed her brother Pat Buchanan's presidential campaigns in 1992, 1996, and again in 2000. She was a coanchor on *Equal Time,* a political talk show carried by CNBC and MSNBC.[12] During the 1992 national elections, she was a political analyst for *Good Morning America.* Bay is currently president of The American Cause, an educational foundation dedicated to advancing conservative issues; cochair of Team America, a political action committee dedicated to opposing amnesty for illegal aliens; and a political analyst for CNN.

As Bay tours the country, she encourages audiences to stand up for conservative beliefs, reminding them that boldness and courage in the defense of the unborn can save lives. She also encourages young people to learn more about others' beliefs. "What do you believe?" she asks. "Start talking to people—not people who agree with you, but people who disagree with you because they're the ones who are going to make you feel uncomfortable. . . . Then you know both sides: you know their side, and you will know what you believe, and you will know it with conviction."

She tells Church members, "Work to be bold—spokespeople, spokesmen, for our beliefs."[13] Through Bay's take-charge attitude, she has created a niche for herself in the conservative realm of national politics.

1   Interview with Angela "Bay" Buchanan by Mary Jane Woodger, July 2, 2010, Salt Lake City; transcription in author's possession.
2   Paul Alexander, "The 20 Most Fascinating Women in Politics," *George,* September 1996, 103.
3   Interview.
4   Ibid.
5   Ibid.
6   Ibid.
7   Rob Howe, "Her Brother's Keeper," *People,* March 4, 1996.
8   Alexander, 103.
9   Interview with Thomas Jackson by Melissa Rehon, July 22, 2010, Los Angeles; interview notes in author's possession.
10   Interview with Angela "Bay" Buchanan.
11   Interview with Thomas Jackson.
12   Alexander, 103.
13   Interview with Angela "Bay" Buchanan.

CLAUDIA LAUPER BUSHMAN

Assertiveness

In 2000 Claudia Lauper Bushman was named New York State Mother of the Year[1]—but, ironically, it was activities outside of her home that led to the recognition. In receiving the honor, Claudia said, "I have come to believe that a woman should never give up on her outside interests, no matter how weary she is or how pruned her life seems to be during the heavy years of childcare. She should keep one foot in her own life."[2]

Though there were times when Claudia felt weary with the many demands on her time, her husband, Richard Bushman, reflects, "She's always had more energy and need for expression than there were outlets." And though Claudia had a "shopping gene that demanded fulfillment at regular intervals," she needed more outlets for expression.[3] In an era when most women settled down to exclusive mothering, Claudia became a role model as a woman who successfully magnified talents both at home and in the community.

Born in 1934, Claudia considers herself part of "the second Mormon diaspora from Utah. The first went to Canada and Mexico with polygamous families, and the next went to the West coast."[4] Her parents joined those leaving Utah to seek their fortune in California, and it was in northern California that Claudia gained her testimony of the gospel of Jesus Christ and determined to be a lifetime member of the LDS Church. "Everything I ever needed to know, I learned at Church," she said.[5]

But academics played a large role for this bright LDS youth. She received a scholarship to study at Wellesley College in Boston, where she studied English literature; more important to her future, it was there that she was introduced to Richard Bushman, a promising young Harvard student. Claudia and Richard were married on August 19, 1955, and they became the parents of two daughters and four sons. To onlookers, it appeared that Claudia "had everything that she had really hoped for—she was married, she had lovely children."[6] She was not rich, but she and Richard were stable and had good friends. Yet Claudia knew that she was restless. Something was missing in her life. One day she was struck by what she called a "morbid feeling":

> What good am I? What use is my life? . . . I would go to parties with intellectual people and just feel stupid. I felt I had nothing to say—nothing to contribute—and that I was probably the best-read housewife in town. I had many good things in my life, but it was just not enough for me. It was then that I started back to school again for about the fifteenth time and began working on my doctorate.[7]

School was vital for Claudia, giving her "an escape, as well as something to escape from." She found that:

> [S]chool made housework a pleasure. I was glad to make cookies or sew Easter dresses or read stories. All those things became more precious and desirable. To have interests outside of childcare or housework doesn't necessarily mean being a

career woman. There is lots of space between being a devoted stay-at-home mom and being an executive in a Fortune 500 company. Mothers are encouraged by the Church to raise their own children, but a woman has years before and after children, and even hours during children when she can read or write something. We don't have to milk our cows, stoke our coal stoves, or spin our wool unless we want to. Even with many children there is time for choices and compromises.[8]

Claudia jumped into many projects outside her home. While Richard served as stake president in Boston, she joined other LDS women in writing a guidebook for newcomers to town. She prepared an institute class and started *Exponent II,* an LDS newspaper for women. After moving to Delaware, Claudia taught classes in women's studies at the University of Delaware, founded the Newark Historical Society, and was the director of the Delaware Heritage Commission.

Yet it was in her home that Claudia found in her husband a partner in historical research and writing. Of his help in her acclaimed endeavors, Richard says, "Claudia has this marvelous gift for seeing things intuitively, but she doesn't have a conscious control of what her idea is. So my task is in a way to tell her what she really thinks. Giving structure."[9] Under his watchful tutelage, Claudia has written seven scholarly books, including *Contemporary Mormonism: Latter-day Saints in Modern America.*[10]

Claudia has also been highly involved in academic instruction. She taught American studies at Columbia University and served as director of the Joseph Fielding Smith Institute for Church History's Summer Scholars Program at Brigham Young University. For the 2007–2008 academic year, she taught Mormon women's studies classes at Claremont Graduate University. "These are great days for women," says Claudia. If a woman is "well-prepared and single-minded, she can rise to the top like cream."

Claudia believes that as women in the Church "we are socialized against careers. . . . It is essential that every woman be able to support herself, hopefully by doing something she enjoys doing and that pays very well."[11] For the next generation, Claudia is a role model of a wife and mother and of a woman who has developed her God-given talents for the benefit of society. She foresees a new ideal for the Latter-day Saint woman of future generations:

> Women will cease to leave their monuments in bounteous feasts to be daily destroyed, in sewn goods to be worn out by lively families, or in icing sugar on ornamental cakes. They will follow the admonition given to Emma Smith, and their time will be given to writing and to learning much. They will each be given a golden pencil at birth to record their thoughts and experiences. . . . In short, a new world will be opened to us and everything will be possible.[12]

1   "National Convention Recognizes 18 LDS Mothers," *LDS Church News,* May 13, 2000, Z7.

2   www.fairlds.org/FAIR_Conferences/2006_Lives_of_Mormon_Women.html.

3   Dennis Lythgoe, "Meeting of the Minds: Richard and Claudia Bushman: Couple have written many books and are still making scholarly contributions," *Deseret News,* November 7, 1999.

4   Dennis Lythgoe, "Meeting of the Minds—Richard and Claudia Bushman," *Exponent II* 23 (Winter 2000), 1.

5   www.fairlds.org/FAIR_Conferences/2006_Lives_of_Mormon_Women.html.

6   Lythgoe, *Exponent II,* 3.

7   Claudia L. Bushman, "The Best of Both Worlds," *Best Lectures 1973–1974* (Provo, Utah: ASBYU Academics, 1974), 88.

8   www.fairlds.org/FAIR_Conferences/2006_Lives_of_Mormon_Women.html.

9   Lythgoe, *Exponent II,* 5.

10   Claudia Bushman, *Contemporary Mormonism: Latter-day Saints in Modern America* (Westport, Connecticut: Praeger Publishers, 2006).

11   Bushman, "The Best of Both Worlds," 86.

12   Jeff Needle, "The Future of Mormon," *The Mormon,* March 21, 2008.

ARIEL BYBEE

Talent

Courtesy of the Church History Library, The Church
of Jesus Christ of Latter-day Saints.

"Five minutes, Miss Bybee!" calls the stage manager through the door of Ariel Bybee's dressing room deep in the bowels of the Metropolitan Opera. At that point she kneels and asks Heavenly Father to help her use her talents to the best of her ability. While that's not what usually happens behind the scenes at major opera houses, it has been the experience for Ariel during thirty-five years as an opera singer—eighteen seasons of them (1977–1995) at the Metropolitan Opera. For Ariel, the answer to her prayer always came with "feelings of light and calm . . . almost as if the Spirit, as audience, is applauding a successful performance!"[1]

Born January 9, 1943, into a family that valued membership in The Church of Jesus Christ of Latter-day Saints, Ariel Bybee learned from her family that "when my actions were in harmony with the teachings of the Church, I felt calmly happy; when they were not, I felt miserable. It was pretty black and white."[2] With that same process, Ariel chose a career in which she could magnify her talents.

Her road to the Metropolitan Opera began as a student at Brigham Young University. Maddalena in the student production of *Rigoletta* and the first Lady in *The Magic Flute* were her very first opera roles. Afterward, Ariel declared, "I was addicted to opera forever."[3]

For five years after receiving a bachelor's degree from BYU, she taught music in junior high schools. Although she enjoyed teaching, she really missed opera. When Ariel won the San Francisco Opera auditions, San Francisco Opera Impressario Kurt Herbert Adler cast her in roles that propelled her to stardom. Adler cast Ariel in leading roles in *Carmen, La Boheme,* and *La Favorita.* The Regional Metropolitan Opera auditions led to the role of wild Jenny in *The Rise and Fall of the City of Mahagonny,* a portrayal that caused opera critics to sit up and take notice. One critic wrote, "Bybee was sensational, not only vocally but in her look and her grasp of the role. . . . From now on the role of Jenny will have to be judged against her definitive interpretation."[4] Another critic penned, "When Miss Bybee sang, we felt Jenny's presence. When she stopped singing, Jenny seemed to vanish from the stage."[5]

Ariel was all too soon caught up in praise for her performance, as well as the temptation to lose herself in the character she portrayed. "I found that I didn't want the show to end with the curtain," she said. "It was my LDS perspective telling me such feelings were stupidly immature that helped me grow up into my true identity—that of an LDS woman," said Ariel. "What was interesting to me was how this realization brought with it a mutually reinforcing seriousness toward both my art and my religion."[6]

In 2000, soon after her retirement from the Met, *Opera News* labeled her "a prominent mezzo at the Metropolitan Opera for eighteen seasons," recognizing her more than 450 performances—including the lead role as Hansel in *Hansel and Gretel,* Nicklausse in *Les Contes d'Hoffmann,* and Suzuki in *Madama Butterfly.* Other newspapers said more. Critics described her leaving audiences speechless with her amazing debut at the Washington DC Opera in Menotti's *The Consul* and in *Bulgaria* as Melisande. She received standing ovations for her performance with the Vienna Philharmonic and the New York City

Ballet. It is little wonder that Franco Zeffirelli selected her to sing the role of Flora in his film *La Traviata* or that she had two solo albums: *O Divine Redeemer* and *Eternal Day,* as well as many *Live at the Lincoln Center* telecasts.

In 1988, she began a new stage in her career as a professor of voice and director of university opera productions. Her production of Frank Loesser's *The Most Happy Fella* won the International Trophy (Grand Prize) in competition at the Waterford (Ireland) International Festival of Light Opera. Upon her retirement from the University of Nebraska-Lincoln Opera Program, the university honored her by endowing the Ariel Bybee Chair of Opera Performance.

Most important to Ariel is that she has never lost sight of her religious commitment. She has served as a ward Primary president and a member of the Church's International Affairs Committee in New York City. She has given numerous vocal performances in Church settings. Through these performances, she sees her life as one of service—even "musical service." Such notices as "Ariel Bybee, world-famous mezzo soprano, to perform at Washington DC Temple Visitors Center" are typical of her decades of musical service. Many will remember that Ariel was featured as a soloist in the annual Missionary Satellite Fireside,[7] the annual Festival of Lights in Salt Lake City, at President Gordon B. Hinckley's ninetieth birthday celebration, and at the dedication of the Winter Quarters Temple.

Ariel willingly gives of her talent because she knows that her talent is a "gift to me from God." When she sings, she views herself as an "actualizer of a worshipful atmosphere for the members of the congregation." Ariel says, "In order to perform well in this role, I must control myself, no matter how moved I may be. If I lose control and indulge myself with my own emotions, I will become vocally tied up, physically restricted. Such a self-centered condition results in the inability to express oneself freely, as is required if the singer is to do justice to both the music and the text."

Perhaps most telling of her character is that it is still the case that before each performance, whether at church or on stage in a famous opera hall, she calls upon the Lord in prayer and asks for Heavenly Father's help in using her talents to the best of her ability.[8]

1   *Why I Believe* (Salt Lake City: Bookcraft, 2002), 85, 88.

2   *Why I Believe*, 87.

3   "Crescendo!" *McKay Today Magazine,* Spring 2008, cover page.

4   Bartin Wimble, *New York Daily News* review of *The Rise and Fall of the City of Mahagonny,* Metropolitan Opera, 1981. (See www.music.utah.edu/faculty/faculty_a-z/ariel_bybee). See additional comment by Tim Page: "The fresh, centered voices of Dawn Upshaw and Ariel Bybee, in tandem with the skillful conducting of James Levine, provided most of the joy at the Metropolitan Opera Tuesday night," in *New York Times* review of *Carmen,* 1986.

5   Bernard Holland, "Opera: Ariel Bybee in 'Mahagonny,'" *New York Times,* April 1, 981.

6   *Why I Believe*, 86.

7   "Prominent members share deep feelings at satellite fireside," *LDS Church News,* March 2, 1996.

8   *Why I Believe*, 87–88.

CHERIE CALL

Hope

I am not the only one who has ever been friendless
Or lost in a wilderness place
I am not the only one who's been rescued by mercy
In exchange for my slivers of perfect faith
I'm not the only one.

These lyrics express songwriter Cherie Call's powerful message of hope—a hope that has blessed her life and the lives of countless listeners. By sharing insights and life experiences through music, Cherie gives LDS listeners hope and peace in troubled times. Her folklike music has set new standards for religious composition in the LDS market.

Daughter of Wynn Call and LaRene Jensen, Cherie was born in 1974 in Mesa, Arizona. At the age of three she began to sing in front of audiences and as a teenager began to write her own songs. By the time she was in high school Cherie was writing songs for all of her friends and constantly performing them at church, school, and at local community events.[1]

As Cherie graduated from high school she had a desire to write and perform music but did not think that such interests would lead to a real career. She thought such a dream seemed more like "when kids say they want to be a super hero."[2] Cherie's father felt that if she was to study music it would be best for her to eventually teach music, but at Brigham Young University she contemplated majoring in media music, which would lead to recording and song writing. She was leery of telling her father about her decision not to major in music education—and considers it a miracle that after praying really hard, her subsequent conversation with her father went really well. She now says of her father, "He'll stick up for me more than anyone."[3]

It was while attending BYU that Cherie picked up the guitar for the first time. The guitar seemed a "perfect fit for her vivid, storytelling lyrics."[4] During the time Cherie attended BYU, the Music Department was rather dismissive about LDS music, an attitude that shaped Cherie's desire to write regular contemporary music. She has reflected on this experience: "I think the songwriting I learned with that type of focus really made me a better writer of religious music when I eventually went that way."[5]

After obtaining her bachelor's degree, Cherie worked for Southwest Airlines. Saving enough from her wages, along with the help of her parents, she produced two albums—*Taken* and *One Star.* While working on her third album, *Heart Made of Wind,* which was paid for by a generous investor, she also submitted an original song, "Promises I Keep," for the 1999 *Especially for Youth* album.[6] Acceptance of that song not only significantly advanced her career, but was the beginning of her shift from contemporary music to LDS music.

This new direction led her to join a traveling tour with Jericho Road, a performing group specializing in LDS entertainment. On her first tour with the group, Cherie and the "sound guy," Joe Anderson, started dating and fell in love. They were married, and today Joe is her biggest fan.

Cherie's most recent musical compositions are a combination of spiritual insights and life experiences; with her unique style, she incorporates religious ideas while being careful not to sound "preachy."[7] She has turned to the Lord in prayer for help in striking that proper balance and with other aspects of her career. "When I am going to do a performance, the first thing that happens is I get nervous and start forgetting the words," she says. "But if I say a little prayer before the performance, then I don't forget. When I am working on a song and I'm praying about it, that really does help the whole process of songwriting."[8]

As for her inspiration, Cherie looks to everyday incidents that occur in her life and that of her family. "Motherhood has continued to be a powerful muse for Cherie."[9] The inspiration for "Already a Butterfly" came from her daughter, Sydney. While Sydney was wearing huge butterfly wings, she begged to also wear a superhero cape. When she realized the cape was crumpling her wings, Cherie's daughter said, "You don't need a cape if you're already a butterfly." Cherie heard a poignant message in her daughter's words. To Cherie, the message was, "If you know who you are, that is enough." She says, "It brings tears to my eyes when I hear [my daughter] singing [the song] because I hope that's a message that she remembers in her life. I never really expected that message would go shooting right back at her even though it came from her. It's neat to see that music has an impact on their lives."[10]

Through her music, Cherie uses life experiences to bless her family and reach out to others. For example, her song "Family Tree" is a response to her parents' divorce. "[It] has been really healing personally to me to write this song," she says. The song consistently brings the greatest response from others who have also gone through a divorce in their family. "It's been a really comforting and healing song for a lot of other people too. It's been neat for me to be able to write a song that could help me work through something that was a hard thing for me to face in my life and to see it help other people too."[11]

Cherie's music—both contemporary and religious—has inspired listeners with courage to face each day. Her songs strengthen testimony as she emphasizes that no one is ever really alone. She shares that challenges can be met straight on if we turn to the Savior. To her, hope and happiness is found in music written and performed from the heart.

1   "Long Biography," chericall.com (assessed December 6, 2010).
2   Email with Cherie Call, December 5, 2010.
3   Diana Vanegas interview of Cherie Call, September 17, 2010, Salt Lake City, 5, transcript in author's possession; Email with Cherie Call.
4   "Long Biography."
5   Email with Cherie Call.
6   "Long Biography"; Email with Cherie Call.
7   Vanegas interview, 3.
8   Ibid., 2.
9   "Long Biography"; Email with Cherie Call.
10   Vanegas interview, 4.
11   Ibid.

BEVERLY CAMPBELL

Hospitality

Courtesy of the Church History Library, The Church
of Jesus Christ of Latter-day Saints.

"Does the Church of Jesus Christ of Latter-day Saints believe in equality for both men and women?" a reporter asked Beverly Campbell. She replied, "The answer has always been yes. The Church is solid and firm and steady. Eighty years ago, when it was a very unpopular view, the Church believed in equality for women. And we were criticized for our stand. We still believe in equality."[1] It was not the first time Beverly was asked about equality between men and women, and it was certainly not the last. She spent a significant part of her career defending the stance of the Church on the Equal Rights Amendment (ERA) and educating the media on the role of Latter-day Saint women.

Daughter of Thomas James Brough and Julia Frances Slagowski, Beverly was born May 15, 1931, the youngest of ten children. Her mother was the president of the Wyoming Association of Women and the Relief Society president, while her father was stake president, legislator, and an advisor to the governor. Her parents instilled the mindset of "if you think it, you dream it, go do it, whatever you want."[2] Beverly listened to this ideal as she went out into the world and accomplished great things.

Beverly enrolled at Brigham Young University, where her talents shone. There she met A. Pierce Campbell, who had just returned from fighting in the Korean War; they were married January 22, 1953, in the Salt Lake Temple.[3]

After several entrepreneurial experiences, the Campbells moved to Washington, DC, in 1967, where Pierce accepted a position as director of acquisitions of a large national firm while Beverly was asked to join the Joseph P. Kennedy Jr. Foundation to help develop a project for the mentally handicapped. At her suggestion the program was named the Special Olympics, and it continues to serve millions of special-needs people around the world. Working closely with Eunice Kennedy Shriver, Beverly was asked to be the coordinating director of the foundation, a position she held until 1976.

At that time the national ERA debate was escalating. Beverly had earned the reputation of being a hard-working, intelligent woman in the nation's capitol, and pro-ERA associates asked that she lend her support and voice to its passage. Beverly declined. She remembers, "As I studied the amendment, I came to feel that it would codify a doctrine of sameness rather than equality between men and women. I determined I could not support it."[4]

As the debate heated, Beverly spearheaded a statewide coalition in Virginia to work with the legislature, media, and other entities. Her strong anti-ERA views and public persona led to appearances on radio and television talk shows, including the Chicago-based *Phil Donahue Show*. Reflecting on that and other national television appearances, she mused, "If there was anything in my life I did not want to do, nor felt prepared to do, it was that. However, I had made covenants with the Lord that I would help at any time and anywhere I was needed in the kingdom, and so with great trepidation, I said yes."[5]

After her appearance on *Donahue*, she was asked by LDS leaders to be an official spokesperson for the Church on the role of women in society. On *Larry King Live* she was articulate in refuting the claim that

the LDS Church is male dominated. She said, "A quarter-of-a-million people join the church every year, attesting to the fact that it appeals to the businessman in Germany, the farmer in the Philippines, the opera star at the Kirov, and the Alabama school teacher. It is not male-dominated. I have never been dominated in my life. I am totally equal."[6]

Beverly's anti-ERA opinions caused her professional difficulties, and she was not surprised when associates, friends, and business interests in Washington withdrew from her. As her involvement with the ERA escalated, she left her successful public relations firm because "all of [her] clients were pro-[ERA]."[7] Beverly found, "Those experiences taught me to trust in the Lord, and they gave me a sure testimony of the doctrine of divine guidance and of the wisdom granted to those called by God to positions of responsibility."[8]

In the early 1980s Beverly served as the Church's regional public affairs director for the northeast region, which covered a wide swath of the country and allowed her to work extensively with the national and other forms of media in those large population centers. She felt all that preceded was but preparatory training for her most important assignments for the Lord.

In 1984 she was asked to create an office in Washington, DC, that would allow previously closed doors to be opened to the Church. Her work was to be directed primarily to that part of the world known as the International Mission, which at that time represented nearly two-thirds of the world's countries and included eastern Europe, much of Asia, and Africa. It was essential that the Church leaders might enter into these countries, that the Church receive official recognition, that they be allowed to register, that its members have freedom to assemble, and that missionaries be allowed to enter and stay. She was also asked to work with the national and international media in acquainting them with the Church and correcting misrepresentations.

She soon realized she would have to come to know and be trusted by the ambassadors who represented their countries in Washington and at the United Nations in New York City. Through her work, along with that of Church leaders, key LDS businessmen, members of Congress, and others, much was accomplished.

The large home Beverly and Pierce had built was put to good use for the Lord's purposes, as it became a sort of "embassy" for the Church where dinners and meetings were held. Beverly also served as director of International Affairs for the Church for twelve years.

Beverly's belief in equality, not sameness, of women was shared at a time when the role of women was being hotly debated across America. Her willingness to defend and advocate the stance of the Church in public settings and on national television placed her in a unique role among women, and her unusual ability to open doors of understanding at the national and international levels benefited many.

1   Beverly Campbell, "Challenges of the '80s," *New Era,* April 1981, 20–21.
2   Interview with Beverly Campbell by Mary Jane Woodger, October 8, 2010, Salt Lake City, Utah; transcription in author's possession.
3   Interview with Beverly Campbell.
4   Beverly Campbell, *Eve and the Mortal Journey* (Salt Lake City: Deseret Book, 2005), xv.
5   Campbell, xv–xvi.
6   Larry King interview with Beverly Campbell, *Larry King Live,* CNN, June 2, 1993.
7   Interview with Beverly Campbell.
8   Campbell, xvii.

ELAINE CANNON

Communication

Courtesy of the Church History Library, The Church
of Jesus Christ of Latter-day Saints.

As a child, Elaine Cannon was mindful of the historic significance
of Salt Lake City and of her own pioneer heritage: oft-repeated stories
about her ancestors and required attendance at parades commemorating
their triumphs taught Elaine that the sacrifices of yesteryear meant
that much was expected of her.[1] She also learned of the great worth of
people, both young and old. "People always have affected me deeply
one way or the other, chilling or warming my sensitive soul either by
their suffering or their joy, or mine," she penned. "You can't say I'm an
expert at anything except at loving people. I'm so interested in people,
and I do ache for everybody who is suffering."[2]

Daughter of Aldon Joseph Cannon and Minnie Egan Anderson,
Elaine was born April 9, 1922, in Salt Lake City. As she grew to
womanhood, Elaine loved to hear her father pray using the "best
language he knew." For her, some of the "best language" was found
in great literature. As a youth she read *Woman's Home Companion,*
Anne of Green Gables, Tarzan, Alice in Wonderland, Heidi, and Dale
Carnegie's *How to Win Friends and Influence People.* She also delved
into the writings of Browning, Shakespeare, Wordsworth, Longfellow,

Dickens, Stevenson, and Emerson, freely admitting that she "loved all these books unabashedly."[3]

With that same zeal, Elaine enjoyed expressing herself through the written word, a way of getting in touch with her own emotions and those of others. She wrote a high school report for the *Salt Lake Telegram* and became a regular columnist for the University of Utah campus paper, *Daily Utah Chronicle*. Later she was employed as a daily newspaper columnist and women's editor for the *Telegram*. She also enjoyed her years as a daily columnist for the *Deseret News*, becoming an editor of the society pages. Elaine also wrote as a freelance reporter for popular magazines such as *Seventeen* and *Better Homes and Gardens*, receiving awards for "her ability to communicate with young people and their families without losing her role as representative of old-fashioned, solid values."[4]

Not surprisingly, much of Elaine's Church service centered on writing. She contributed to the *Improvement Era* as an associate editor of the "Era of Youth" section. Later, her section became the *New Era*.[5] Elder Marion D. Hanks of the First Quorum of Seventy characterized Elaine as "the one person in the world who did the most to perpetuate a magazine for youth."[6] More than fifty gospel-centered books were authored by Elaine.

Elaine also developed many other talents. She was a competent pianist and a master at sewing and needlework. Cooking over campfires and swimming in the Great Salt Lake brought her hours of joy. Art, music, drama, and speech came as second nature to her.[7]

When it came time for marriage, many suitors found more than one reason to be interested in the talented Elaine. But for her there was only one: Donald James Cannon, the son of Elder Sylvester Cannon, presiding bishop of the Church. Elaine was married to "Jim" on March 25, 1943, in the Salt Lake Temple. Shortly after their marriage, she graduated from the University of Utah with a degree in sociology. Jim and Elaine became the parents of six children—James, Carla, Christine, Susan, Holly, and Anthony.

Elaine and her husband supported each other in all their endeavors. Elaine was by his side when Jim served in the Utah House of Representatives from 1957 to 1959. She also stood by him through his unsuccessful bids as governor of Utah and mayor of Salt Lake City. She encouraged him in his position as executive director of the Utah Travel Council, where he coined Utah's slogan, "Greatest Snow on Earth."

Jim likewise encouraged Elaine in her professional writing—but her busy professional life did not replace or diminish her influence as a mother. She proudly claimed that she never missed a column in twenty-five years, but woke up at 4 A.M. to write before her children were awake. Jim also supported her in many Church callings, through which she helped establish the LDS sorority Lambda Delta Sigma and served on the ward, stake, and general levels of the YWMIA.[8]

In 1978 President Spencer W. Kimball called Elaine to be the eighth president of the YWMIA. During her presidency, the first general meeting of young women and their mothers was held in September 1978 in the Salt Lake Tabernacle, a meeting now held annually for young women and their mothers and broadcast by satellite to the world. Throughout her presidency, Elaine sought to simplify and strengthen the Young Women program. She streamlined supervision by reducing general board membership from sixty members to twelve; invited the young women to repeat a spiritual theme each week and strengthen their testimonies; and helped young women transition to Sunday classes as part of the LDS Church's consolidated worship services.

After being released from the YWMIA presidency on April 7, 1984, Elaine devoted her time to her family. Her husband was ill for many years, and she was a great comfort both to him and to her children and grandchildren. During these later years she also continued to write. Some of her most popular books were *Adversity*, *The Truth about Angels*, and *Called to Serve Him*. Elaine died in May 2003 at age eighty-one.

Elaine is remembered for her unique ability to reach youth of all ages through her written words; seeing the best in others and reaching out to make a wonderful difference in their lives, she taught generations of Latter-day Saints that they were important and appreciated.

1   Elaine Cannon, *The Seasoning* (Salt Lake City: Bookcraft, 1981), 42, 52, 54.
2   Janet Peterson and LaRene Gaunt, *Keepers of the Flame* (Salt Lake City: Deseret Book Company, 1993), 129.
3   Cannon, 5, 19–20, 47–49, 57.
4   Peterson and Gaunt, 133.
5   Ibid., 121–122, 125–126, 129, 133.
6   Ibid.
7   Cannon, 40–41, 61, 62–63; Peterson and Gaunt, 120–121.
8   Peterson and Gaunt, 127, 129.

MARTHA HUGHES CANNON

Independence

Was independence thrust upon Martha Hughes Cannon, or did she choose it? Her early years suggest that she had little choice other than to be independent, but her later years suggest that she chose independence as a way of life.

Daughter of Peter Hughes and Elizabeth Evans, Martha was born July 1, 1857, in Great Ormes Head, Wales. When she was one, her parents converted to The Church of Jesus Christ of Latter-day Saints and immigrated to New York City.[1] At age three, "Mattie," as she was called, crossed the nation with her family to reach the Salt Lake Valley. Her father died just a few days later.[2]

Losing her father at such a young age and growing up in pioneering Utah contributed to Martha's early sense of independence. By age fourteen she was supporting herself as a school teacher and working part time as a typesetter on the *Young Women's Exponent* and the *Deseret News.* But for Martha, employment was a means to an end. She had an insatiable desire for knowledge and dreamed of one day becoming a medical doctor.

In 1875 she earned a degree in chemistry from the University of Utah and entered medical school at the University of Michigan. She put herself through medical school washing dishes, making beds, and working as a secretary. At age twenty-three she graduated on July 1, 1880, as a full-fledged medical doctor. She then enrolled in pharmacological studies at the University of Pennsylvania, the only woman in a class of seventy-five students. There she cut her hair short to save time and wore men's boots to keep her feet dry.[3] Martha received a bachelor of science degree in pharmacology from the university and simultaneously earned a diploma from the National School of Elocution and Oratory by successfully completing evening classes.

At twenty-five Martha returned to Salt Lake City as one of the most educated women in the Church. Hoping to give women in Utah opportunities that mirrored her experiences in the East, Martha founded the first training school for nurses in Utah.

While working at Deseret Hospital, she met Angus M. Cannon, twenty-three years her senior. At the time Angus was superintendent of the hospital and president of the Salt Lake Stake, which included all of the wards in the city. Martha and Angus were married October 6, 1884, in the Endowment House; Martha was his fourth wife under the law of plural marriage.[4]

Some aspects of plural marriage suited Martha's personality well, but other aspects of plural marriage were uncomfortable, such as trying to avoid federal marshals.[5] She once described her marriage as "a few stolen interviews thoroughly tinctured with dread of discovery." In her medical practice she was in constant fear of being forced to testify against polygamist fathers.[6]

After giving birth to her first child, Martha wrote, "I would rather be a stranger in a strange land and be able to hold my head up among my fellow beings than to be a sneaking captive at home."[7] Relying on her own ingenuity, in April 1886 Martha left the Salt Lake Valley with her infant daughter, Elizabeth. During her two years of volunteer exile, when few women traveled alone, Martha and her baby lived in

England, Switzerland, and Michigan. It was not until June 1888 that she and her child returned to Salt Lake City.

Martha took an active role in the women's suffrage movement. When called on to speak before a Congressional committee about the political activity of women in Utah, she said, "I know that women who stay home all the time have the most unpleasant homes there are. You give me a woman who thinks about something besides cook stoves and wash tubs and baby [flannels, and I'll show you, nine times out of ten, a successful mother]."[8]

In 1896, partly through Martha's efforts, women in Utah were given the right to vote in state and national elections; Martha ran for Utah State Senator against her husband—Angus on the Republican ticket, Martha on the Democratic. The *New York Times* reported, "[Martha] showed her intense independence by declining to follow the political convictions of her husband, who is one of the staunchest Republicans in the State."[9] In truth, Martha and Angus were not running head to head against each other. Both could have won the election with ten candidates nominated, five Republicans and five Democrats for the five at-large seats in the Senate. The fact that Martha defeated her husband by almost 3,000 votes, however, places her in a unique position in the annals of Utah history.[10]

It is little wonder that the election caused a rift between Angus and Martha. The *Salt Lake Herald* editorialized, "Mrs. Mattie Hughes Cannon, his wife, is a better man of the two. Send Mrs. Cannon to the State Senate and let Mr. Cannon, as a Republican, remain at home to manage home industry."[11] Angus "met the situation with outward humor, [but] he did not find it easy to accept his wife's effrontery."[12]

On November 3, 1896, Martha Hughes Cannon became the first woman to be elected state senator in the United States. As a senator she supported funding for a state board of health and helped pass laws regulating working conditions for women and young girls. After retiring from the legislature, Martha served on the Utah Board of Health and on the Utah State School Board for the Deaf and Dumb.

When her husband died in 1915, Martha moved to Los Angeles to be near her son. There she worked for the Graves Clinic, becoming a noted authority on narcotic addiction until her death on July 10, 1932, in Los Angeles.[13] The Martha Hughes Cannon Health Building in Salt Lake City, which houses the Utah State Department of Health, was dedicated in her honor in 1986. An heroic-size bronze statue of Martha is housed in the Utah capitol rotunda.

Whether it was the circumstances of her life or her own choice, Martha's independence impacted the lives of women in her generation and in generations to come as she pioneered the path for female physicians and politicians.

1   Andrew Jenson, *LDS Biographical Encyclopedia* (Salt Lake City: Andrew Jenson Memorial Association, 1936), 4:86.

2   Marc Haddock, "Utah Woman Blazed Trail in State Politics," *Deseret News,* December 14, 2009.

3   "Doctor Martha Hughes Cannon (1857–1932), Utah Suffragist, State Senator, and Physician," n.p., Utah State Historical Society, Salt Lake City.

4   Haddock.

5   Richard S. Van Wagoner and Steven C. Walker, *A Book of Mormons* (Salt Lake City: Signature Books, 1982); John Sillito and Constance Lieber, "Martha Hughes Cannon," in *Utah History Encyclopedia,* ed. Allan Kent Powell (Salt Lake City: University of Utah Press, 1994), 72.

6   Constance L. Lieber and John Sillito, eds., *Letters from Exile: The Correspondence of Martha Hughes Cannon and Angus M. Cannon, 1886–1888* (Salt Lake City: Signature Books, 1993), xv.

7   Lieber and Sillito, 269.

8   Annie Laurie Black, "Our Woman Senator," *San Francisco Examiner,* November 8, 1896, reprinted in the *Salt Lake Herald,* November 11, 1896, 95.

9   "Women Office Seekers," *The New York Times,* November 1, 1896.

10 Holly Melissa Cox, "From Suffragettes to Grandmothers: A Qualitative Textual Analysis of Newspaper Coverage of Five Female Politicians in Utah's *Deseret News* and *Salt Lake Tribune*," Master's Thesis, Brigham Young University, 2008, 33.

11 *Salt Lake Herald,* October 31, 1896, 4.

12 *Deseret News,* September 28, 1968, as cited in Haddock.

13 Jenson, 4:88.

ERIN CHAMBERS

Faithfulness

While pursuing her passion for acting, Erin Chambers remains faithful to her Latter-day Saint values. She has appeared in several movies and national television shows such as *Without a Trace, Medium, Miami Medical, Ghost Whisperer, Cold Case, Happy Feet, Alvin and the Chipmunks,* and NBC's *Days of Our Lives.*[1] She is currently recurring her role as Siobhan on ABC's *General Hospital.*[2] Erin is a person who remains faithful to her values as a Latter-day Saint as she pursues her passion for acting.

Erin was born September 24, 1979, in Portland, Oregon.[3] She began acting at age eight when she played a royal child in *The King and I.* The director of *The King and I* recruited her two years later to play Amaryllis in *The Music Man.*[4] When she was fifteen, she appeared in Free Willy II, her first on-camera job. During high school she had leading roles in several school productions. "By the time I graduated from high school," Erin says, "I knew acting would be a huge part of my life."[5]

Erin moved from Oregon to Provo, Utah, to receive her BFA in acting from Brigham Young University. At BYU she performed in *The Three Sisters, Cyrano,* Disney's *Don't Look Under the Bed,* and on national television as a Disney Channel presenter.[6] Her agent, Carole Turcotte of the Eastman Agency in Salt Lake City, said, "[Erin] managed to do well in school despite her busy acting career. Her professors have been understanding of her situation. . . . There have been times when Erin will have to miss class because she has an audition, but she will also miss auditions because she feels she has missed too much school."[7]

Her acting career took a major leap during her sophomore year at BYU when Erin played the "lead role in a Halloween Disney movie called *Don't Look Under the Bed* . . . as a sister who must help her younger brother deal with a prank-playing boogey man." The show premiered in October 1999 on the Disney Channel. Her youthful appearance allowed her to "play 15- or 16-year-old parts realistically," which was "helpful for directors because federal laws prohibit children from working too many hours, which hinders film progress."[8]

After graduating from BYU in June 2002, she played Johanna in the musical *Sweeney Todd* at the Pacific Conservatory of the Performing Arts in Santa Maria and Solvang, California.[9] The busy year ended with her marriage to Carson McKay on December 21, 2002.

From 2002 to 2007, Erin appeared in many popular television shows, such as *Drake & Josh, CSI: Crime Scene Investigation, Joan of Arcadia, Stargate: Atlantis, Veronica Mars, ER, CSI: NY,* and *Bones.*[10]

In 2007 Erin had a major part in *The Singles 2nd Ward,* a sequel to *The Singles Ward.* She played Christine, a young LDS woman who falls in love with a young man who shares her goal of a temple marriage. When the couple becomes engaged, problems ensue when Christine's parents, who are not Mormon, realize they can't attend their daughter's wedding. The movie was released on DVD in December 2007.[11]

Erin also had a major role in *The Errand of Angels,* which debuted in Utah theaters on August 22, 2008. She played the role of "Sister Taylor, a sister missionary who struggles with food, missionary life, and language during the first part of her mission. . . . In the film, [Erin's] character questions her reasons for going on a mission, and finds answers to her prayers in scriptures and in her companions." For her role in the film she learned "phonetics and memorized German dialogues."[12]

Erin has "decided what she will and will not do as an actress and a member of the LDS Church," and she sees "her faith as something that sets her apart from other actors."[13] For instance, Erin refuses to accept roles that require nudity. When a director's team changed her role in one film to include a scene where she would not be fully clothed, instead of accepting the change, Erin withdrew from the film.[14]

Erin will socialize with her non-LDS friends but chooses not to drink when she is with them. On the last night of shooting *Don't Look Under the Bed,* producers brought alcohol to the celebration party. One of them offered her a bottle of expensive wine purchased especially for her. When she politely refused the wine it caused the producer to ask why she would not drink on a special occasion. She then explained the Word of Wisdom. The producer accepted her values and understood even more when she had difficulties with scripts that were not wholesome.[15]

As Erin continues to build a promising acting career, she explains, "My managers and agents know . . . I live to be a good example. If the Church comes up, I talk about it. I think being a good example is what I try to do the most."[16]

1   Jaclyn Anderson, "BYU Actors Maintain LDS Standards," *The Daily Universe,* January 11, 2007; Erin Chambers Interview by Jeff Milone, June 4, 2009; Elio Valenzuela, "Film Portrays Sister Missionary," *The Daily Universe,* August 18, 2008.
2   Erin Chambers, "Filmography," http://www.imdb.com/namenm0150326, accessed November 17, 2010.
3   Ariel Cassady, "Brigham Young U. Student Lands Lead Role in Upcoming Disney Flick," *The Daily Universe,* June 3, 1999; Erin Chambers Interview.
4   Anne Bradshaw, "BYU Student, Erin Chambers, Storms Show Business World," mahonri.org, May 8, 2002.
5   Erin Chambers Interview.
6   Bradshaw.
7   Cassady.
8   Ibid.
9   Bradshaw.
10 Chambers, "Filmography."
11 Alyssa Moses, "'Singles Ward' Sequel Released," *The Daily Universe,* December 10, 2007.
12 Valenzuela.
13 Anderson.
14 Erin Chambers Interview, *Light Refreshments Served,* http://lightrefreshmentsserved.com/2008/07/18/guest-erin-chambers, July 18, 2008.
15 Bradshaw.
16 Erin Chambers interview.

WYNETTA WILLIS
MARTIN CLARK

Conversion

Courtesy of the Church History Library, The Church
of Jesus Christ of Latter-day Saints.

One of the first African-Americans to sing with the Mormon
Tabernacle Choir, Wynetta Willis Martin Clark says, "I think many
times the acceptance has been more difficult on my part, acceptance
of myself for what I am, obviously, colored; and accepting white
people's kindness and friendship, inside the Church." She laments,
"The hurts of many, many small slights, both imagined and real, heal,
but always I feel faced with new wounds opening, as I try to turn
away from snubs, and from derision, from forced toleration that is
suffocation and an insult to me."[1]

Wynetta was born and reared in the greater Los Angeles area at a
time of racial upheaval and cultural prejudice. Wanting as a child to
sort out where she fit in the larger picture of racism, Wynetta tried to
find God so that He could explain the turmoil she felt. "Somehow my
hunger was never filled, and I began a grasping, groping, and frantic
search for my fulfillment," she said. Fortunately, Wynetta had loving
parents who were very religious. "They gave me their share of goodness
in the simple wisdom of their lives," she recalls. Yet as her friends spoke
of finding God and being saved, Wynetta had to confess, "I wasn't even

sure I wanted to be saved while I was growing up, and I was even more sure I wouldn't be!"[2]

The bond that held her close was a caring family and their love of music, and a few family members even became professional musicians. The Willis & Johnson Quartet—composed of Wynetta, a brother, a sister, and a cousin—sang for a variety of church congregations in the Los Angeles metropolitan area. Although performing often consumed her days, at night Wynetta found herself dreaming of one day becoming a missionary. In attempting to explain her dreams and ambitions, she said, "I knew I had something to do in life, that I must help to ease the ever present, always growing torment of a searching heart."[3]

By the time Wynetta was twenty-four, she had been in and out of so many churches that she "felt like a tourist in Italy." She made many friends along the way, but as her interest in one church group after another dwindled or dulled, the friendships made in those congregations also faded. After years of searching for truth, she reached the conclusion that "all churches were relatively void of meaning for me, and I nearly lost all faith."[4]

This was a disturbing time in her life. The family quartet had stopped performing; she had married, but the marriage had failed. Seeking solace, Wynetta turned to music but still did not find the gospel truths she had longed to embrace since childhood. There remained in her an emptiness—a void even though she was now the mother to two little girls.

It was at this difficult time that Wynetta met Barbara Weston, who introduced her to the word *Mormonism*. When Wynetta first heard the word, she recalls, "I thought she meant something to do with her dietary habits, like a vegetarian or something, so I shrugged and said, 'Me, I eat anything!'" Nevertheless, her curiosity was piqued, and Wynetta investigated the Church; soon she was baptized. "My life from the moment of my baptism, to state a gross understatement, was changed," she said. "I attended church faithfully, I restored a lost ego,

I became a better mother, a better daughter, and I learned to truly love my neighbor."[5]

As she learned more about the Church, Wynetta developed a strong desire to take her daughters to Salt Lake City and audition for a position in the Mormon Tabernacle Choir. "I knew I could sing, but I did not know whether I could sing well enough for this magnificent choir," she said. To her surprise, she was invited to join the choir after her audition. The first time she sat in the choir at a general conference session, it was like a dream come true.[6]

Wynetta toured with the choir for two years. During the choir's many performances throughout the nation and in various countries of the world, Wynetta believed her "personal mission was to prove to the world" that the Church welcomed African-Americans. During those tours, she was also instrumental in sharing the gospel in word and song with those of differing nationalities and cultures.

In 1970 Wynetta was hired by Brigham Young University to help in the training of nurses, becoming the first African-American faculty/staff member at the institution. As she shared her experiences, she sensitized future nurses to cultural differences between races. She also served as a research consultant on Black culture.[7]

During her life, Wynetta was recognized as "an exuberant, happy, adult member of the Mormon Church." As to how she felt about her quest and embrace of gospel truths, she said, "This is my life and this is my peace."[8]

1   Wynetta Willis Martin, *Black Mormon Tells Her Story* (Salt Lake City: Hawkes Publications, 1972), 12.
2   Ibid., 15–16, 18–19.
3   Ibid., 23.
4   Ibid., 29.
5   Ibid., 51, 56.
6   Ibid., 59, 61.
7   Erin Howarth, "The Lives of African American Mormons and the Evolution of Church Policy," Senior Thesis, Brigham Young University, 1995, L. Tom Perry Special Collections, Harold B. Lee Library, Brigham Young University, Provo, Utah.
8   Martin, 34.

MARTHA JANE CORAY

Devotion

Used by permission from Daughters of Utah Pioneers.

Martha Jane Coray is known among Latter-day Saints as the woman Lucy Mack Smith chose to write her memoirs. Yet to her husband, Howard Coray, Martha was the choice companion that Joseph Smith promised "will be suited to your condition and whom you will be satisfied with." In his mind, Martha had been sent from God to complete his life.

Daughter of Sidney Algernon Knowlton and Harriet Burnham, Martha was born June 3, 1822, in Covington, Kentucky. When her family moved to Bear Creek, Illinois, they were introduced to Mormonism by George A. Smith. Martha was baptized in January 1840 in the icy Mississippi River.

Near the time of her baptism, Howard Coray was serving as a clerk for the Prophet Joseph Smith. One day Joseph said to Howard, "Brother Coray, I wish you were a little larger, I would like to have some fun with you." Not realizing that Joseph was speaking of wrestling, 130-pound Howard replied, "Perhaps you can." During the wrestling match that ensued, Joseph accidentally broke Howard's leg. The next day, Howard said to him, "Brother Joseph, when Jacob wrested with the angel and was lamed by him, the angel blessed him; now I think I am also entitled to a blessing." In the priesthood blessing that followed, Howard was promised, as mentioned above, "that [he] should find a companion, one that will be suited to your condition and whom you will be satisfied with. She will cling to you, like to cords of death, and you will have a good many children."[1]

At a Church gathering held three or four weeks later, Howard scanned the congregation to see if "possibly the fair one promised might be present." He wrote, "My eyes settled upon a young lady sitting in a one-horse buggy. She was an entire stranger to me and a resident of some other place. I concluded to approach near enough to her to scan her features well and thus be able to decide in my own mind whether her looks would satisfy my taste." He described Martha as having "dark brown eyes, very bright and penetrating, at least they penetrated me, and I said to myself, she will do. The fact is, I was decidedly struck."[2]

That very day Howard made the acquaintance of Martha Knowlton. "I discovered at once that she was . . . inclined to be witty; also, that her mind took a wider range than was common of young ladies of her age. This interview, though short, was indeed very enjoyable, and closed with the hope that she might be the one whom the Lord had picked for me; and thus it proved to be."[3]

Martha and Howard were married February 6, 1841, in Nauvoo; they were sealed for eternity July 22, 1843. They became the parents of thirteen children—eight sons and five daughters—all of whom grew to maturity.

In addition to family life, Martha and Howard shared a profound interest in preserving records of important speeches given in Nauvoo. When Martha attended a Church meeting and saw that a clerk was not present, she wrote down the words of such leaders as Joseph Smith, John Taylor, Brigham Young, and George A. Smith. Wilford Woodruff "consulted her notes, when he was Church Historian, for items not to be obtained elsewhere."[4] Martha also taught school with her husband in Nauvoo. Her favorite subjects to teach were law, philosophy, history, poetry, chemistry, and geology.

Their joint teaching efforts ended in the winter of 1844 when Lucy Mack Smith asked for Martha's help in writing the history of Joseph Smith.[5] As sixty-nine-year-old Lucy Mack Smith told her life story to twenty-three-year-old Martha Coray, Martha noted that Lucy was suffering from rheumatism and had difficulty breathing at the time. Within a few months Howard was asked to help Martha with the manuscript. They worked together "until the work was accomplished, which took us until nearly the close of 1845," wrote Howard.[6] The Corays created two holographic copies of the manuscript—one given to Mother Smith and the other retained by Church leaders.

In May 1846 Martha and Howard left Nauvoo and joined thousands of Mormon exiles in Iowa; stopping to earn funds for the journey, they did not arrive in the Salt Lake Valley until 1850. Once Howard acquired additional funds, he took his family to Mona, where he raised livestock and Martha sold liniments and medicines made from herbs gathered and grown on their land. Although the herbs brought medicinal relief to many, Martha was unable to solve her own health issues. The Corays moved to Provo, hoping to find solutions for her persistent cough.

In spite of health issues, Martha was appointed the first dean of students and a member of the board of trustees of Brigham Young Academy in Provo. In accepting these appointments, she wrote to Brigham Young, "My principle of education has been God's laws of religion first, Man's laws of honor and morality second, Science of every attainable kind" third. Knowing that her views may not match the educational thoughts of Brigham Young, she concluded her letter, "I am mainly desirous to know your will and that shall be my pleasure in everything touching this establishment."[7]

Her tenure as dean and as a member of the board ended all too soon. Despite all that medicine could do, Martha died December 14,

1881, at age fifty-nine. Hundreds attended her funeral, including Church leaders Wilford Woodruff and Joseph F. Smith. Her obituary read, "She was a woman among ten thousand. . . . Sister Coray was intensely beloved by her children, to whose training she had devoted the greater portion of her life's best energies." But more important, her husband, Howard, said of her, "A more intelligent, self-sacrificing, and devoted wife, and mother, few men have been blessed with. . . . She lived a consistent Latter-day Saint life up to the time of her demise."⁸

1   *Autobiography of Howard Coray,* Church History Library.
2   Ibid.
3   Ibid.
4   Martha J. C. Lewis, "Martha Jane Knowlton Coray," *Improvement Era,* April 1902, 440.
5   *Autobiography of Howard Coray.*
6   Ibid.
7   Martha Jane Coray to Brigham Young, April 10, 1876, Brigham Young Papers, Church History Library.
8   *Autobiography of Howard Coray.*

VIRGINIA CUTLER

Overcoming Obstacles

In 1922 Virginia Cutler was promised in her patriarchal blessing that she would become "a teacher of young and old and of friends and strangers, and that the way would be opened for her to obtain her education."[1] That blessing was fulfilled as she overcame obstacles, eventually teaching in public schools and universities in Utah as well as in Asia and Africa.

Daughter of Robert and Mary Farrer, Virginia Grace was born in Park City, Utah, and was reared on a six-acre farm in Murray. Her parents, hard-working farmers, taught Virginia to embrace their work ethic and to worship God. When her younger brother Art was stricken with polio, four-year-old Virginia prayed for his recovery. She described herself being confused about God when her brother was not immediately healed. It was not long, however, before she received confirmation of the Lord's love: "I could scarcely control myself when a light came through the bedroom window, and I felt the presence of a heavenly being—I knew not what—but the influence was overpowering, and I felt peace within my soul and assurance that all was well with Art."[2]

Before graduating from Murray High School in 1922, Virginia entered a home economics competition in which she won a four-year tuition scholarship to the University of Utah. At the university her interest in and understanding of the study of home management grew. After graduating in 1926, she was employed as a high school home economics teacher in Manti, Utah, before accepting a teaching position in the Jordan School District.[3]

While working in Jordan, Virginia met Ralph Garr Cutler; they were married July 10, 1929, in the Salt Lake Temple. For a brief period Virginia and Ralph lived on the Cutler farm in Salt Lake, where they were self-sufficient and protected from the economic perils so prevalent in the Great Depression. Virginia gave birth to a son, Robert Garr Cutler, on April 23, 1930. In November 1931, Virginia's husband died from septicemia. Rather than sit back and feel helpless, Virginia found employment as a substitute teacher at South High in Salt Lake City. A month later, when she discovered she was pregnant, Virginia resigned, since expectant mothers were not allowed to teach at that time. Virginia gave birth to her second son, Ralph Garr Cutler, on July 27, 1932.[4] Soon after his birth, she found employment as a teacher in Taylorsville.

Although she loved being a teacher, Virginia concluded that she needed more education to better support her family. With an academic scholarship in hand, she enrolled in Stanford University in 1935. She graduated with a master's degree in 1937 and was hired as a home demonstration agent for the University of California Extension Service at double her former salary. Virginia and her two sons lived in a large house in Colusa County for the next eight years.[5]

Realizing that more schooling would better provide for her sons' educational aspirations, Virginia moved to Ithaca, New York, and enrolled in a doctorate program at Cornell University. "The head of my department welcomed me with open arms and urged me to accept a teaching assistantship," recalled Virginia. "My patriarchal blessing was still being fulfilled!" After graduating with a PhD in 1946, Virginia and her sons moved back to Utah. Virginia secured a professorship in the Department of Home Economics at the University of Utah. Later, under the jurisdiction of the United States Point Four Program with the Foreign Operations Administration, she taught in Southeast Asia. She said, "I knew that my patriarchal blessing directed me to go, even against the advice of well-meaning friends who thought it was a terrible risk."[6] From 1954 to 1961, Virginia taught home management—two years in Thailand and five years in Indonesia. In Thailand she helped establish a national home economics program, and in Indonesia she set up a standard pattern project to make clothing in conjunction with McCall's patterns.

When Virginia returned to the states, she was appointed dean of the College of Family Living at Brigham Young University. In the mid-1960s, she was approached to establish a College of Home Economics at the University of Ghana, where in 1966 she founded the Department of Home Science in the Faculty of Agriculture at the university. At the time she had eight students, no facilities, and no faculty. Within two years she had a teaching laboratory, a child study center, three offices, and a home science court. Virginia stayed in Ghana for three years to help ensure the program she established functioned properly;[7] she returned to BYU to teach for two more years before retiring.

In the years that followed Virginia served on the White House Consumer Committee and as the first chair of the Major Appliance Consumer Action Panel, serving more than two hundred manufacturers of home products in the United States.

During her lifetime, Virginia's commitment to the Church never waned. She had a personal goal to perform 2,500 endowments, which she reached. As she did so, she "wondered if my husband was aware of my efforts and if he was preparing the sisters to receive their blessings. As those thoughts passed through my mind, I suddenly knew he was there. I knew that he knew of my work and that he was assisting sisters on the other side of the veil. I was so glad to be in the temple that day.

I can hardly wait to greet him and the sisters he will introduce to me."[8] Virginia died on May 20, 1993, of Alzheimer's disease.

As a widow with two young sons to support, Virginia educated herself, supported her family, and accomplished her goals. Opposition did not slow Virginia down; it seemed to encourage her on. Best of all, Virginia fulfilled her patriarchal blessing as she taught others about the importance of creating a home and filling it with love.

1   Cynthia M. Gardner, "Virginia Cutler—Her Heart Is Where the Home Is," *Ensign*, July 1985, 36.
2   Ibid., 36.
3   Ibid., 37.
4   Ibid.
5   Ibid., 38.
6   Ibid., 38–39.
7   Ibid., 39.
8   Merrill J. Bateman, "Becoming a Disciple of Christ," *Ensign*, April 2006, 23.

LARAINE DAY
Taking Risks

"Too many of us are tentative, dipping our toes into the waters of life, fearful that the waters are too cold," said Laraine Day. As for Laraine, she lived the advice of poet John Keats: "I leaped headlong into the sea, and thereby have become better acquainted with the soundings, the quick sands, and the rocks, than if I had stayed upon the green shores, and piped a silly pipe, and took tea and comfortable advice."[1] Laraine played roles in more than four dozen Hollywood films, working alongside rising stars Cary Grant, Robert Mitchum, Lana Turner, John Wayne, Spencer Tracy, and Kirk Douglas. But stardom had its price. Laraine wanted to be a Hollywood superstar, but studio executives at Metro-Goldwyn-Mayer (MGM) pigeonholed her as "attractive ordinary."[2]

LaRaine Johnson, better known to movie buffs as Laraine Day, was born October 13, 1920, in Roosevelt, Utah. When her family moved to Long Beach, California, six-year-old Laraine saw her first movie and concluded that one day she would be a star on the silver screen. Hoping to help, her parents enrolled her in acting classes under the tutelage of Elias Day (whose surname she later took). When a talent scout came looking for a "fresh face" and a "demure-looking young lady," Laraine was discovered.

In 1937, seventeen-year-old Laraine was cast in several westerns until her talents captured the attention of MGM producers, who signed her to a six-year contract, but did little to boost her career. Her big break came when MGM loaned her to competing studios. She starred in Alfred Hitchcock's spy thriller, *Foreign Correspondent,* and her performance in an Irish melodrama, *My Son, My Son!,* led *Life* magazine to name her "a major young Hollywood personality."[3] She was almost the victim of an ax murderer in *Fingers at the Window,* and played opposite Cary Grant in *Mr. Lucky.* Of Grant, she said, "Cary would arrive on the set and everybody's morale immediately lifted. The crew were crazy about him and so was I. But, curiously, I never felt the male-female chemistry that you sometimes experience on a set. I could have been talking to my best girl-friend."[4] She starred opposite Robert Mitchum as a destructive psychotic in the disturbing drama *The Locket,* in which the *New York Sun* critic claimed she transformed a "sweet-faced wanton" into "a very real person" in the drama.[5] She played an attentive nurse in seven *Dr. Kildare* television episodes. Her last major film was an airplane melodrama, *The High and the Mighty,* starring John Wayne.

After a first marriage failed, Laraine married baseball manager Leo Durocher. Laraine said, "My life as Mrs. Leo Durocher and baseball come first." In 1950 she told a *New York Times* reporter, "I'd rather win a pennant than an Academy Award."[6] She added, "I'll be the world's greatest baseball fan."[7] In 1950 Laraine hosted a fifteen-minute television interview show with baseball players before home games. The show was taped at the Polo Grounds and carried by New York's WPIX. In so doing, Laraine became "The First Lady of Baseball" and the first woman to host a television show. In 1952 she wrote *Day with the Giants,* which the *New York Herald Tribune* called "an amusing, informative book, the first to report on baseball from the viewpoint of the wife."[8]

Aside from her baseball shows, she hosted two short-lived television variety shows and spent a year as a panelist on the TV show *I've Got a*

Secret. In 1960 she divorced Durocher and abandoned baseball. Laraine explained to a reporter, "When our relationship was over, so was my relationship with baseball."[9]

In 1961 Laraine married Michael M. Grilikhes, an LDS convert and television producer. For the next forty-seven years, she enjoyed life within the confines of the gospel. She enjoyed motherhood, supporting missionaries, and helping advance the Polynesian Cultural Center. She continued to be in the limelight with occasional appearances on *Wagon Train, Murder She Wrote, Fantasy Island, Love Boat, G.E. Theater,* and other television serials. In between roles, she began a playhouse for LDS actors in Los Angeles. In 1971 she wrote *The America We Love,* and she became a goodwill ambassador for the National Association of Real Estate. She traveled the country for the realtor board, encouraging citizens to improve their environment: "Making the community better is everybody's business. We are all in this together. . . . We are under obligation as decent human beings, responsible citizens, and God-fearing people to clean up our environment, not only in the physical sense, but in our speech, in our daily work, and in our attitudes."[10] Laraine died a few months after her husband, Michael, on November 10, 2007, at the home of her daughter, Gigi Bell, in Ivins, Utah.

For Laraine Day, life was never about "dipping our toes into the waters of life, fearful that the waters are too cold."[11] For her, life was about leaping headlong into the deep where quicksands and rocks too often hide. By so living, she found that the tinsel of Hollywood does not always shine. Yet she picked herself up and started anew, knowing that there was a wonderful life ahead. She received her hoped-for dream of a star on the Hollywood Walk of Fame—but more important to her descendants, she found happiness with loved ones.

1   From John Keats's epic poem "Endymion," as quoted in Laraine Day, "Improving Our Environment," *Ensign,* October 1971, 48.

2   Myrna Oliver, "Laraine Day, 87; 'Dr. Kildare' Film Actress had Love of Baseball," *Los Angeles Times,* November 12, 2007.

3   Aljean Harmetz, "Laraine Day, 'B+ Movie' Star, Dies at 87," *The New York Times,* November 13, 2007.

4   Tom Vallance, "Laraine Day," *The Independent,* November 13, 2007.

5   "Laraine Day, 87, Film Actress and 'First Lady of Baseball,'" *The New York Sun,* November 13, 2007.

6   Ibid.

7   Oliver.

8   See Oliver.

9   Harmetz.

10   Day, 48.

11   From Keats, as quoted in Day.

DONNA STRINGHAM DEWBERRY

Creativity

Donna Stringham Dewberry remembers that her father always told her, "Never say can't. YOU can do anything. And NEVER forget that."

"It wasn't that dad was a proud man," she remembers. "He just knew he could do anything and so could we if we believed we could. You know what, he was right."[1]

Donna remembers that her father liked to ask her, "Who are you?" When she replied, "I'm a Stringham," he always told her, "You have a name you should be proud of. You should always remember your name at all times and in all places and never do anything to harm your name."[2] Since 2002 Donna's name has been widely broadcast to the world on *The Donna Dewberry Show,* a weekly PBS television program, and on more than seventy books and thirty self-instruction DVDs. To those outside her family circle, Donna has lived up to her name and more.

Donna, daughter of Gerald and Doris Stringham, was born November 6, 1953, in Fort Pierce, Florida. At an early age her creativity was nurtured; she regularly sewed next to her mother and grandmother, and for Christmas each year everyone in her family made handmade gifts to exchange with each other. Donna recalls with fondness her father creating wooden gifts for each child. As an adult, Donna expanded on the family tradition by making and selling handmade gifts for the holidays, which allowed her to help support her family while being a stay-at-home mom.

One of her most important contributions was actually serendipitous. While trying to paint tinware without smearing the paint, she discovered the One Stroke™ technique, an easy-to-learn painting style for interior design and giftware. Excited about her discovery, she shared her method at entrepreneurial craft productions and demonstrations. From that simple beginning, there are now more than 6,000 people certified in her painting technique. Her more than 200 designs for mailboxes are featured in such high-end American catalogues as Neiman-Marcus, Horchow, and Spiegal. She is also a columnist for *Tole World* and the *Decorative Artist Work Book* and travels throughout the world sharing her techniques with other artists.[3]

Although success follows her wherever she travels, she has been careful to not let her thriving career interrupt family life. Growing up, she looked to her mother as an example of heartfelt kindness and love. She seeks to emulate these qualities in her professional and family life by blending them together. Her husband, Marc, is her marketing director, adviser, and best friend. Her children are involved in the painting, drawing, distribution, and warehouse processes.[4] How do her children feel about mixing family life, Church callings, and work? One child said, "Mom, I'm so grateful Heavenly Father gave me you as a mom."[5]

In spite of her success, Donna says that confidence has taken time to develop—and she still thinks of herself as a stay-at-home "craft mom." It is difficult for her to embrace the fact that she is viewed by worldwide fans as an artist. "In my long painting career, I was challenged to step out of my comfort zone and try something new," she says. "I learned new things that were hard to do at first, but I grew and soon new things felt natural. . . . Now each time I approach my easel I find myself willing to paint something new and different." She adds, "Be glad for

the challenges put before you, for they will truly help you grow."[6]

Donna's influence has extended much further than creating designs and painting techniques. She has been told, "You have saved my life, sharing your life with me and teaching me how to paint. You have given me so much peace! You have brought beauty in my life by sharing your talents."[7]

But her television audiences have been touched by more than the beauty of Donna's work. One of the hardest challenges Donna ever faced was the loss of her twenty-three-year-old daughter to Sudden Adult Death Syndrome in 2000. Difficult as it was and continues to be, Donna has publicly spoken of the peace that is hers knowing that one day she will see her daughter again. She wrote *I Believe in Angels* in honor of her daughter, and through her public broadcasts she has been a comfort to those experiencing similar challenges by assuring them that they will see their loved ones again.[8]

Donna gives others the same advice she received years ago from her father. "Believe in yourself," she says. "Share all you can with others. . . . And never say 'I can't,' because what you think you can, you can in life."[9] Donna's conviction that anything is possible, a conviction learned in childhood, inspires thousands across Asia, Europe, and the Americas. Many now realize that if Donna can find peace in life and achieve her potential, so can they. Donna has given new meaning to her father's question, "Who are you?"

1   Donna Dewberry, "Questionnaire," September 13, 2010, 2; transcription in author's possession.

2   Dewberry, 2.

3   Donna Dewberry, http://www.dewberrycrafts.com/about-one-stroke/about-the-creator.html [accessed 2 September 2010].

4   Donna Dewberry, "About One Stroke," http://www.dewberrycrafts.com/about-one-stroke/about-the-creator.html [accessed 2 September 2010].

5   Dewberry, "Questionnaire," 3.

6   Donna Dewberry, *Fast & Fun Landscape Painting with Donna Dewberry* (Cincinnati, Ohio: North Light Books, 2007), 5.

7   Dewberry, "Questionnaire," 4.

8   Ibid., 2.

9   Ibid., 4.

LIRIEL DOMICIANO
Following Your Dreams

Courtesy of the Church History Library, The Church of Jesus Christ of Latter-day Saints.

On April 4, 2004, twenty-two-year-old Brazilian convert Liriel Domiciano became the first soloist in seventy-two years to sing with the Mormon Tabernacle Choir at a session of general conference. "I felt that a dream had happened. . . . And I continue to pray to my Father in Heaven that he can help and teach me to sing with the Spirit like the Choir, so that perhaps I, too, could help His children."[1]

Born in December 1981 in São Paulo, Liriel was an unusually talented child who became aware of her unique gifts at the age of three when she expressed a desire to be a singer.[2] Music lessons were out of the question because of her family's financial struggles, but Liriel did her best to imitate what she heard and began to sing classical arias at age five.[3] Nevertheless, her dream of becoming a lyric soprano looked doubtful. "I was impatient. But a voice would come to my mind saying, 'Be calm. It isn't your time yet. . . . God will try us, but all these things are for our growth," she explained.[4]

As Liriel matured she didn't feel that her Catholic religion gave her the direction needed to find more happiness, and she couldn't figure out how the lifestyle she observed "fit with God's plan."[5] Joy came

when she listened to the LDS missionaries and was baptized.[6] It was then that her mother shared her own conversion story with Liriel.

When Liriel was young, a family friend and member of the LDS Church worked at their house. The friend sang Primary songs as she worked and talked with Liriel's mother about Mormonism. She said that if her mother would "pray with a pure heart and real intent, that God would answer her prayers and tell her that the Church was the true Church."

Willing to accept the challenge, Liriel's mother prayed to know if the Church was true. One night she had a dream in which she saw herself near the Salt Lake Temple. A man she knew to be the Savior invited her to come with Him and showed her through the beautiful temple, telling her she was worthy to partake. Liriel said, "I didn't have one doubt that my mother was telling me the truth. I thought, 'Why didn't she tell me about this dream before? I would have entered the Church before the age of 14.'"[7]

Liriel became an icon for Brazilian youth after applying to be a seamstress for a bridal fashion show and auditioning as a wedding singer for the show at the same time. Within forty-eight hours, nineteen-year-old Liriel received ten job offers to sing. Learning of her fortune, friends encouraged her to try out for Brazil's largest televised talent competition, the *Raul Gil Amateur Show* (a Brazilian equivalent to *American Idol*). She passed the stress-filled audition and was given the opportunity to share her talent on national television.

Liriel wanted very much to let the television audience know that she was a Latter-day Saint—standing as a witness of God at all times and in all places—but she had been told she could not say anything about her religion on the air. After praying in her stage room before her first performance, she looked up and saw her Young Women medallion. It was the answer she had been looking for. "Earning my Young Women medallion was an accomplishment," she says. "To me it means that I am spiritually prepared for temple marriage and a family."[8] She wore her medallion during television performances and in this subtle way let viewers know that she was a member of the Church. In front of millions of viewers, she stood as a witness for Christ.

Liriel wore her Young Women medallion at each level of the competition on the *Raul Gil Amateur Show.* She and her partner, tenor Rinaldo Viana, won the contest and became an overnight sensation. They signed a recording contract and watched as their first CD became the second-highest classical bestseller in Brazil's history, with more than one million copies sold.[9] Her name has become a household word in Brazilian homes.

Liriel still wears her Young Women medallion attached to whatever necklace she is wearing at the time. Many of her fans have noticed and wondered where they can purchase such a medallion for themselves. Wearing her medallion is just one way she demonstrates to fans what it means to be a Latter-day Saint. She hopes her story will inspire others and that she can be a good role model not only for Latter-day Saints, but for young people all over Brazil as she appears on Brazilian television.[10]

In 2004 Liriel performed in a program held to celebrate the rededication of the São Paulo Temple. President Gordon B. Hinckley heard her performance and was so impressed that he invited her to sing in general conference with the Mormon Tabernacle Choir.[11] When a producer learned that Liriel would be turning down his offer to perform without pay with the Tabernacle Choir, he became irate and warned her that his offer "wouldn't be there when she returned." Liriel said, "To sing for money is one thing, but the choir sings for no money, just the spirit."[12] She performed magnificently.

As Liriel gains popularity as one of Brazil's most sought-after celebrities, she continues to stand as a witness for Christ. Her example of a faithful Latter-day Saint woman blesses the lives of youth throughout her nation and the world.

1   Robb Cundick, "Singing Before the Saints: The Stories of Lulu and Liriel," *Meridian Magazine,* January 26, 2002.

2   R. Scott Lloyd, "Longtime Dream to Sing with Choir," *LDS Church News,* March 27, 2004, 6.

3   Cundick.

4   Jeanette N. Oakes, "A Voice for Values," *New Era,* August 2004, 14.

5   Cundick.

6   Ibid.

7   Lloyd, 6.

8   Oakes, 13.

9   Ibid.

10   Lloyd, 6.

11   Ibid.

12   Peggy Fletcher Stack, "Singing with Spirit," *Salt Lake Tribune,* March 14, 2004, C1.

CHRISTINE MEADERS DURHAM

Education

To those still holding a single-minded view of women in society, meet Utah Supreme Court Chief Justice Christine Durham. She not only fulfills her role as wife and mother, but is making her mark in the professional world. As a Latter-day Saint, she "has always been aware of the Church's emphasis on excellence, learning, and academic value,"[1] using her quality education to make a difference in legal discussions and judgments in Utah.

Daughter of William Anderson Meaders and Louise Christensen, Christine was born August 3, 1945, and even as a child was always interested in school and academic pursuits. Christine was an "early decision" admission to Wellesley College in 1963. At Wellesley she had many opportunities to interact with "enormously bright, active women," an association that led to her lifelong effort to encourage women to develop their intellect.[2] Four years later, she was denied admission to Harvard University Law School, which she had hoped to attend, due to a 10 percent quota for acceptance of female applicants at the time.

While pursuing her studies in religion and philosophy at Wellesley, she met Harvard freshman George H. Durham II, one of the few

men she had ever met who admired her mind and ambition. While Christine continued her studies, George served an LDS mission in England. After he returned from his mission, George and Christine were married in December 1966.

In 1967, Christine graduated from Wellesley College. Fifteen months later she entered law school at Boston College just ten days after her first child was born. At this same time George was completing his undergraduate work at Harvard. She transferred her studies to Arizona State University and then to Duke, following George throughout the country as he taught chemistry in Arizona prior to beginning medical studies at Duke University in 1969. Christine was the "first pregnant law student in the [school's] history" and graduated in 1971 from Duke.[3] George graduated from Duke in 1973.

She taught legal medicine at Duke, where she is still a trustee, from 1971 to 1973. In 1973 she and her family moved to Salt Lake City, where George began his pediatric residency at the University of Utah Affiliated Hospitals. She and George enjoyed themselves so much in Utah that they decided to permanently locate there.[4]

In Utah, Christine struggled to find her niche in society because Utah's legal profession was still viewed as a traditional male-dominated field. Yet she pressed forward and found enjoyment in her career. "I was right all those years ago to fantasize about [being a judge] because it is the best job in the world," Christine says.[5] From 1973 to 1978 she worked as an adjunct professor at Brigham Young University,[6] and from 1978 to 1982 she was a judge in the Third Judicial District Court. "If I had failed as a trial or an appellate judge," says Christine, "it would have redounded not just to my detriment but also to that of women lawyers across the board."[7] As a result of her extraordinary legal skills, she was appointed an Associate Justice of the Utah Supreme Court in 1982 and was elected Chief Justice of Utah's Supreme Court in 2002.

She enjoys the "intellectual stimulation of being a judge. It's kind of like solving puzzles," says Christine. "I do enjoy being a problem solver."[8] In all of her various legal capacities—founder of the Leadership Institute in Judicial Education and a member of Utah Judicial Council's Education Committee, the Council of the American Law Institute, the Conference of Chief Justices, and the American Judicature Society—Christine has always been a recognized leader.

Amid education and career goals, Christine and George have raised five children, including a child with Down syndrome and an adopted nephew.[9] Christine confesses, "Being a judge is challenging, but it is not as hard as being a parent." She shows great enthusiasm as a wife and mother, proving that family and professional life need not be mutually exclusive. Without the help of her husband, however, Christine may not have pursued her career goals. George has always been Christine's greatest support.[10] George has "forgone many professional opportunities in order to meet his children's needs and to allow his wife the time she needs to work."[11] Christine has also given up time in her career to give her husband time to pursue his work as a pediatrician. Through the years, Christine and George's relationship has been strengthened by their resolve to sacrifice for one another as equal partners, a reversal of traditional roles that has given the couple "a foundation for conversation, for empathy and understanding."[12]

Christine explains that the way she and George manage their professional and family responsibilities is "by having very much a fifty-fifty partnership. The house and kids were not 'my' responsibility—they were 'our' responsibility," she says. If she could not make it to a parent-teacher conference, George would be there.[13] She recalls that her children would occasionally complain about her nontraditional role as a mother: "My son claims I never made him cookies," says Christine. "Well, it's not true. I made him cookies, and when I wasn't there his father made him cookies. And at a very young age, he figured out he could make better cookies than either of us. And ever since he's made his own cookies."[14]

Christine has worked to successfully fuse her desire to develop professional skills and intelligence with her love of and responsibility to her family. Christine maintains that "the most significant role I have ever played in life—and the one that has been the most significant to my personal growth and development—has been my role as a wife and mother. On the other hand, I never saw any conflict in the performance of that role with also pursuing professional pursuits."[15]

1   Jim Christensen, *A Biographical History of Mormon Women Lawyers,* December 19, 1978, 12.
2   James N. Kimball and Kent Miles, *Mormon Women: Portraits & Conversations* (Salt Lake City: Handcraft Books, 2009), 192.
3   Ibid., 199.
4   Christensen, 8; Christine Meaders Durham Interview by John Jensen, February 26–27, 2002, 1–2, 5–6, 14.
5   Christine Meaders Durham Interview, 32.
6   Kimball and Miles, 185, 205.
7   Vicki Donlan and Helen French Graves, *Her Turn: Why It's Time for Women to Lead in America* (Westport, Connecticut: Praeger Publishers, 2007), 20.
8   Kimball and Miles, 208.
9   Christine Meaders Durham Interview, 27–28.
10   Kimball and Miles, 195.
11   Christensen, 15.
12   Kimball and Miles, 194–195.
13   Christine Meaders Durham Interview, 27–28.
14   Kimball and Miles, 195.
15   Christine Meaders Durham Interview, 27.

MARY ELLEN EDMUNDS

Happiness

Courtesy of the Church History Library, The Church
of Jesus Christ of Latter-day Saints.

Mary Ellen Edmunds is a popular speaker who entertains large LDS audiences with homespun stories and gospel wit. Standing-room-only crowds laugh and cry with her at Education Week and at women's conferences across the country. People who kept asking where to get copies of her speeches led Mary Ellen to write a dozen Deseret Book titles—among them, *Love Is a Verb, Thoughts for a Bad Hair Day, Keeping it Together in a Pull Apart World,* and *MEE Thinks: Random Thoughts on Life's Wrinkles.*

"I just am kind of a zany person," she says, "but I do think deeply, and I weep a lot. And it's in there."[1] Take for instance her 14th Article of Faith:

> We believe in meetings—all that have been scheduled, all that are now scheduled, and we believe that there will yet be scheduled many great and important meetings. We have endured many meetings and hope to be able to endure all meetings. Indeed we may say that if there is a meeting, or anything that resembles a meeting, or anything that we might possibly turn into a meeting, we seek after these things.[2]

Born in 1940 in Los Angeles, Mary Ellen recalls an incredibly wonderful childhood with lots of opportunities to play her violin.[3] In 1943 she moved with her family from balmy southern California to Cedar City, Utah, where she lived for fourteen years. Just before her senior year in high school, her family moved from Cedar City to Mapleton. Mary Ellen enrolled in Brigham Young High School, where she was recognized for her writing for the school newspaper, yearbook, and the Quill & Scroll Club. After high school graduation, she attended Brigham Young University and majored in nursing.[4]

After graduating from the College of Nursing in 1962, she received a mission call to the "Southern Far East"—which she interpreted to be Florida. Mary Ellen and her companion were the first sister missionaries to serve in the Philippines, where they entered homes "without electricity, indoor toilets, even toilet paper." What she discovered was that those who had little material wealth had much love to share. She was so overcome by their love for her that she "could not imagine heaven without everyone being there."[5]

After returning home, Mary Ellen taught at the mission home in Salt Lake City and as a BYU instructor of nursing at local hospitals. Her next full-time mission was in the Philippines Manila Mission from 1972 to 1973, where she was called as the first health missionary to that country.

Upon returning from her second mission, Mary Ellen was employed as the Coordinator of Health Missionaries for the Church until a third mission call sent her to the Indonesia Djakarta Mission from 1976 to 1978. She was the first sister missionary and the first welfare service missionary in Indonesia, where she "learned much more about the meaning of relief, compassion, and service." For example, in Central Java she witnessed sisters setting "aside a spoonful of rice each morning before they began their cooking. They kept the rice in plastic bags, which they brought to Relief Society each week. After the meeting, they would gather and prayerfully consider who needed a visit. Together, they would visit someone in need, taking a few of the bags with them." From these thoughtful sisters, Mary Ellen "learned so much about sacrifice" that she wondered aloud "what my equivalent of a spoonful of rice would be."[6]

When Mary Ellen got home, she worked as a coordinator of training for welfare missionaries until becoming one of the directors of training at the Missionary Training Center (MTC) in Provo, where she had oversight for training all Asian-language and welfare missionaries. "What a blessing!" she wrote of the assignment.[7] "There is no place like the MTC on earth. It was an incredible journey working there," she said.

In 1984 she became director of the Thrasher International Program for Children in Nigeria. Although she had hoped to spend three years there, she returned home earlier than planned due to illness. But there may have been more than one reason for her return: in 1986, she was called to serve on the general board of the Relief Society.[8]

When Mary Ellen retired from the MTC in September 1995, she began to devote more time to writing. Most of what she writes is cheerful and filled with suggestions for a happier life. She believes that "miracles [are] all around us, every day. And maybe we don't look at them and realize, maybe we get used to some things." For example, "We get used to the feeling that our prayers are being listened to. We get used to this brand new little baby." She says, "It's a miracle that our heart beats for a hundred years or eighty." And she adds, "it's a miracle that so many things go so right and so many people are so kind, responsive when there's a need." She believes that Heavenly Father "sees us down here working hard, and He just puts a moving walkway in our path and, you know, enhances our ability to do what we're doing, going through our lists, going through our day, going through our deep water and fiery trials."[9]

For her homespun stories, humor, and impact on missionaries throughout the world, Mary Ellen has been honored as the recipient of the BYU Alumni Distinguished Service Award, the BYU Exemplary

Womanhood Award, and a BYU Presidential Citation in recognition of extraordinary Christlike service. In 2005 the Mary Ellen Edmunds Nursing Endowment for the Healer's Art was established by the College of Nursing at BYU.[10]

"I have SO MUCH for which to be grateful," says Mary Ellen. "Not everything has turned the way I had dreamed and hoped, but I suppose it's that way for most if not all of us."[11] In the meanwhile, she will continue to bring happiness to many. As for personal satisfaction, she says, "It's wonderful to help people understand how to live the gospel. . . . It is our duty to respond to people who are hungry, sick, naked, and imprisoned."[12]

1   "Everyday Lives, Everyday Values: Interview with Mary Ellen Edmunds," August 29, 2004.

2   "MEE: Mary Ellen Edmunds, Popular Speaker and Author, Brigham Young High School Class of 1958," http://byhigh.org/Alumni _A_to_E/Edmunds/MaryEllen.html.

3   Mary Ellen Edmunds, "One Thing After Another," http://byhigh.org/Alumni _A_to_E/Edmunds/MaryEllen.html.

4   "MEE: Mary Ellen Edmunds, Popular Speaker and Author."

5   "Mentors Show Mary Ellen Edmunds a New Way of Thinking," *BYU Alumni Association,* 2008.

6   Edmunds, "A Daily Spoonful of Rice."

7   Edmunds, "One Thing After Another."

8   See Mary Ellen Edmunds, *You Can Never Get Enough of What You Don't Need: The Quest for Contentment* (Salt Lake City: Deseret Book, 2005), book cover.

9   "Everyday Lives, Everyday Values Interview with Mary Ellen Edmunds."

10 Edmunds, "One Thing After Another.

11 Ibid.

12 Edmunds, "A Daily Spoonful of Rice."

KIMBERLY FLETCHER

Homemaking

Most Americans can remember exactly where they were and what they were doing on September 11, 2001, when terrorists attacked U.S. citizens on American soil. Kimberly Fletcher's memories are more vivid than most: her life was completely turned upside down when a 757 passenger jet flew into the United States Pentagon where her husband was stationed. She was one of the lucky ones—her husband survived the attack. When he returned home later that day, Kimberly determined that she would do everything in her power to ensure that her children remained safe. This resolve led to an intense study of American history and public policy and active involvement in government and civic affairs.[1]

Daughter of William and Joyce Tregaskes, Kimberly was born March 19, 1966, in a small rural Pennsylvania town where she felt protected, safe, and loved as a young child. She recalls many happy memories in the care of extended family homemakers who had a positive influence on her life. One was her grandmother; Kimberly still carries out the traditional Christmas meal she enjoyed at her grandmother's house, which still holds wonderful memories long after her grandmother's death.[2]

Another homemaker who greatly influenced Kimberly was her great-grandmother Jesse, who helped her through some very difficult

times in her childhood. She remembers the unique gifts this matriarch shared: "When I was with her I could be a child; I was treated like a child—it was a magical time when I stayed with her at her house—the things that storybooks are made of." Kimberly remembers those times as a wonderful blessing that she really needed to hold on to.[3]

Kimberly wants all children to have the same safety net provided by the homemakers who influenced her as a child—and especially wants that same sense of protection and love for her eight children. After the 9/11 attack on the United States, Kimberly made it her personal mission to educate and inspire the women of America on America's history and heritage; she also hoped to empower women to take an active role as citizens in their homes, communities, and the nation, ensuring "that the legacy of freedom our Founders left us continues on to the next generation and for generations to come."[4] With this goal in mind, she founded Homemakers for America and serves as president of the organization, "a national membership-based, nonprofit corporation focused on education, citizenship and empowerment."

The organization consists of "a diverse group of women who share core values of God, freedom, and family." Its goal is to help women recognize the great legacy our founders provided as they established the nation and constructed the constitution—and to help women respect our freedom documents and what they stand for. The organization's desire is "to preserve this great legacy through influence in homes, communities and in the nation."[5] In its first year Homemakers for America grew from twenty-seven original members who met on November 11, 2004, in Dayton, Ohio, to a national membership of thousands in all fifty states.[6]

Kimberly believes that the organization was not solely her idea. "There is no doubt that I was directly inspired by the Lord to start this organization because the idea was so far removed from anything I had ever considered and I had no idea where it would lead me. . . . My family is my eternal calling. But this is definitely my earthly mission."[7]

Founding Homemakers for America and continuing to work toward its goals has not been easy for Kimberly. Many have criticized her efforts, even mocking her use of the word *homemaker*, but Kimberly is not deterred. Coming from a rich heritage of homemakers, she is adamant about the name of the organization. "For centuries homemakers have been honored and revered. . . . We ARE homemakers. It is time we stand together, support each other and recognize our influence and impact on society."[8]

In a short decade Kimberly has become an acclaimed author, columnist, and public speaker, appearing regularly on regional and national television and radio programs. Her articles have appeared in several print and online publications, including *American Thinker, WorldNet Daily,* and *Citizen USA Newspaper.* For Kimberly, it has been very hard to be put in a position where so many women look up to her for guidance and strength. She often wonders if she is falling short. She claims that she doesn't like "being so public" but has been pleasantly surprised at her ability to respond in such a wide forum.[9]

Kimberly's current interests include spearheading the 9-12 Project, intended to bring us "back to the place we were on September 11, 2001." She explains that "the day after the U.S. was attacked we weren't obsessed with Red States, Blue States, or political parties. We were united as Americans, standing together to protect the values and principles of the greatest nation ever created."[10] Though the world was turned upside down on 9/11, Kimberly used the catastrophe as the ignition to support women in the same way generations of homemakers supported her as a child.

1 "Kimberly Fletcher: President and Founder of Homemakers for America," Homemakers for America, http://www.homemakersforamerica.com/Kimberly-Fletcher.html (accessed August 16, 2010).
2 Kimberly Fletcher, "Questionnaire," August 19, 2010; transcription in author's possession.
3 Fletcher, "Questionnaire."
4 "Kimberly Fletcher: President and Founder of Homemakers for America."
5 Ibid.
6 Ibid.
7 Fletcher, "Questionnaire."
8 Kimberly Fletcher, "Feminism Is Dying. Let's Give It A Boost!" Homemakers for America, http://www.homemakersforamerica.com/Feminism-Is-Dying.html.
9 Fletcher, "Questionnaire."
10 "Kimberly Fletcher: President and Founder of Homemakers for America."

RUTH MAY FOX

Equality

When Ruth May Fox penned the lyrics to the popular hymn "Carry On" as an anthem for youth in her day, little could she have imagined that her words would be applicable to generations of LDS youth—and to her own life. The hymn speaks volumes about Ruth, who courageously met trials head-on, pressed forward to accomplish much good, and refused to let the problems of life define who she would become.

Daughter of James and Mary Ann Harding, Ruth was born November 16, 1853, in Wiltshire, England. Her parents joined the LDS Church five months after she was born. When Ruth was just sixteen months old, her mother died in childbirth—and at almost the same time, her father was called to be a traveling elder for the Church. Ruth was placed in the homes of extended family members so that her father could fulfill his mission call.[1]

Moves from one house to another proved difficult for Ruth, and she began to misbehave at an early age. Among other antics, she took a bite out of a china saucer, caught her own hair on fire with a candle, and stepped in front of an oncoming train.[2] It was not until her father returned from his mission that Ruth calmed down.

Soon she and her father moved to Yorkshire, England, where they lived in a boarding house run by Latter-day Saint Mary Saxton, whom he married; it was with Mary that Ruth and her father found happiness.[3] In September 1865, Ruth immigrated to America with Mary—following her father, who had immigrated months earlier. In America, Ruth worked alongside her father in a cotton mill to earn necessary funds to continue their journey to the Salt Lake Valley. It was not until 1867 that the family, which now included Mary, trekked to the valley.[4]

The family settled in the Ogden area, where Ruth was employed as a mill worker until entering John Morgan's College in Salt Lake City. In 1870 when her father purchased a mill in Salt Lake, Ruth left college to join him. At the mill, Ruth's feelings about equality between men and women surfaced when she was assigned to operate equipment that was meant to be run by men. "I should have had a man's wages for this," Ruth told her father. "[My] father thought that his partner would object since I was a girl. . . . I was given only $10.00 a week; but that was very good [wages] for a girl at the time."[5]

At age nineteen Ruth married twenty-year-old Jesse W. Fox, Jr., on May 8, 1873. Ruth and Jesse flourished financially in their marriage for the next decade. Ruth was happy in her marriage and with her children. In 1888 difficulties quickly arose when Jesse married a plural wife without telling Ruth. The two families lived in separate households, and when Jesse was living with the other household, Ruth was left alone to care for their twelve children. The difficult living situation for Ruth was compounded when Jesse lost his business and incurred such large debts that her home was sold. To help solve their indebtedness, Ruth managed the St. Omer Boarding House in 1900. Once again, she faced the issue of equal pay.

Hoping to make a difference for all women in Utah's workforce, Ruth helped draft the suffrage clause of the Utah Constitution during the 1895 Constitutional Convention. She served as president of the Utah Woman's Press Club and as treasurer of the Utah Woman Suffrage Association.[6]

In 1914 Ruth was hired as a typist for the Young Ladies' Mutual Improvement Association (YLMIA).[7] The menial job turned into years of devoted and unpaid service to the YLMIA when Ruth became first counselor to President Martha Horne Tingey from 1905 to 1929.

Even though she had served for twenty-four years as a counselor, Ruth was surprised to be called as president of the YLMIA in 1929. At the time of her call, she was seventy-five years old. When President Heber J. Grant set her apart for the calling, he promised Ruth that she would have "the same vigor of body and mind in the future" that she enjoyed in the past and "great joy, peace and happiness." In her eight years as president of YLMIA, Ruth wrote many poems. The most remembered is "Carry On," written for the June 1930 centennial celebration of the LDS Church. For the celebration, LDS youth chose the theme "Onward with Mormon Ideals," a theme that inspired Ruth to write "Carry On." When the youth sang her hymn at the conference held on June 8, 1930, in the Salt Lake Tabernacle, Ruth said, "I was thrilled to hear an army of young men and women vocalizing the pledge to continue the work of their noble fathers."[8]

Ruth's long life included the pioneer era and the era of women's suffrage. As time passed, Ruth saw both eras end. She died on April 12, 1958, in Salt Lake City at age 104.[9] Throughout a lifetime of meeting challenges head-on, Ruth demonstrated to admiring LDS youth that the correct course to choose is to "carry on," no matter the circumstance.

1   Linda Thatcher, "'I Care Nothing for Politics': Ruth May Fox, Forgotten Suffragist," *Utah Historical Quarterly,* Vol. 49, no. 3 (Summer 1981), 240.
2   Janet Peterson, "Carry On! Carry On!," *Ensign,* August 2004, 34.
3   Ibid.
4   Thatcher, 240.
5   Ibid., 241.
6   Ibid., 243.
7   Ibid., 241–242.
8   Peterson, 33.
9   Thatcher, 243.

MARY FIELD GARNER

Being a Witness

Used by permission from Daughters of Utah Pioneers.

Mary Field Garner was the last surviving person to have known the Prophet Joseph Smith, living ninety-nine years after his martyrdom. Born when Andrew Jackson was president of the United States, she lived through twenty-six presidential administrations. She saw the beginning of steamboats, the cotton gin, the reaper, and the telegraph. She lived to use the telephone, electric lights, and the television. When asked if she had ridden in an airplane, she said that "she'd rather keep one foot on the ground."[1] When Mary was 100 years old, her descendants numbered 465. She lived to welcome six generations of her own posterity, which numbered more than 600 descendants at her death.

Daughter of William Field and Mary Harding, Mary was born February 1, 1836, in Stanley Hill, Bosbury, Herefordshire, England. Her parents were members of the United Brethren in Herefordshire when Mormon missionary Wilford Woodruff taught them the gospel of Jesus Christ. Her father and mother were baptized in 1840; along with their children, including four-year-old Mary, they journeyed to America and settled in Nauvoo. In Nauvoo, Mary recalled, "My father did not have enough money to buy a home, so we rented a house from one of the Saints." After his death, her family's poverty deepened. "We were very poor and had very little to eat—corn meal being our main food," said Mary. "Oh how hungry we were for something else to eat!"[2]

Mary recalled being in the presence of the Prophet Joseph Smith, saying, "No greater words have ever been uttered by man than the teachings of the Prophet Joseph." To her, Joseph was a "very dignified looking man and in his uniform of a general he was noble and kingly looking."[3]

When Joseph was martyred, Mary recalled trying to "be as calm as possible, although we were very grieved over the terrible tragedy. The bodies of Joseph and Hyrum were placed in rude lumber boxes and put in a wagon and each was covered with an Indian blanket and then with brushes to protect them from the hot sun. I was with the Saints who met them outside the city and followed them to the Nauvoo Mansion House. . . . Mother took us children to view the bodies after they were prepared for burial."[4]

Mary and her family followed the leadership of Brigham Young. "I, with my mother, was present at the meeting in the bowery when the mantle of Joseph fell upon Brigham Young while he was talking with the people," she recalled. "We saw the form of the Prophet Joseph standing before us. Brother Brigham looked and talked so much like Joseph that for a minute we thought it was Joseph."

When mobs drove Mormons from the town in 1846, Mary's mother "had some bread already in the kettles to bake. Of course she did not have time to bake so she hung it on the reach of our wagon and cooked it after we crossed the Mississippi River."

She and her family journeyed from Nauvoo to Council Bluffs, where Mary first met William Garner. They then trekked across the plains to the Salt Lake Valley. On the trek, Mary helped drive a team of oxen. Most memorable, however, was her encounter with Native Americans: "I had long, red, curly hair, in ringlets down my back. This seemed to attract the Redmen." One Indian chief took a fancy to her and "wanted mother to give me to him. He said he would give her many ponies for me."[5] Her mother refused. To keep Mary safe, she hid her in between feather beds in the wagon.

Once in the Salt Lake Valley, Mary and her family were called to settle in Slaterville, Weber County, where Mary became reacquainted with William Garner. They married on November 1, 1856, and became the parents of ten children, five born in Slaterville and five in Hooper, a small town a few miles away. William supported his family as a farmer until being called on a mission to England in 1882.

After William died in 1915, Mary spent many years alone. Asked why she had such a long life, she said, "I always eat good, plain, wholesome foods and have plenty of sleep. I listen to the news broadcasts and especially the war news."[6]

At age ninety-five, Mary's mind was still sound. Up until that advanced age, she had never worn glasses or a hearing aid. She walked erect and had never used a cane. At age 107 she fell and broke her hip; she died shortly after on July 20, 1943, in Hooper. At her funeral, relatives were asked to move to the front of the chapel so that others could find a seat. "All of us are her descendants," was the response.[7]

At age 105, Mary realized that she was the only living witness to have seen and known the Prophet Joseph Smith. With that realization came a deep conviction that she must bear testimony to the world of his prophetic calling. In so doing, Mary spoke often of the truthfulness of the gospel, as revealed by the Prophet Joseph Smith, that Jesus Christ is the Savior of mankind, that Joseph Smith was a true and living prophet of God, that he was divinely called of God to establish His true gospel on the earth in this last dispensation. That he was "a true and faithful leader of the saints and the princip[les] he advocated were true and correct beyond doubt. That he lived the gospel as he taught it to his people, that he did seal his testimony with his blood."[8]

1   Gladys Hobbs, "Very Young Old Lady of 100 Coming to Salt Lake to Ride Merry-Go-Round During Covered Wagon Days," *Deseret News,* June 25, 1936.

2   Anne Garner Bafton, "The Last Leaf on the Tree: The Story of Mary Field Garner," http://earlylds.com/showmedia/php?&mediaID=17&page=20&tngprint=1; Mary Field Garner Autobiography 1880 (typescript), 2.

3   Mary Field Garner Autobiography, 4.

4   Ibid., 7.

5   Mary Field Garner as told to Harold H. Jenson, "The Last Leaf," *LDS Church News,* August 24, 1957; Autobiography, 7.

6   "Life of Mary Field Garner," 11.

7   Ibid., 12.

8   Ibid.

SUSA YOUNG GATES

Ambition

Learning music and ballet was not enough for the talented twelve-year-old Susa Young. She enrolled in a shorthand class, thinking that one day shorthand might come in handy. In her class of fifty students, she excelled. Recognizing her exceptional ability, Brigham Young asked Susa to be his personal secretary in recording the dedication events of the St. George Temple. In April 1893, she was asked to transcribe the official notes of the Salt Lake Temple dedication.

Writing, in any form and on most subjects, came easy to Susa. But when writing in defense of her religious values, few had the tenacity to express conviction in such an unrestrained manner. When writing of the role of LDS women, she was no less tenacious. She did not hesitate to reject societal borders: "Woman's sphere hitherto confined expressly within the four walls of her home, was now to be limited only by the confines of the Kingdom of God itself."[1] In her day, Susa was recognized as the most "versatile and prolific LDS writer ever to take up the pen in defense of her religion."[2]

Daughter of President Brigham Young and Lucy Bigelow, Susa Young Gates was born March 18, 1856, in downtown Salt Lake City.[3]

She grew to womanhood in the Lion House. During her formative years, Susa was recognized for "her talents in many lines of endeavor—domestic science, music, editing, and writing."[4] By age thirteen, she was a beginning student at the University of Deseret, and by age fourteen, named associate editor of the *College Lantern,* one of the first student newspapers in the West.

In 1872, sixteen-year-old Susa married Alma B. Dunford, a dentist. She bore Alma two children—Bailey and Leah. Their marriage ended in divorce in 1877. A custody battle over the children followed. Susa retained custody of her son, Bailey. Alma was awarded custody of the two-year-old daughter, Leah. Although other women would have been bitter over the court decision, Susa wrote to her mother, "God help me to be worthy of the good opinion of all the true Saints." She then penned of her sure knowledge that the Lord still had a great purpose for her: "Oh I know I am young and have a destiny in this Church to fulfill."[5]

Her destiny began to unfold in 1878 when Susa entered Brigham Young Academy at Provo. She was not content to just attend classes as a student. She taught voice lessons and organized a choir as an extracurricular activity.[6] Before the year was out, Principal Karl G. Maeser was extolling her talent. He named twenty-two-year-old Susa head of the Music Department and appointed her a faculty member of the Domestic Science Department.

Two years later, on January 5, 1880, Susa married Jacob F. Gates. She bore Jacob thirteen children, only four living to adulthood. In spite of Susa's repeated pregnancies, she and Jacob served an LDS mission to the Sandwich Islands. After their return to Utah, Susa founded and edited the *Young Woman's Journal,* a periodical for young LDS women. Through the journal, she became known as "Aunt Susa." In 1897 the Young Ladies' Mutual Improvement Association adopted her journal as its official publication.

In 1897 she was employed as a faculty member, teaching classes in "special physiology which treated basic anatomy, hygiene, and sex education" and was appointed to the board of regents of Brigham Young Academy;[7] she was a trustee from 1891 to 1933. She was never intimidated by the male-dominated board. For example, Susa told President Franklin Harris that he needed to "get a new class of teachers: real Latter-day Saint men instead of philosophers and theorists."[8]

In 1900 the strain of academic work and personal sorrow overcame Susa. During the next three years, her emotional struggles were very evident. During this difficult time, she often said, "Keep busy in the face of discouragement." She kept busy by learning to "discipline my taste, my desires and my impulses—severely disciplining my appetite, my tongue, my acts . . . and how I prayed!"[9]

By 1906 her health had returned, and she immediately jumped into self-motivated projects. She organized genealogical sections in *The Inter Mountain Republic* and the *Deseret News,* and wrote columns for both papers over the next ten years. She served on the board of trustees of the Utah State Agricultural College from 1906 to 1912. In 1914 she founded the *Relief Society Magazine,* which later became the official publication of the society. Susa also wrote a biography of her father, *The Life Story of Brigham Young,* and wrote two novels and four nonfiction books.

Susa also served for twenty-two years on the general boards of the YLMIA and the Relief Society, where she was proactive in espousing women's rights, suffrage, and enrollment in high school and college. She helped found the Utah chapters of the Daughters of the American Revolution, Daughters of the Utah Pioneers, and the National Woman's Press Club. She was a delegate to meetings of the International Council of Women in Rome and Copenhagen. She represented the LDS Church and the YLMIA on the National Council of Women. She associated with prominent women in the United States, including Clara Barton of the Red Cross and Susan B. Anthony, a famous suffragette. When Susan B. Anthony offered Susa the presidency of the National Council of Women if only she would abandon Mormonism, Susa countered, "The price was too high."[10]

In her later years, Susa turned her time and talents to genealogy. She served as head of the Research Department and Library of the Genealogical Society of Utah. She cataloged more than 16,000 names for the Young family. She also served as an ordinance worker in the Salt Lake Temple. Susa died on May 27, 1933, in Salt Lake City at age seventy-seven.

Few women rival the accomplishments, energy, or pace of Susa Young Gates. She did not confine herself to "the four walls of her home," and her life was defined by "the confines of the Kingdom of God."[11] Neither domestic sorrow nor personal heartache slowed down her contributions. She pressed forward, often at great personal sacrifice, to become the most prolific LDS writer of her time.

1   *The Relief Society Magazine,* Vol. VI, no. 3 (Salt Lake City: General Board of the Relief Society, March 1919), 139.
2   Ralph Paul Cracroft, "Susa Young Gates: Her Life and Literary Work," Master's Thesis, University of Utah, 1951, 73.
3   Louise Plummer, "Gates, Susa Young," in *Encyclopedia of Mormonism* 2:535–536; "Discover Your Heritage: Susa Young Gates," *New Era,* November 1973, 13.
4   Ernest L. Wilkinson, ed., *Brigham Young University: The First Hundred Years* (Provo, Utah: Brigham Young University Press, 1975), 2:730.
5   Susan Evans McCloud, "'An Extraordinary Initiative Power': Susa Young Gates, 1856–1933," in Barbara B. Smith and Blythe Darlyn Thatcher, eds., *Heroines of the Restoration* (Salt Lake City: Bookcraft, 1997), 235.
6   See Zina Young Card, "Sketch of School Life in the Brigham Young Academy, 1878-1884," 5, as cited in Wilkinson, 1:185.
7   Wilkinson, 1:484.
8   Susa Young Gates to Franklin Harris, February 27, 1930, as cited in Wilkinson, 2:221.
9   Carolyn W. D. Person, "Susa Young Gates," in Claudia L. Bushman, ed., *Mormon Sisters: Women in Early Utah* (Cambridge, Massachusetts: Emmeline Press, 1976), 208, 212.
10   Wilkinson, 2:768.
11   *The Relief Society Magazine,* 139.

RACHEL IVINS GRANT

Service

Rachel Ivins Grant faced many struggles in her life, yet viewed herself blessed of God. "Poverty, widowhood, obscurity in office, and total deafness," wrote Susa Young Gates, "soul-handicaps which would have crushed or stultified a weaker woman—these were but ladder-steps on which the angels flitted up and down between Aunt Rachel Grant and God."[1] She became the mother of Heber J. Grant, the seventh president of The Church of Jesus Christ of Latter-day Saints.

Daughter of Caleb and Edith Ridgway Ivins, Rachel was born March 7, 1821, in Hornerstown, New Jersey. When she was four, her father suffered sunstroke; for the next two years, he was like a little child and had to be fed and cared for like an infant. He died when Rachel was six; three years later, her mother died. These early hardships, too difficult for most children to bear, were just the beginning of the trials that beset Rachel throughout her life. She grew to adulthood in the home of grandparents and cousins, where she learned domestic skills that would serve her well the remainder of her life.

In her youth, Rachel was "religiously inclined but not of the long-faced variety" like her Quaker cousins. She said, "I thought religion

ought to make people happier and that was the kind of religion I was looking for."[2] With the consent of her cousins, she joined the Baptists. "The singing pleased me and the prayers were somewhat inspiring, but the sermons were not much more satisfactory than the none-at-all of the Quakers."[3] When Rachel attended her first Mormon service, she wrote, "Upon returning home I went to my room, knelt down, and asked the Lord to forgive me for thus breaking the Sabbath day."[4]

Yet she and other family members accepted the Mormon faith and gathered with the Latter-day Saints in Nauvoo, Illinois. As Emmeline B. Wells recalled, "One could easily discern the subdued Quaker pride in her method of using it, for Sister Rachel had the air, the tone, and mannerisms of the Quakers."[5] For Rachel, her time in Nauvoo proved to be turbulent. Her cousin Charles Ivins took part in the *Nauvoo Expositor* conspiracy. Her cousin James Ivins and family chose to join with apostate James Strang. As for Rachel, her future seemed uncertain. She returned to New Jersey, but did not cast aside her faith in the Restoration.

By spring 1853, Rachel knew she needed to join Latter-day Saints in the Salt Lake Valley. Although family members tried to dissuade her, she journeyed west. For her, the trek was very pleasant; dry air and outdoor life cured her of a persistent cough and she enjoyed the ever-changing scenery.

Once in the valley, Rachel received several offers of marriage, but none suited her fancy until Jedediah Morgan Grant asked her to marry him. "Without a love story, but with mutual respect and common aspirations,"[6] she married Jedediah on November 29, 1855, and became his seventh and last wife. At the time, she was thirty-four and Jedediah was thirty-nine.

Just twelve months and two days after their marriage, Rachel gave birth to her only child, Heber Jeddy Grant; nine days later, Jedediah died. Rachel then married George D. Grant, an older brother of Jedediah, but the marriage ended in divorce. Fortunately, she had enough funds to purchase a small adobe house on 14 South and 200

East in Salt Lake City, where she and Heber lived. To support herself and her son, Rachel did custom sewing for the Salt Lake Theater and also took in boarders. "I never felt humiliated at having to work and support myself and [Heber]," penned Rachel, "and I thanked my heavenly Father for giving me the strength and ability to do it." [7]

When Bishop Edwin D. Wooley visited her home and saw a half dozen or so buckets on the floor to catch rain from the roof, he said, "Why, Widow Grant, this will never do. I shall take some of the money from the fast offering and put a new roof on this house." "Oh, no, you won't," said Rachel. "No relief money will ever put a roof on my house. I have sewing here, and I have supported myself and my son with a needle and thread for many years. . . . When I get through with this sewing that I'm doing now, I will buy some shingles and patch the holes in the roof."[8]

In 1868, when Heber was only twelve, Rachel lost her hearing. Her last forty years were spent in almost total silence. She contended that being deaf meant that "she missed a great deal of unpleasantness, because people didn't bother to tell her scandal, while they always brought her any good news."[9] For thirty-five of those forty years of silence, she was president of her ward Relief Society. In that capacity, she presided over meetings and supervised sewing projects, including the making of carpets for the Salt Lake Temple. As a tribute to her service, Susa Young Gates wrote, "For many, many years she meekly, grandly stood as leader of her sex in one small ward."[10] To perhaps cheer up her spirits, "she kept a hymn book under her pillow, and sometimes, when she couldn't sleep, she would turn on the light and read hymn after hymn."[11]

Although Rachel was often alone, she "had good books and pleasant memories to keep her company."[12] She died in her eighty-seventh year on January 27, 1909. Just before her death, she said, "I have far more friends and loved ones on the other side than I have here."[13]

In the life of Rachel Grant is found a belief in the goodness of God and a willingness to serve others when her own needs were great. Her

greatest need was to prepare Heber for the important work that would be his in the kingdom of God. Acting as both father and mother, she loved him and showed him the way to greater happiness through looking to God for support and giving service to others. Heber said of her, "Mother was indeed a lovable character, always looking for the good in others."[14]

1   Susa Young Gates, "A Tribute to Rachel Ivins Grant," *Young Woman's Journal* 21, January 1910, 30. (See also May Booth Talmage, "Coronets of Age: Rachel R. Grant," *Young Woman's Journal* 19, April 1908, 182–185; "Rachel Ridgeway Ivins Grant," *Improvement Era,* June 1909, 585–599; Ronald W. Walker, "Rachel R. Grant: The Continuing Legacy of the Feminine Ideal," *Dialogue: A Journal of Mormon Thought* 15, Autumn 1982, 105–121.)

2   Leonard J. Arrington, Susan Arrington Madsen, and Emily Madsen Jones, *Mothers of the Prophets* (Salt Lake City: Bookcraft, 2001), 114.

3   Mary Grant Judd, "Rachel Ridgway Ivins Grant," *Relief Society Magazine* 30, April 1943, 228–229; Leon R. Hartshorn, comp., *Remarkable Stories from the Lives of Latter-day Saint Women,* Vol. 1 (Salt Lake City: Deseret Book, 1973), 37.

4   Frances Bennett Jeppson, "With Joy Wend Your Way: The Life of Rachel Ivins Grant, My Great-Grandmother," n. p., 1952, L. Tom Perry Special Collections, Harold B. Lee Library, Brigham Young University, Provo, Utah, 3.

5   Arrington, Madsen, and Jones, 115.

6   Jeppson, 10–11.

7   Arrington, Madsen, and Jones, 122–123.

8   Bryant S. Hinckley, *Heber J. Grant, Highlights in the Life of a Great Leader* (Salt Lake City: Deseret Book, 1951), 38–39.

9   Jeppson, 13.

10   Gates, 30

11   Jeppson, 19.

12   Ibid.

13   Arrington, Madsen, and Jones, 124.

14   Ibid., 110.

SHANNON HALE

Humility

Newberry Award winner and *New York Times* bestselling author Shannon Hale has an interesting persepective on rejection: it's not always "a bad thing. It isn't a condemnation of you or your book. It's just saying you haven't found the right home yet, and keep trying until you find the right place."[1] For Shannon, perseverance and a willingness to overcome rejection were necessary as she pursued her dream to become a writer.

Shannon Bryner Hale was born January 26, 1974, in Salt Lake City and had a childhood filled with imagination. At first she had to beg her older sisters to participate in her games and plays, but by the time she was in third grade, her teacher recognized Shannon's talents and encouraged classmates to read her original poetry and act in her creative plays. Her fourth-grade teacher, Mrs. Spackman, suggested that Shannon write fictional stories and poetry.[2] And at age ten, Shannon announced that one day she would be a writer.

Shannon took creative writing as an elective in high school and served as a fictional editor for the school's literary magazine. She also participated in the community theater production of *The Secret*

Garden. "Theater is very good for relationships. It's also very helpful for a writer," she says. "Acting is about character creation; directing is about world creation. I feel the benefit of those skills when I sit down alone to write."[3]

Shannon attended the University of Utah with a double major of English and theater—until realizing that she had "two impossible dreams—being a writer and an actor." She reflected:

> My writing was going nowhere. I was never able to finish any book I started, and I felt that my poems and short stories were weak. So I had to decide—what's my real passion? Acting came close, but in the end, I knew that I didn't have "it." That sparkle, that presence, that look. As hard as I worked, so much of acting is out of your hands—you have to be cast. And I realized that writing books truly was my utmost desire, even though I didn't know what kinds of books I wanted to write.[4]

Shannon stepped away from making a career choice while serving an LDS mission in Paraguay. She reflected:

> It was very, very hard being away from family and friends and working so hard, but it was also so wonderful. Besides being a spiritual experience, it was marvelous to take myself out of myself, to not think about what I wanted and to focus on other people. As a writer, it was wonderful training to imagine new cultures. It was also intensely educating in humanity—people are people wherever you go.[5]

Home from her mission, Shanon started dating Dean Hale, an old friend from high school; a year later, they ended their relationship. Shannon decided to move on with her life and attend graduate school at the University of Montana, but she was disappointed when she was the only student in her graduate program that was not offered a teaching assistant position—positions that, according to her professor, went to only the best writers. "I was never considered the best or the brightest at any stage in my education," she said, "and that's never a good indication of whether or not you've got what it takes."[6]

After her first year at the university, she decided to become a short-story writer. She wrote a hundred stories hoping that several would be published; all were rejected. Shannon said, "I still have all the rejection letters for my short stories laminated into a long roll I show during high school visits."[7] Despite that setback, she was happy: she became engaged to Dean Hale before returning for her second year of graduate studies. The couple lived in Utah; Shannon took a job as an instructional designer, spending her lunch breaks on a fairytale she had begun in graduate school.

By the summer of 2001, the fairytale was finished. A literary agent agreed to shop her book, but she again faced rejection until UK-based Bloomsbury made an offer on her manuscript. Shannon was elated that *The Goose Girl*—like many of her other books, written for children—would be published.[8] Of her inspiration for these books, she says:

> I think the stories of our childhood have the most power. They're the ones we think and wonder about when we're at that stage where we wonder most. And as we grow up, they're still there, in the deepest parts of our brains, still being worked out. . . . As a writer, my greatest interest is in the story. . . . So when I set out to write a book, for me it's got to be a story that's engaging, fathomless, and worth telling.[9]

Shannon's books have won many awards. *The Goose Girl* is an ALA Teens' Top Ten and Josette Frank Award winner. *Princess Academy* is a Newberry Honor Book and a *New York Times* bestseller. *Book of a Thousand Days* has received the CYBILS award. Shannon has

also authored two adult novels—*Austenland* and *The Actor and the Housewife*—and two novels with her husband, *Rapunzel's Revenge* and *Calamity Jack.*

A strong determination to pursue her dreams has paid off in a big way—something that would not have happened if Shannon had recoiled at the first sign of rejection. Instead, she pressed forward in spite of repeated disappointments. *The Goose Girl,* which was initially repeatedly rejected, went on to be one of her most successful books, with hundreds of thousands of books in print in fifteen languages.[10]

1   Matthew Peterson interview of Shannon Hale, "The Author Hour.com: Shannon Hale," October 22, 2009, http://theauthorhour.com/shannon-hale/.

2   "Shannon Hale," interview by *Kids Reads,* Kidsreads.com, August 2005, www.kidsreads.com/authors/au-hale-shannon.asp.

3   Shannon Hale, "Ridiculously Long Bio," www.squeetus.com/stage/shannon_longbio.htm (accessed September 1, 2010).

4   Ibid.

5   Ibid.

6   Ibid.

7   Dennis Lythgoe, "Life is Hectic for Novelist," *Deseret News,* July 8, 2007.

8   Hale.

9   Shannon Hale, interview by *Embracing the Child,* Embracingthechild.org, July 2003.

10 Peterson interview of Shannon Hale.

PAULA HAWKINS

Activism

Courtesy United States Congress.

A devoted Latter-day Saint and self-described "housewife" from
Maitland, Florida, Paula Hawkins was the first woman elected to the U.S.
Senate from the southern states. Florida Governor Charlie Crist praised
her for being a pioneer in the political arena, saying, "Paula Hawkins'
pioneering spirit earned her the respect of Floridians, fellow senators
and all who worked alongside her."[1] History books will record her many
firsts—first female Florida Public Service Commissioner, first female U.S.
Senator from Florida, and first female Senator from the entire South.

Daughter of Paul and Leone Fickes, Paula was born January 24, 1927,
in Salt Lake City. Her father worked as a Naval chief warrant officer in
Salt Lake before accepting employment with Georgia Tech in Atlanta in
1934, when Paula was six. Paula attended public school in Atlanta until
her parents divorced when she was in high school; she then returned to
Utah with her mother and finished her schooling in Richmond.

From 1944 to 1947 Paula attended Utah State University in Logan,
Utah, where she met Walter Eugene (Gene) Hawkins. They married
September 5, 1947, and became the parents of three children.

After ten years of marriage and with the encouragement of Gene,

Paula began her political career. In the late 1950s she fought Maitland City Hall to get sewers put in her neighborhood. Her victory as a community activist had a lasting impact on Paula's political aspirations. In 1972 she was the first woman elected to a statewide office in Florida when she won a seat on the Florida Public Service Commission. She ran for the U.S. Senate in 1974 and lost. She ran for Lieutenant Governor in 1978 and lost again. Believing the third time would be the charm, Paula again ran for the U.S. Senate in 1980. To the surprise of many constituents, she garnered 52 percent of the vote.

Washington, DC, was not prepared for a female senator from the South, let alone her husband. Paula was the first senator to bring her husband with her to Washington. This forced the exclusive Senate Wives' Club to change its name to the Senate Spouses' Club and embrace Gene as a member.

During her single six-year term as the junior Republican senator from Florida, Paula was visible and outspoken. She positioned herself as an enemy of drug dealers and as a champion of working mothers and children. She helped push through legislation to cut aid to all foreign countries that refused to reduce drug production. She helped create the Senate Caucus on International Narcotics Control and served as the U.S. representative to the Organization of International-American Drug Abuse Commission.

Paula also supported legislation that helped women enter the work force after divorce or widowhood. She voted for equalizing pension benefits for women by taking into account years spent rearing children in the home. She fought for tax breaks on childcare expenses and pushed through the Missing Children's Act of 1982, helping to establish a national clearinghouse for information about missing children. Why was Paula such a strong advocate for children? In 1984 at a Congressional hearing, she disclosed that she had been sexually molested as a child. In 1986 she wrote *Child at Risk, My Fight against Child Abuse.*[2]

With such a strong emphasis on women and children, it surprised her constituents that Paula opposed abortion-on-demand and the Equal Rights Amendment. "I did not like the Equal Rights Amendment," she said. "I predicted that it would bring about the downfall of the father's responsibility to support the family."[3]

In 1986 Paula lost her bid for a second term in the Senate to Democratic contender Florida Governor Bob Graham. "I want you all to know that I look back, not with regret," she said. "But to six years ago when we promised the people of Florida that if I went to Washington, you'd know I was there and I would make a difference."[4]

Although never again elected to a political position, Paula remained in public service. In 1987 she was a delegate to the United Nations Drug Conference in Vienna, and in 1989 she served as a delegate to the United Kingdom/United Nations Cocaine Summit in London. Such service was curbed, however, when a studio partition toppled during one of her television interviews. She was knocked unconscious by the partition, and over the next several years she made regular visits to physical therapists and spent much time in traction. After suffering a stroke in 1998, she was confined to a wheelchair. Paula died on December 4, 2009, in a hospital in Orlando at age eighty-two.[5]

As Paula recalled the path-breaking course she set in the U.S. Senate, she said, "I think it showed other women that you could do this."[6] President Ronald Reagan viewed her accomplishments in the Senate as more than projecting a clear political path for women: "Paula's been a leader on many issues. She championed using diplomacy against drugs as well as issues like missing children and child abuse." He claimed that "in her work against illegal drugs and for children, she's making a difference for an entire generation."[7]

1   Mike Schneider, "First Mormon Woman Elected to Senate Dies," *Mormon Times,* December 12, 2009, 4.
2   See Paula Hawkins, *Child at Risk, My Fight against Child Abuse: A Personal Story and a Public Plea* (Bethesda, Maryland: Alder and Alder, 1986).
3   Schneider, 4.
4   Ibid.
5   See "Former Sen. Paula Hawkins dies at 82," Associated press via *Orlando Sentinel,* December 4, 2009.
6   Schneider 4.
7   President Ronald Reagan, "Remarks at a Campaign Rally for Senator Paula Hawkins in Tampa, Florida, October 24, 1986," http://www.reagan.utexas.edu/archives/speeches/1986/102486b.htm.

DRUSILLA DORRIS HENDRICKS

Courage

Soon after the death of her husband, sixty-seven-year-old Drusilla Dorris Hendricks wrote her life story. At the time she did not realize that family and historians alike would view her first and foremost as a Latter-day Saint woman who courageously held fast to the truths of the gospel when her circumstances in life were difficult to the extreme.[1]

Drusilla Dorris, daughter of William Dorris and Catherine Frost, was born February 8, 1810, in Sumner County, Tennessee. Her parents were Baptists and her neighbors were Methodists and Presbyterians; she recalled hearing "much contention on religion" in her home and neighborhood. She was an eyewitness to the "jerks and dancing" symbolic of the spirit of revivalism spreading through the South in the early nineteenth century.[2] Reading the Bible led Drusilla to conclude that she was a sinner: "Lord, have mercy on me and save me from the Awful place I had heard so much about."[3]

At age seventeen Drusilla married James Hendricks,[4] and they soon joined the Baptist church. Disappointed at not finding greater religious truths in worship services of the Baptists, Drusilla penned, "I was no better satisfied than before." Two years later when Elders James

Emmet and Peter Dustin came to Simpson, Kentucky, her brother-in-law insisted that Drusilla listen to the Mormon elders. "You have read so much that you can catch their errors in the scriptures," he told her. Drusilla was curious and went to hear them preach. "Those Elders brought the same light that Jesus had in the days of John the Baptist," she said. She returned home rejoicing, although her "brother-in-law was so mad he could not talk decent."[5]

Drusilla wrote of her baptism, "I arose to walk in the newness of life. That fear of death and Hell was all gone from me, and I was a new creature. Such a feeling of calmness pervaded me for months, and my husband had the same feelings."[6] In spring 1836 James and Drusilla sold out their interest in Simpson, Kentucky, and moved to northern Missouri to be with other Latter-day Saints. Drusilla wrote, "I never lived happier in my life."[7]

But the fight on election day at Gallatin, Missouri, between Mormons and their neighbors ended much of her happiness.[8] On Thursday, October 25, 1838, in the Battle of Crooked River, James was shot in the neck. When Drusilla reached James, "He could speak but could not move any more than if he were dead." In an attempt to revive his muscles Drusilla "rubbed and steamed him but could get no circulation. He was dead from his neck down."[9]

After a series of other mishaps, Drusilla paused to wonder aloud if she were sorry for the decision she had made to become a Mormon. She concluded, "I am not, I did what was right, if I die I am glad I was baptized for the remission of my sins, for I have an answer of a good conscience." It was then that she heard a still, small voice say, "Hold on, for the Lord will provide."[10]

The Lord did provide for James and Drusilla and their family. Each time Drusilla began to despair, the Lord sent someone to provide for her needs. "I have just found out how the widow's crust and barrel held out through the famine," wrote Drusilla. "Just as it was out someone was sent to fill it." James slowly received strength; though he was still an invalid,

Drusilla remarked, "My husband by this time could turn on his elbows, turn his feet out of bed and begin to take things in one hand."[11]

To provide financially for her family, Drusilla took in washing and sewing. On January 19, 1840, "the High Council at Nauvoo voted to donate a city lot to Brother James Hendrix *[sic]*, who was shot in Missouri." Church leaders encouraged brethren to build a log house for the family, an act that was greatly appreciated.[12] Drusilla, of necessity, turned her attention to making money for the family.[13] She made and sold gingerbread and took in carpenters and mason who had come to Nauvoo to work on the temple. In exchange for rent, the boarders built a brick house for James and Drusilla.

In 1846, James and Drusilla left their house and most of their belongings to join the Mormon exodus to Iowa. They were en route when they encountered federal officers seeking LDS recruits to join a Mormon Battalion and fight in the Mexican War. Drusilla did not want her son William, the only eligible member of her family, to join the Mormon Battalion; he was all she had to depend on, since her husband was an invalid and her other son was only nine. Yet when Drusilla was alone, "whisperings of the spirit" suggested that William should join the battalion. "Be you afraid to trust the God of Israel? Has he not been with you in all your trials? Has he not provided for your wants?" she heard. She also heard a voice ask, "If I did not want the greatest glory." She answered, "Yes I did." "Then how can you get it without making the greatest sacrifice?" asked the voice. Upon answering, "Lord what lack I yet?" the voice said, "Let your son go in the battalion."[14] Believing these words were from God, Drusilla encouraged her oldest son, William, to join the epic march.

"I cannot tell the hardships we endured by his going," penned Drusilla.[15] During his absence of fifteen months the rest of the family journeyed with the Jedediah M. Grant wagon train to the Rockies, reaching the Salt Lake Valley on October 4, 1847.[16] The family settled temporarily in Fort Salt Lake before moving to Warm Springs to manage a bathhouse property of the LDS Church. These were happy days for Drusilla. "We made good gardens and the Lord blessed every move we made," she wrote. "I still wove, made gloves and rope and kept boarders for to gain a living." [17]

When James died in 1870, Drusilla viewed him as a "martyr for the cause of truth." Of him, she penned, "He often wanted the bretheren [sic] to lay hands on him to ease him from pain, but I could not ask the Lord to spare his life any longer, for I thought he had suffered long enough."[18] Her testimony, born in the crucible of affliction, was sure: "The Gospel is true. I have rejoiced in it through all my trials, for the Spirit of the Lord has buoyed me up, or I should have failed."[19]

1   "Historical Sketch of James Hendricks and Drusilla Dorris Hendricks (His Wife) [typescript]", 47, Mss. Sc. 2409 (Dictated by Drusilla Dorris Hendricks after the death of her husband. Copied by James Roskelley, grandson through Rebecca, from the original work, February 1904, Smithfield, Utah. Copied by Lela H. Johnson. L. Tom Perry Special Collections, Harold B. Lee Library, Brigham Young University, Provo, Utah); Kenneth W. Godfrey, Audrey M. Godfrey, and Jill Mulvay Derr, *Women's Voices: An Untold History of the Latter-day Saints, 1830-1900* (Salt Lake City: Deseret Book, 1982), 84–96.

2   "Historical Sketch," 2.

3   Ibid., 3–5.

4   See Andrew Jenson, *LDS Biographical Encyclopedia* (Salt Lake City: Western Epics, 1971), 2:403; Marguerite H. Allen, comp., *Henry Hendricks Genealogy* (Salt Lake City: The Hendricks Family Organization, 1963).

5   "Historical Sketch," 7–10.

6   Ibid., 13–14.

7   Ibid., 25.

8   For information on the election day fight in Gallatin, see Joseph Smith, *History the Church,* 3:56–58.

9   "Historical Sketch," 28–29.

10   Ibid., 29, 32–33.

11   Ibid., 33–34.

12   See *History of the Church,* 4:76, 312, 354.

13   "Historical Sketch," 34–35.

14   Ibid., 38–41.

15   Ibid., 42.

16   Mormon Pioneer Overland Trail, Church History Library.

17   B. H. Roberts, *A Comprehensive History of The Church of Jesus Christ of Latter-day Saints,* 6 vols. (Provo, Utah: Brigham Young University Press, 1961), 3:428

18   "Historical Sketch," 47.

19   Ibid.

MARJORIE PAY HINCKLEY

Optimism

Courtesy of the Church History Library, The Church
of Jesus Christ of Latter-day Saints.

Twenty-five-year-old Marjorie Pay was anticipating her wedding day when the telephone rang. "I think we had better go to lunch today," her fiancé, Gordon B. Hinckley, said. He did not tell her on the phone that he had cold feet and was trying to find a way out of the engagement. While ordering lunch Gordon warned his bride-to-be, "I think you should know that I only have $150 to my name." Marjorie's response was not what Gordon had expected: "Oh, that will work out just fine; if you've got $150, we're set!" Reflecting on her thoughts that day, Marjorie said, "Well, $150 sounded like a small fortune to me. I had hoped for a husband and now I was getting $150 too!"[1]

Born November 23, 1911, in Nephi, Utah, Marjorie had an ability to "see the good in any situation—and to see it instantly—mak[ing] Pollyanna look like an amateur." Her optimistic attitude included "a willingness to be flexible and adaptive, to not overreact to daily irritations." Her basic philosophy, "Things always work out somehow," proved a blessing in her life and the lives of those who knew her best.[2]

Marjorie never learned to ride a bicycle or swim, never went to college, and never viewed herself destined for fame.[3] Early in her marriage she realized it would be better if "we worked harder at getting accustomed to one another than constantly trying to change each other—which [she] discovered was impossible." She believed, "It is the artful duty of a woman to adjust."[4] And adjust she did, although Gordon never insisted that she do anything his way—or any way for that matter. He gave her space and "let her fly."[5]

She was a low-stress mother who tried not to over-schedule herself or her children. One day her oldest son came up missing when there were lawns to be mowed and irrigation ditches to be cleaned. When he showed up just in time for dinner she asked him, "Where have you been?" He replied, "Down in the hollow." She asked, "And what have you been doing down in the hollow?" He said, "Nothing." Years later when this same son returned from a mission he said to his mother, "Mom I had a wonderful childhood, didn't I?" Marjorie replied, "Oh, it was wonderful—those long summer days when you could lie on your back in the hollow and listen to the birds sing and watch the ants build their castles."[6]

Marjorie's willingness to look on the bright side of life was a constant source of strength to Gordon as he served in the leading councils of the LDS Church. After his call to the Quorum of the Twelve, Gordon was asked to travel extensively throughout the world. The night before a trip to South America that would take him away for several weeks, Marjorie asked whether she should plan to go with him. He replied, "Can't we decide that in the morning?"[7]

As Marjorie traveled with her husband, Gordon would often call on her to speak extemporaneously. "I can tell you why my husband has called on me," she would say. "It is because he is still trying to figure out what to say and I'm supposed to stall."[8] Audiences immediately responded to her humor because they felt "in Sister Hinckley, what you see is what you get—and that is what everyone wants to get! Her love, her honest interest in you as a person, her lack of affectation and self-aggrandizement, her faith—she is the real thing."[9] She once told

Church members, "I have a new project to read one chapter a day from each of the standard works. I've been on it four days and I'm only three days behind."[10] Another time when she and Gordon were informed by a Church security officer of a possible danger, Marjorie smiled and said, "It will be all right" and kept reading a book. When asked how she could remain so calm, she replied, "I stopped worrying about Gordon a long time ago because I knew it couldn't do much good. I just pray for him, ask him to be careful, and trust that the Lord knows every situation we are in."[11]

When her husband was sustained as president of the Church, Marjorie's easy-going manner and humor not only blessed him, it endeared her to Church members. Marjorie once told an audience that "sometimes as she is doing her housework the thought occurs to her of the reality that she is married to the prophet of the Lord. . . . Her first reaction is to think, 'I want my mother!'" In explaining what it is like to live with a prophet, she said, "He leaves his towels on the floor and his tie over the couch."[12]

Whether speaking to an audience or just one person, Marjorie always put others at ease because she was at ease with herself and never fussed over her appearance. Once when she was getting ready for a formal occasion her daughter dropped in to see her. When Marjorie started to put on a pleated skirt and white cotton blouse her daughter protested. "Mother, this is a huge thing. . . .The reception is in honor of Dad and you. He's probably going to wear a tux. Every woman there will have on sequins and diamonds." Continuing to dress, completely unruffled by her comment, Marjorie said, "Well, I don't have any sequins in my closet. But this skirt is black, and the blouse does have a lace collar. And besides that, if we're the guests of honor, whatever I wear will have to be right!"[13]

Marjorie died on April 6, 2004, in Salt Lake City. Did she ever imagine where her life would take her? "Absolutely not," she insisted.[14] It has been said that "Marjorie was faith, hope and charity personified.

It is the pure love of Christ everyone felt in her presence. It was the pure love of Christ that allowed her to stop worrying how the world saw and treated her and let her focus on how she treated others. She simply chose to see the best in any situation."[15]

1   Virginia H. Pearce, ed. *Glimpses into the Life and Heart of Marjorie Pay Hinckley* (Salt Lake City: Deseret Book, 1999), 77.
2   Ibid., 77, 145.
3   Doug Robinson, "Marjorie Hinckley—'Every bit his equal': The low-profile woman behind the high-profile man," *LDS Church News,* April 5, 2003.
4   Pearce, 184, 186.
5   "Til We Meet Again: Marjorie Hinckley's Funeral," *Meridian Magazine,* 2.
6   Ibid., 3.
7   Sheri L. Dew, *Go Forward with Faith: The Biography of Gordon B. Hinckley* (Salt Lake City: Deseret Book, 1996), 338.
8   Ibid.
9   Pearce, 40.
10   L. Tom Perry, "An Elect Lady," *Ensign,* May 1995, 73–75.
11   Deseretbook.com/mormon-life/news/story?story_id=3999.
12   Pearce, 108–109.
13   Deseretbook.com/mormon-life/news/strory?story_id=3999.
14   Ibid.
15   "Til We Meet Again," 4.

ALICE MERRILL HORNE

Culture

Courtesy of the Church History Library, The Church
of Jesus Christ of Latter-day Saints.

To Alice Merrill Horne, good taste and beauty made life more abundant. "God has created gifts, and men work so that we're not without poets, painters, sculptors, architects, craftsmen, gardeners and homemakers," she said. "So long as talent and industry unite there will be art—original, spontaneous, inspirational—the kind that lives."[1] Alice devoted her life to ennobling art in everyday life in Utah.

Daughter of Clarence Merrill and Bathsheba Smith, Alice was born January 2, 1868, in a log cabin in Fillmore, Utah. She began her schooling at age six in the old rock schoolhouse in Fillmore. By age eight, she left school and her family to be a companion to her grandmother, Bathsheba Smith, general president of the Relief Society and widow of George A. Smith. The remainder of Alice's childhood and youthful years were spent in Salt Lake City, where her doting grandmother introduced her to the leading women in town and encouraged her interest in art.

By age fourteen, Alice was ready to enter the University of Deseret. There she showed interest in art, art education, writing, and literature. She organized a Shakespearean Society on campus and invited George

Henry Horne, a fellow student, to attend. When she graduated in 1887, she was invited to speak at the commencement exercises; ever true to the arts, she read from Shakespeare.[2]

Alice became a teacher at Washington School in Salt Lake City before her marriage in 1890 to George Horne, then a Salt Lake banker. They became the parents of six children.

During her years of motherhood, Alice always kept one hand in the arts, if not two. In 1893 she represented Utah on the Liberal Arts Committee at the Chicago World's Fair. She also published a book of poems written by Utah poets, hoping to show an emerging cultural tone in the state.

From 1894 to 1896, while George served an LDS mission in the Southern States Mission, Alice returned to teaching at Washington School and took classes in art. It was during this time that she directly challenged the prescribed art program in the Salt Lake City School District. Twenty-six-year-old Alice used her well-placed connections in Salt Lake City to convince a member of the state board of education to replace the district's worn-out art training with a course in drawing by J. Leo Fairbanks, a Utah impressionist trained in Paris.

By the time George returned from his mission, Alice had launched a political career. When plans to widen State Street in downtown Salt Lake City included tearing down the Eagle Gate landmark, Alice convinced the highway commission to incorporate the Eagle Gate Monument in their plans for State Street.

In 1898 Alice announced that she would run for the Utah House of Representatives as a Democrat in Salt Lake's Eighth District. She was elected by a thousand-vote margin and served one term—the second woman to serve in that legislative body. Her main objective as a legislator was to "establish a state agency that would hold an annual art exhibition and make annual purchases of paintings to begin a permanent collection of art" in the state.[3] In her honor the state collection is still called the Alice Art Collection. That same bill was later used to establish a state orchestra known today as the Utah Symphony.

While in the legislature, Alice chaired the University Land Sites Committee that chose the present location of the University of Utah. She sponsored a bill to provide four-year tuition teaching scholarships for students at the University of Utah. Alice was also instrumental in pushing through legislation to stop smoking in the House chambers and cloakrooms during legislative sessions.[4]

When it came time for re-election in 1900, Alice chose not to run. She never again held an elective office in the state, but she kept herself in the public arena. She served as chair of the Salt Lake County Democratic Party for several years and as the Utah chair of the International Peace Committee. She also served as the second president of the Daughters of the Utah Pioneers and was a state regent of the Daughters of the Revolution. She was also chair of the Utah branch of the National Peace Society.

From 1902 to 1916 she was a member of the Relief Society general board, where she directed the society's art committee and helped prepare lessons on art appreciation for LDS sisters throughout the world. In 1904 she represented the Relief Society at the International Congress of Women in Berlin, Germany, where she spoke on the progress of art in Utah and on women in politics. In the 1930s she organized the Smokeless Fuel Federation, hoping to end the hazard of using coal as a home heating fuel. She and her friends set up a coal cook stove at the corner of Main Street and South Temple and baked rolls and pies to show that great food comes from cooking with smokeless coal—a type of coal in which oil and gas is removed.[5] In 1934 she was inducted into the Hall of Fame of the Salt Lake Council of Women.

Of her many contributions, none has had a bigger impact than her contributions to Utah art. She sponsored permanent art exhibits in Utah's schools[6] and also wrote a book, a children's play, and a periodical featuring news of art in Utah.

Alice died on October 7, 1948, of a heart attack at age eighty. Artist Minerva Teichert, who had been encouraged by Alice to continue her own artistic endeavors, spoke at her funeral: "Always was this great woman looking after the welfare of the artists, hoping they would be able to 'make a go of it' financially and still grow in spirit. Few people are so forgetful of self."[7] In 1954 Horne Hall, one of the Heritage Halls dormitories at Brigham Young University, was named in her honor.[8]

To Alice, art was not just an expression of self—it was a way of life. It communicated, inspired, and ennobled the onlooker. She believed that every home, no matter how small, deserved a good picture, for beauty could enhance even the humblest abode. Without equivocation, Alice made art a lifetime commitment; by so doing, she brought a greater sense of culture and the fine arts to the state of Utah.

1   Alice Merrill Horne, *Devotees and Their Shrines: A Handbook of Utah Art* (Salt Lake City: Deseret News, 1914), 8.
2   See Harriet Horne Arrington and Leonord J. Arrington, "Alice Merrill Horne, Cultural Entrepreneur," in Mary E. Stovall and Carol Cornwall Madsen, eds., *A Heritage of Faith* (Salt Lake City: Deseret Book, 1988), 128–129.
3   Harriet Horne Arrington, "Alice Merrill Horne: Art Promoter and Early Utah Legislature," in Colleen Whitley, ed., *Worth Their Salt: Notable but Often Unnoted Women of Utah* (Logan, Utah: Utah State University Press, 1996), 178.
4   See S. A. Kenner, *Utah As It Is* (Salt Lake City: Deseret News, 1904); *House Journal of the Third Session of the Legislature of the State of Utah* (Salt Lake City: Tribune Job Printing, 1899); Ralph V. Chamberlin, *The University of Utah: A History of Its First Hundred Years, 1850–1950* (Salt Lake City: University of Utah Press, 1960), 184–185.
5   Arrington, "Alice Merrill Horne: Art Promoter and Early Utah Legislature," 185–186.
6   See Robert S. Olpin, *Dictionary of Utah Art* (Salt Lake City: Salt Lake Art Center, 1980), 126–128; Raye Price, "Utah's Leading Ladies of the Arts," *Utah Historical Quarterly* Vol. 38, no. 1 (Winter 1970), 65–85.
7   Minerva K. Teichert, "Remarks at Funeral of Alice Merrill Horne, 10 October 1948," as cited in Whitley, 185.
8   Brigham Young University, "Alice Merrill Horne," *Dedication and Naming of 22 Buildings* (Provo, Utah: Brigham Young University, 1954), 50–51.

FLORENCE JACOBSEN

Happiness

Courtesy of the Church History Library, The Church
of Jesus Christ of Latter-day Saints.

"I have a marvelous heritage," says Florence Jacobsen. "I have two presidents of the Church as my grandfathers—President Joseph F. Smith and President Heber J. Grant." She laughingly adds, "I inherited my Grandfather Grant's nose, and it has taken me a long time to be proud of it." But she says that the most important gift she received from her ancestors is The Church of Jesus Christ of Latter-day Saints, because "the Church is designed to bring to you in your life everything that is worthwhile and the greatest happiness that is possible for mankind."[1] She found that happiness.

Florence was born April 7, 1913, and says, "I had the most wonderful parents that ever lived and am one of eight children—a large marvelous family—and I was taught the gospel from my babyhood."[2] She recalls being awakened at six each morning by her father, saying, "It's a beautiful morning! Time to get up." Before school or other activities, she was expected to work around the house; her job was to dust the living and dining rooms and make lunches for her father, her brothers, and herself. To her, the work was an opportunity to share in the responsibility of the home.

That attitude led Florence to major in home economics at the University of Utah, where she graduated in 1934. The next year she began a home of her own, marrying Ted Jacobsen, an engineering graduate from Utah State University, in the Salt Lake Temple. They became the parents of three sons. Ted supported Florence and the children as the leader of Jacobsen Construction, most noted for building the University of Utah Special Events Center, the Los Angeles Temple, and the Oakland Temple. He also served as chair of the Salt Lake City Chamber of Commerce, president of the Associated General Contractors, a member of the Utah State House of Representatives, and president of Temple Square, supervising hundreds of volunteer guides.

When Ted was called in 1955 to be president of the Eastern States Mission, Florence joined him in New York City.[3] Upon completion of that mission, Florence was called to serve on the general board of the Young Women's Mutual Improvement Association (YWMIA). Within one year, she was called as the sixth general president of that organization, serving from 1961 to 1972. (Her aunt and next-door neighbor, Lucy Grant Cannon, held the same position from 1937 to 1948.)

Florence remembers well the day she received that calling from President David O. McKay. Bertha Reeder, the YWMIA president, had lost her husband only a few weeks earlier. Florence said to President McKay, "Oh, President McKay, do you know what you are doing?" President McKay smiled and said, "I usually do."[4] During her tenure, the YWMIA celebrated its centennial in 1969 and launched the *New Era,* an LDS magazine for youth in 1971. Florence emphasized during her administration that each young girl was "born to be something special." She said to LDS girls throughout the world, "You have a special obligation in life to be an example to all the world in your high goals, actions, attitudes and accomplishments."[5] She taught the girls that it was important to plan, prepare, and conduct annual leadership conferences, set personal goals, meet with bishops in youth councils,

and plan their own activities.[6] Her leadership of the young led Stephen R. Covey, renowned author, to say, "[Florence] is undoubtedly one of the great women in our Church—a remarkable woman."[7]

Under her watch, the Lion House, which was operated by the YWMIA, was saved from the wrecking ball. Florence supervised the splendid restoration with meticulous care. She noted that the "ingrained carpet pattern copied for the Lion House carpet was originally made with seventeen colors and the manufacturer's largest looms had only twelve. To be able to restore it accurately, Sister Jacobsen negotiated—but did not compromise."[8] She and her husband went to England and negotiated with weavers to lay the extra colors by hand to assure the carpet was more authentic.

Florence was called to be the LDS Church curator by President Spencer W. Kimball. As curator, she was a key figure in the construction of the Museum of Church History and Art in Salt Lake City. She supervised the restoration of the Promised Valley Playhouse in Salt Lake City, the E. B. Grandin building in Palmyra, the Brigham Young home in St. George, the Jacob Hamblin home in Santa Clara, and the Newel K. Whitney store in Kirtland. Of all that she supervised, it was the refinished Manti Temple that gave her the greatest personal satisfaction. After all, it was her philosophy, "If you're going to produce anything beautiful—a beautiful dinner, a beautiful building, a beautiful life—it's going to take time."[9]

Through these efforts, Florence became known as a "lady in love with excellence." This unique reputation led to her call as director of the Church Arts and Sites Division. In this capacity, she supervised the first systematic catalogue of the artworks and historic artifacts of the Church. By collecting and displaying historic artifacts, she is credited with preserving the most significant artifacts of the Restoration. As to why she cared enough to preserve the past, she says, "We want members to see in the Church museum artifacts that reaffirm that the gospel has been restored. We want to enlarge the testimonies of members with the art and artifacts that were part of the Restoration and develop the desire in nonmembers to know more."[10]

Although there were many other accomplishments for Florence—including representing the United States at four international conferences, establishing an endowed scholarship, and generous donations to the Perpetual Education Fund—her work with young women and the preservation of Church artifacts is a lasting contribution to the worldwide Church. Why has she given so much of herself to these worthy causes? It has brought her great happiness and has provided an opportunity to remember her heritage. She says, "Each generation should improve on the previous generation and pass on a more immense, great, inspirational and positive heritage than was received."[11]

1   Florence S. Jacobsen, "Earning Your Own Heritage," *Speeches of the Year* (Provo, Utah: Extension Publications, Division of Continuing Education, Brigham Young University, 1967), 2, 7
2   Ibid., 2.
3   Scott R. Lloyd, "Life of Building," *LDS Church News,* May 1, 2010.
4   Jacobsen, 2.
5   Julie Dockstader Heaps, "Forever 'Young,'" *LDS Church News,* November 22, 2008.
6   Lavina Fielding, "Florence Smith Jacobsen: In Love with Excellence" *Ensign,* June 1977, 27.
7   Jacobsen, 1.
8   Fielding, 26.
9   Ibid.
10 Ibid., 25, 29.
11 Jacobsen, 2.

VIENNA JACQUES

Discretion

Courtesy of the Church History Library, The Church
of Jesus Christ of Latter-day Saints.

There are only two nineteenth-century women named in the Doctrine and Covenants. The first is Emma Smith, the wife of the Prophet Joseph Smith, and the second is Vienna Jacques (or Jaques). Much is known of Emma, but what of Vienna? Why was she named in scripture? Was it because of her "strict economy"?[1]

By the 1830s, Vienna was a nurse in the greater Boston area, where she attended Methodist services at the Bromfield Street Church in Boston until becoming dissatisfied with that religion. While investigating other Christian denominations, she learned of the Book of Mormon and sent for a copy.[2] After glancing through the book, she laid it aside until a vision of the book convinced her to pick it up and read the new witness of Jesus Christ. As she read, her mind became "illuminated."[3] Convinced of the truthfulness of the book, forty-three-year-old Vienna cast "strict economy" aside to travel by canal boat and then by stage to Kirtland, Ohio, to meet the translator of the Book of Mormon, Joseph Smith. Her meeting with Joseph led her to enter the waters of baptism.

Vienna remained in Ohio with fellow believers for about six weeks before returning to Boston, where she was instrumental in converting several family members to the Latter-day Saint faith. She again journeyed alone to Kirtland. This time she brought with her precious valuables, including $1,400 that she had carefully saved. On March 8, 1833, Joseph Smith directed Vienna to give all of her savings to the Church. Without hesitation, she offered the entire amount. For her unselfish consecration, the Lord through the Prophet Joseph told Vienna that she would "be rewarded in mine own due time." The Lord promised her "an inheritance from the hand of the bishop; That she may settle down in peace inasmuch as she is faithful."[4]

Joyful about possessing an inheritance in Zion (Jackson County, Missouri), Vienna planned to leave Kirtland immediately to secure that promised land—but being advised on April 20, 1833, to wait and journey with William Hobert, she delayed her departure. When Vienna and William finally reached Jackson County, word was sent to Joseph of their safe arrival. On July 2, 1833, he penned, "We rejoiced greatly to hear of the safe arrival of Sister Vienna Jacques and Brother William Hobart, and thank our Heavenly Father that their lives have been spared them till their arrival."[5]

Vienna received the promised inheritance but did not hold the land long before mobs forced her to abandon it. Although nearly penniless, she continued to give—this time with other talents. Near Fishing River she ministered to the needs of Heber C. Kimball, who penned, "I received great kindness . . . from sister Vienna Jaques, who administered to my wants and also to my brethren—may the Lord reward [her] kindness."[6]

On September 4, 1833, Joseph wrote to Vienna:

I have often felt a whispering since I received your letter, like this: "Joseph, thou art indebted to thy God for the offering of thy sister Vienna, which proved a savor of life as pertaining to thy pecuniary concerns. Therefore she should not be forgotten of thee, for the Lord hath done this, and thou shouldst remember her in all thy prayers and also by letter, for she often times calleth on the Lord, saying, O Lord, inspire thy servant Joseph to communicate by letter some word to thine unworthy handmaiden."[7]

In the same letter, Joseph told of being forewarned of the struggles that Vienna would experience in Missouri: "I was aware when you left Kirtland that the Lord would chasten you, but I prayed fervently in the name of Jesus that you might live to receive your inheritance. . . . I am not at all astonished at what has happened to you."[8] Unfortunately, other problems followed. A few years after her marriage to widower Daniel Shearer, marital discord led to a separation.

At age sixty, Vienna drove a wagon across the plains in the Charles C. Rich Company, arriving in the Salt Lake Valley on October 2, 1847. When she was given a city lot in the Salt Lake 12th Ward, Vienna believed the lot was her new land of inheritance. On this land, she lived out her days away from family. Friends said of Vienna that she lived a life of "strict obedience to the commandments of God."[9] Her obedience was noted by Church leaders, who took ninety-year-old Vienna to speak to a gathering of more than six hundred "old folk" in Provo.[10]

One year later, Vienna was interviewed by a *Woman's Exponent* reporter, who marveled that she "milked her own cow" and made sixty-one pounds of butter that spring. The butter was not for herself—it was freely given to the needy. Did she consider herself among the needy? The reporter observed, "She lives entirely alone . . . does all her own housework, including washing, ironing and cooking, writes many letters, and does a great deal of reading. Sister Vienna is very familiar with the Scriptures."[11] When Vienna was ninety-four, another reporter wrote, "The erectness of her carriage is sufficient to fill many of the Misses of the nineteenth century with envy."[12] Vienna died on February 7, 1884, in her own home at age ninety-six. Her faithfulness was extolled in her obituary: "She was true to her covenants and esteemed the restoration of the Gospel as a priceless treasure."[13]

The life of Vienna Jacques was marked by strict attention to economic matters. She did not accumulate funds to appease her every whim; her funds became a means to an end. They helped her travel from Boston to Kirtland to meet the Prophet Joseph. They helped the Prophet meet financial obligations of the Church in Ohio and in later years were used to relieve the hunger of the poor. For the woman whose "strict economy" made such a significant difference to Joseph Smith, verses in the Doctrine and Covenants held great meaning: "My handmaid Vienna Jaques should receive money to bear her expenses, and go up unto the land of Zion."[14]

1   *Woman's Exponent,* Vol. 12, no. 19, March 1, 1884, 152.
2   Ibid.
3   Ibid.
4   D&C 90:29–31.
5   Joseph Smith, *History of the Church,* 1:368.
6   Heber C. Kimball, "Extract from Journal," *Times and Seasons* 5, March 15, 1845, 839–840.
7   *History of the Church,* 1:408.
8   Ibid.
9   Ibid.
10   Jerrie W. Hurd, *Our Sisters in the Latter-day Scriptures* (Salt Lake City: Deseret Book, 1987), 69.
11   *Woman's Exponent* 7, July 1, 1878, 21.
12   *Woman's Exponent* 9, June 15, 1880, 13.
13   *Woman's Exponent* 12, March 1, 1884, 152.
14   D&C 90:28.

JANE ELIZABETH MANNING JAMES

Faith

Courtesy of the Church History Library, The Church
of Jesus Christ of Latter-day Saints.

When Jane Manning James was in her late eighties, she dictated "a concise but true sketch" of her life to biographer Elizabeth J. D. Roundy.[1] Although the life sketch is less than five pages, the sincerity—if not urgency—of her words reveal a life devoted to God no matter the affliction. This sketch is particularly poignant as Jane was one of only a few African-Americans to join the Church in the 1840s.

At the age of fourteen, Jane joined the Presbyterian Church—yet did not feel satisfied. Within eighteen months, she learned that Mormon missionaries would soon be preaching in her town. Even though the Presbyterian pastor forbade her from going to hear them, she went. Jane was "fully convinced" that the elders preached the "true gospel."[2] She was baptized and confirmed a member of The Church of Jesus Christ of Latter-day Saints in 1841.

"One year after I was baptized, I started for Nauvoo," recalled Jane.[3] In October 1842, she and eight members of her family left Wilton, Connecticut, and traveled by canal boat to Buffalo, New York. Unable to meet the demand for fares in Buffalo, Jane and her family left the boat and started on foot to travel the more than eight hundred miles to Nauvoo. "We walked until our shoes were worn out, and our feet became sore and cracked open and bled until you could see the whole print of our feet with blood on the ground," Jane said. "We stopped and united in prayer to the Lord; we asked God the Eternal Father to heal our feet. Our prayers were answered and our feet were healed forthwith."[4]

When Jane and her family reached Peoria, Illinois, a government official threatened to put them in jail if they did not show "free papers." Jane explained, "We didn't know at first what he meant, for we had never been slaves." After much discussion, a disgruntled official let her and her family pass on. "We traveled on until we came to a river, and as there was no bridge, we walked right into the stream. When we got to the middle, the water was up to our necks but we got safely across." After sleeping in a forest, she and her family awoke to find that frost had fallen heavy in the night and a light snow was falling. Jane recalled that they walked "through that frost with our bare feet, until the sun rose and melted it away." In recalling these trials, she remarked, "We went on our way rejoicing, singing hymns, and thanking God for his infinite goodness and mercy to us—in blessing us as he had, protecting us from all harm, answering our prayers, and healing our feet."[5]

Jane and her family finally reached Nauvoo, where Emma Smith saw them approaching her house and exclaimed, "Come in, come in!" That evening several listened as the Prophet Joseph Smith said to Jane, "You have been the head of this little band haven't you!" She answered, "Yes sir!" After listening to her recall incidents from the journey, the Prophet said, "God bless you. You are among friends now and you will be protected."[6]

For several months, Jane lived in the Smith home, where she learned from Joseph Smith and viewed him as one of the finest men she had ever known. After the martyrdom of Joseph, Jane resided in the Brigham Young home until her marriage to Isaac James, a free black man from rural Marmouth County, New Jersey.

In 1847 Jane and Isaac journeyed to the Salt Lake Valley in the Ira Eldredge Company. Early days in the valley were difficult for Jane

and the children that blessed her marriage: "Oh how I suffered of cold and hunger, and the keenest of all was to hear my little ones crying for bread, and I had none to give them; but in all, the Lord was with us and gave us grace and faith to stand it all."[7]

For more than sixty years, Jane lived in the Salt Lake Valley, participating in ward Relief Society events and contributing to the building funds of the St. George, Manti, and Logan temples. A seat was reserved for her in the front/center of the Salt Lake Tabernacle during general conferences.

Near the end of her life, Jane had lost her husband and six of her eight children. But she said, "I want to say right here that my faith in the gospel of Jesus Christ of Latter-day Saints is as strong today—nay it is if possible stronger—than it was the day I was first baptized."[8]

On Thursday, April 16, 1908, the *Deseret News* reported her death: "Jane Manning James, an aged colored woman familiarly known as 'Aunt Jane,' passed away about noon today. . . . She was in her ninety-fifth year. . . . Few persons were more noted for faith and faithfulness than was Jane Manning James, and though of the humble of the earth she numbered friends and acquaintances by the hundreds. Many persons will regret to learn that the kind and generous soul has passed from earth."[9]

The life sketch of Jane Manning James has preserved for future generations the faith of a noble African-American pioneer. Although the sketch is a simple review of the life of a humble woman, the faith conveyed in her brief vignettes stand as a beacon for women today.

1   Jane Elizabeth Manning James dictated a brief life story to Utah biographer Elizabeth J. D. Roundy. Kate B. Carter, *The Story of the Negro Pioneer* (Salt Lake City: Utah Printing Co., 1965), 9–10.
2   J. D. Roundy, "Jane Manning James: Life history of Jane Elizabeth Manning James as Transcribed by Elizabeth J. D. Roundy," http://www.blacklds.org/manning.
3   She traveled with "my mother, Eliza Manning, my brothers, Isaac Lewis, and Peter, my sisters, Sarah Stebbins and Angeline Manning, my brother-in-law Anthony Stebbins, Lucinda Manning (a sister-in-law)." Roundy.
4   Ibid.
5   Ibid.
6   Ibid.
7   Ibid.
8   Ibid.
9   Carter, 11.

JANE CLAYSON JOHNSON

Decision-Making

Jane Clayson's interest in broadcasting was almost an accident: arriving at Brigham Young University in 1985 on a violin scholarship, she was sure her future would be in music and that she would marry before ever graduating. When graduation came without an engagement, a series of unplanned events led her to become a major network news anchor—but in the end she chose motherhood as her career.[1]

Jane Clayson was born August 25, 1967, in Sacramento, California. When Jane ran into a friend who worked for KBYU, the university's television station, he encouraged her to visit the studios and learn about broadcasting—a chance conversation that led Jane to a job at KBYU-FM, BYU's classical radio station.

Jane changed her major to broadcast journalism, and her part-time stint at KBYU eventually led to a part-time position reporting local news for KSL television in Salt Lake City during her senior year. At the time, she didn't realize exactly how unusual it was for a student to get a job at a local station in such a large market. She told herself she would work for KSL for fun until "real life" kicked in; upon graduation, however, KSL offered her a full-time job.

The accolades Jane earned during her six years at KSL were unusual for a rookie reporter. She won several awards, including an Emmy for her story about a boy from Park City with cancer who traveled to California to die and an Edward R. Murrow Award for her coverage of Utah doctors donating services to children with disabilities in China. Her biggest recognition came from a New York talent agent who recognized national potential in Jane; within a matter of weeks she was working in Los Angeles as an ABC News correspondent for *Good Morning America* and *World News Tonight with Peter Jennings*. Her first major assignment was the O. J. Simpson murder trial. More high-profile assignments followed.[2]

Though her professional life thrived, there were unexpected struggles, personally. She had married and soon divorced. It was a painful and challenging period. Jane remembers wondering what lessons she needed to be taught. "I had this career, which I had never planned on and, frankly, didn't always want. . . . I had to learn to put everything I had on the altar of God—my fears, my anxiety, my hopes, my dreams—give it all to Him. When I did that, things changed. . . . It was a very pivotal moment for me."[3]

Jane was hired by CBS to cohost The Early Show. While she was packing to move to New York City, she received a phone call from Elder Neal A. Maxwell of the Quorum of the Twelve Apostles. At the time, he supervised the Church's public affairs work. Elder Maxwell told Jane he had felt prompted to offer her a blessing before she began her coanchor position in New York City. One directive in his blessing was particularly poignant for Jane: "You must allow the Lord to use you. Sometimes you will not understand what He is doing or why He is doing it, but do not question. You must allow Him to guide you and direct you."[4]

Jane soon found herself in a position where she needed the promised direction. The routine of being a coanchor was physically and emotionally taxing. Her day started at 3:45 A.M. During the two-hour show she conducted interviews with politicians, celebrities, and newsmakers; afternoons and evenings were filled with speaking engagements, interviews, promotional appearances, and research. She dropped into bed at 10 P.M. and started all over when the alarm rang.

Issues about her religious beliefs often surfaced at work, and Jane found many opportunities to stand as a witness for what she believed. She felt passionate about her work and believed that she was "fulfilling a particular mission she had been called to serve."[5] But at the same time she still had deep longings to be a wife and mother.

During the summer of 2003 Jane's sister set her up on a blind date with Mark Johnson, a former Naval officer, Harvard Business School graduate, and recent convert to the Church. After a short courtship Mark proposed marriage and Jane accepted. The very next morning Jane's agent called with a job offer at another network that included a four-year contract, prime-time opportunities, and a big paycheck. Her wedding was set for September, and her contract with CBS would not expire until January.

Jane turned down the lucrative offer, let her contract with CBS expire, and left her television career. Colleagues told her she was nuts. One told her she was making a terrible decision that she would regret the rest of her life. "'What will you be without your job?' he said. 'If you leave television now, you're done.' Then knowing of Jane's faith he asked, 'What are you going to do? Move up [to Boston] and teach Sunday School?'" As it turned out, the first Sunday in her new ward Jane was called to teach Sunday School.[6]

The day after Jane moved to Boston she learned she was pregnant. Today, as a full-time mother of two children, Jane looks back on her decision without regret. As she reflects on her past life as a broadcast journalist, she says, "I know what it's like to live what many people would call a glamorous, interesting, intellectually stimulating life, and I can say with the full conviction of my heart—with full power in my soul—that nothing is more important than the work I'm doing

within the four walls of my own home, with my children. Nothing. No interview, no award, no network TV program—nothing." Jane says, "Most people won't remember Jane Clayson the news anchor or network correspondent, but Mark and [my] children will be changed forever because of Jane the wife and mother."[7]

1   Lisa Ann Thomson, "Reporting on the Home Front," *BYU Magazine,* Summer 2007.
2   Ibid.
3   Ibid.
4   Jane Clayson Johnson, "Reporting on the Home Front," Guest Lecture for the College of Fine Arts and Communications, March 29, 2007.
5   Ibid.
6   Ibid.
7   Thomson.

LUCILE JOHNSON
Reaching Out

Lucile Johnson describes herself as "a gray-haired grandmother, a colonel's wife."[1] But she is far from being a typical grandmother or colonel's wife—in her seventies and eighties, she lived by the motto that "by pushing one's limits that life gets bigger and better."[2] In her seventies she went back to school and took advanced coursework in sociology, then put her new talents to work as a counselor. She dubs herself a marriage counselor, not a divorce counselor. Her sage advice has become legendary as she changes lives for the better.

Lucile Fern Short was born in 1919 in Idaho and grew up in California's beautiful San Fernando Valley. She grew up with a father who thought "she could do no wrong." He instilled in her a sense of confidence that has grown brighter through the years. For example, when her family attended a local talent contest, eight-year-old Lucile jumped up on the stage, without being named on the program, and danced the Charleston to "Yes Sir, That's My Baby." She won the contest.[3]

Such confidence attracted the attention of college classmate Harold Otto Johnson. "I was attracted to her intellectually before I was ever aware of her physical appearance," he said. But after her smart comment in a psychology class, he turned around to see "a very pretty brunette with hair down past her shoulders."[4] He was smitten.

Soon after their marriage, Harold entered the Army in 1939. As he was browsing through *The Officer's Guide,* he read, "An officer is ever a gentleman, and his wife is his lady." It was then that Harold decided to treat Lucile "like the lady she is. I loved her, and there was something romantic about going through life married to a 'lady.' She has truly fulfilled my expectations, and I hope that I have always been her gentleman."[5]

During the early years of their marriage, Lucile was first and foremost a military wife. She accompanied her husband all over the world while raising five children mostly by herself, as Harold had military obligations that too often meant war. To stay connected with those outside of her home, Lucile joined military wives' clubs and volunteer organizations, but never considered being a speaker at these organizations.

When two of her five children were grown and establishing homes of their own, Lucile got her start as a speaker in Heidelberg, Germany, where Harold was stationed. She was asked to give a twenty-minute talk on the birth of Christ at an officers' wives' Christmas luncheon. She worried about the opportunity and prayed for guidance. To her surprise, her talk was very well received. In fact, the commanding general's wife exclaimed, "My dear, I have just found the keynote speaker for the Protestant Women of the Chapel Conference."[6] Lucile was honored by her request and agreed to be the keynote speaker. At the ensuing conference, she received a standing ovation at the end of her speech.

Many speaking assignments followed. She enjoyed speaking about issues faced by military families. Learning of her effectiveness in helping military personnel, the commander of the U.S. Army Forces in Europe created a staff position for Lucile—Advisor to the Commander of U.S. Army Forces in Europe for Family Affairs.

In her position, Lucile's opportunities to lecture and even counsel troops and their dependents increased. She recalled, "As a professional family therapist, I have conducted dozens of family seminars on countless military bases. And everywhere I go, I meet choice young Latter-day Saint women and men in uniform who are striving to stay close to the Lord. Many are outstanding examples of Mormonism."[7] For her many seminars and speeches to military personnel and their dependents, Lucile received the Bob Hope Five-Star Civilian Award for Service to Country. The award was presented at Valley Forge in 1976.[8]

"I believe she has amazing stamina, grace, and beauty for a woman in her seventies!" wrote Harold. "Lucile followed me around the globe for thirty-five years, and now I am following her around the globe on her speaking assignments, as she continues to use her talents and knowledge to benefit others!"[9] Harold has been with Lucile as she has broadened her audiences to include Latter-day Saint "civilians." She has been a much-sought-after speaker on the BYU Know Your Religion circuit and Education Days, traveling the country to address the Saints. Thousands of Latter-day Saints crowd into chapels and cultural halls to listen to Lucile, whom they call one of the best-loved speakers in the Church.

Lucile speaks of real-life situations, adversities, and trials, but always ends with seeing the bright side of life. She pushes her audiences to consider reaching out and touching "someone with a call, a note, or a visit. You do not know how it might change their day."[10]

To deliver her message of hope to an ever-widening audience, Lucile wrote *Sunny Side Up; Enjoy Life's Journey: Choosing Happiness Along the Way; Mothers, Your Best is Good Enough;* and *Women of Christ: Be of Good Cheer.* At one time, Lucile had more than a dozen different talk tapes on the market that, like her books, were filled with hope and love. For example, she encouraged her listeners to "keep a 'glad' book, not a 'mad' book, to look for rainbows they had not noticed, to know that life is a training ground for imperfect people, and to realize that our growth is what counts more than anything else."[11]

When asked why she is so successful at such an advanced age, Lucile freely admits, "My husband gave me a great deal of encouragement and loving support every step of the way. I am indebted to my husband for his support and patience."[12] Harold and Lucile could have chosen a quieter and more reserved path to follow. After all, they had the means to live comfortably without reaching beyond the walls of their retirement home. But such a lifestyle would not have worked for Lucile. She wanted to be out and about making a difference. Thousands are blessed by her willingness to reach beyond the confines of her home.

1   Lucile Johnson, "Saints in the Military: Conversion and Reconversion," *Ensign,* February 1982, 24.

2   Lucile Johnson, *Sunny Side Up* (American Fork, Utah: Covenant Communications, Inc., 1993), xi.

3   Ibid., ix.

4   Ibid.

5   Ibid., xii.

6   Ibid., xi.

7   Johnson, "Saints in the Military," 24.

8   Johnson, *Sunny Side Up,* xi.

9   Ibid., xii.

10   Lucile Johnson, *Enjoy Life's Journey: Choosing Happiness Along the Way* (American Fork: Covenant Communications, Inc., 2000), 43.

11   Ibid., About the Author.

12   Johnson, *Sunny Side Up,* xii–xiii.

BARBARA
BARRINGTON JONES

Sense of Humor

Barbara Barrington Jones grew to womanhood in a home where propriety was the first priority. Defined strictly by her mother, an etiquette teacher at a private girls' school, *propriety* meant severely limiting laughter and humor. Because her mother found little in life amusing enough to even chuckle about, Barbara struggled to laugh until she realized a healthy sense of humor "is vital to the poise and well-being of the confident woman."[1] Since confidence is imperative in Barbara's line of work, she integrates humor freely into her life.

As a high school student, the introverted Barbara was, in her words, "not popular at all." Public speaking was a huge challenge. As a senior in high school, Barbara remembers that "tears streamed down my cheeks while I was presenting an oral book report; my knees shook and my voice quivered."[2] Adding to her problems, classmates called her "Spider" because of her height and long legs. Little did these classmates realize that those legs would help Barbara realize her dream of becoming a professional dancer.

Her efforts to make the most of poise led her to opportunities to coach beauty queens and to help five pageant candidates win the title of

Miss USA (1985–1989.)[3] But through all the glamour that surrounded Barbara in the 1980s, she was still not as humorous or confident in her speaking as she wanted to be.

After learning of her success with beauty queens, personnel at BYU Conferences and Workshops invited Barbara to speak at a youth conference. Because she was a convert to the Church, Barbara had never attended a youth conference and understandably felt apprehensive about speaking to anyone, let alone teenagers. When she told her mother about the invitation, her mother chided, "Well, I hope you told them you can't speak." She had, in fact, done just the opposite.

The day of her speech, Barbara felt extremely uncomfortable wearing a "fashionable" suit and hat to speak to a roomful of unimpressed teenagers wearing jeans and T-shirts and speaking in jargon she did not comprehend. "They tuned me out after one glance, and I did nothing to change their minds," she said. "To those teenagers that day, I was a living sleeping pill."[4]

Expressing her discouragement to conference coordinators and other youth speakers, she said, "This is my first youth conference and my last. I'll never do this again. I mean it!" One successful speaker told her, "Barbara, don't look at it like that. Try to remember back when you were their age. Think of humorous experiences in your own early life that youth can relate to."[5] She now looks back on that advice as some of the best advice she ever received.

To her credit, Barbara took the challenge and recalled funny experiences from her teenage years. She found that sprinkling humor in her gospel message created a bond between her and her teenage audiences. As they laughed with her about humorous experiences, Barbara's gospel message penetrated the barrier she had once perceived between her and youth. Instead of feeling awkward or out of place among strangers and young people, she felt confident in her ability to speak in front of large groups and to relate to youth.

Humor not only transformed Barbara's speaking ability, it transformed her outlook. While she admits that making others laugh is not a natural gift, she argues that it is a gift that can be developed. Drawing on her own experience, Barbara asserts that attitudes improve when you are "looking for the humor in life, laughing at oneself, and, most definitely, finding the humor in unpleasant situations." Among the positive outcomes of "lightening up" for Barbara has been an increased motivation and excitement about life. Somewhat ironically, it is her confidence and public speaking talent—results of developing her sense of humor—that now defines who she is.

Contrary to what her mother once believed, Barbara found that she could speak in public situations and enjoy the opportunity. A friend said of her, "I've heard Barbara speak, and I've seen the hunger women have for what she has to offer"—a healthy dose of humor with a meaningful message attached.[6] In attempting to explain the difference laughter has made in her life, Barbara says, "There is power in humor. If you can make someone laugh—or, more important, if you can laugh together—life develops a glow. Valuable lessons are learned more easily. Problems seem less frightening."[7]

1   Barbara Barrington Jones and Kris MacKay, *The Confident You: A Woman's Guide to Eternal Beauty* (Salt Lake City: Deseret Book, 1992), 139.
2   Ibid., 139–140.
3   Ibid.
4   Ibid., 140–141.
5   Ibid.
6   Ibid., 141–142.
7   Ibid., 139.

ARDETH GREENE KAPP

Facing Adversity

Courtesy of the Church History Library, The Church
of Jesus Christ of Latter-day Saints.

Growing up in Glenwood, Alberta, Canada, Ardeth Greene learned you cannot rush the seasons. Planting seeds in Canada's soil did not always produce the desired harvest, but it did affirm to Ardeth a dependence on the Lord—a perspective that later defined her response to other challenges, especially the challenge of not becoming a mother. Ardeth confesses that her challenges led to "spiritual growth," for she "wouldn't have prayed as hard or turned to the Lord as much or probably struggled to understand the plan [of salvation] as much" without trials.[1]

Daughter of Ted and June Greene, Ardeth was born March 19, 1931, in Glenwood. As the oldest living daughter in the family, she was given many opportunities to tend and even protect her younger siblings. On June 28, 1950, Ardeth entered the Alberta Temple with her fiancé, Heber Kapp, to be married. The two had met when Heber had visited Ardeth's parents' home as a young missionary. After he was released from his mission, a friendship and then courtship ensued.

Following their marriage, Heber attended the University of Utah, and Ardeth worked for Mountain States Telephone Company. She advanced there, attaining "the highest position possible for a woman in the telephone company at that time." Yet she left to fulfill her own educational goals.[2] In 1964 she received a bachelor's degree in elementary education from the University of Utah and in 1971 a master's degree in curriculum development from Brigham Young University. After teaching school she became a supervisor of teacher education at BYU.

Although Ardeth found joy in her work, she had "envisioned living in a small white house with a picket fence" where she would "take care of the flowers, be active in the Church, friendly with neighbors—and have lots of children." She and Heber were not blessed with children, and prayers about adoption were not confirmed.[3] Ardeth often "found herself in tears just at the sight of the young mother wiping her child's nose. . . . Even the smallest things reminded her of their childless state." It was then that she and Heber made the decision to consciously refuse "to let their own heartache prevent them from sharing in the happiness of others."[4] She admits that "not having any children and living in an LDS community with families is hard. You are either going to pull back and isolate yourself from it or you are going to just try and get into the middle of it and magnify the opportunities that you have to be an influence to others."[5]

Ardeth jumped into the middle to make a difference. She has been a strength—a beacon to those who suffer similar disappointments in life. She takes strength from the words of Paul: "Blessed be God. The God of all comfort; Who comforteth us in our tribulation, that we may be able to comfort them which are in any trouble, by the comfort wherewith we ourselves are comforted."[6] For example, when a stake president sent a childless woman to Ardeth's door, although the woman "came as a stranger . . . sharing deeply personal concerns made [the two women] sisters." Ardeth wrote that as the sister drove away from her home, she "rejoiced in the blessing of being able to ease the burden of another, for I did understand."

Always an active figure in the lives of young women, Ardeth consciously avoids taking the place of their mothers, and speaks of the bond between mothers and daughters. Ardeth promotes the concept of creative motherhood through one of her many popular publications, *All Kinds of Mothers,* which addresses the role all women have in mothering, "whether or not they have children."[7] She explains, "You need not give birth to help another gain eternal life."[8]

As the ninth Young Women general president, Ardeth was ever mindful of the escalating challenges facing young women at that time. Under her leadership the Lord's program for young women, Personal Progress, was changed to help meet the needs of young women, focusing first on an understanding of their true identity as daughters of God; second, the need for a clear sense of direction and how to stay on the path; and, finally, the grand purpose. The Young Women theme addresses these issues of identity: "We are daughters of our Heavenly Father who loves us, and we love Him. We will stand as witnesses of God at all times and in all things and in all places." When the Young Women values (Christ-like attributes) are accepted and acted upon, young women are preparing to make and keep sacred covenants, receive the ordinances of the temple, and enjoy the blessings of exaltation. The values include, in sequence, faith, divine nature, individual worth, knowledge, choice and accountability, good works, integrity, and virtue. The Young Women motto, "Stand for Truth and Righteousness," and logo, featuring the silhouette of a young women's face in the flame of a torch, were also introduced.[9]

In 1985 the first Young Women satellite broadcast introduced the Young Women theme and values. The following year the first Young Women worldwide celebration was observed[10] to "provide every Latter-day Saint young woman with the opportunity to write her testimony expressing her feelings for the Lord and the Church on paper and attach it to a helium-filled balloon. On the designated morning at sunrise all over the world, the balloons were released. A bond of sisterhood, united in a common cause of sharing the gospel, was felt far and wide."[11]

After Ardeth's service in the Young Women program, her husband, Heber, was called to preside over the Canada Vancouver Mission. Their service together in the mission field was a very rich and rewarding time for Heber and Ardeth.

Five years after returning to their home in Utah, they received a call from President Gordon B. Hinckley to serve as president and matron of the Cardston Alberta Temple, just twenty miles from where Ardeth was born and reared. This calling came exactly fifty years from the time of their marriage, when they were sealed in that temple. It was truly a glorious experience to return "home" to that temple, Ardeth says.

"When I was young I thought the noblest thing in this life was to be a mother. I have since learned that the best mission in life is the one the Lord has prepared for *me*. So I have felt a real sense of responsibility to discover and fulfill *my* mission."[13]

1   Jessica Christensen interview with Ardeth Greene Kapp, Bountiful, Utah, December 3, 2009, 3, 10 (Transcription); Anita Thompson, *Stand as a Witness: The Biography of Ardeth Greene Kapp* (Salt Lake City: Deseret Book Company, 2005), 214.

2   Email conversation with Ardeth Kapp by Mary Jane Woodger, November 30, 2010.

3   Thompson, 116, 140–141.

4   Karen Thomas Arnesen, "Ardeth Greene Kapp: A Prairie Girl, a Young Woman Still," *Ensign*, September 1985, 35.

5   Thompson, 128.

6   2 Cor. 1:3–4.

7   Christensen, 10.

8   Email conversation.

9   Email conversation.

10   "Presidents of the Young Women Organization through the Years," *Ensign*, June 2008, 40–45.

11   The Church of Jesus Christ of Latter-day Saints, Young Women Worldwide Celebration, 1985, 1, 3.

12   Thompson, 349, 355.

13   Arnesen, 35.

CAMILLA EYRING KIMBALL

Sacrifice

Courtesy of the Church History Library, The Church
of Jesus Christ of Latter-day Saints.

When her husband, Spencer W. Kimball, was called to be president
of The Church of Jesus Christ of Latter-day Saints, Camilla said that his
calling as "Prophet, Seer, and Revelator of the Church put [them] on
a pedestal" neither chose. To fulfill her role "honorably and humbly,"
Camilla forfeited her quiet, private life. Camilla believed that her life's
work was to "take as much responsibility as I can for [Spencer's] health,
relieve him of the business of the house, and, yes, I try to shelter him."[1]
At that time and throughout her life, Camilla was ever willing to
sacrifice her wants for her husband and family.

Daughter of Edward Christian Eyring and Caroline Cottam
Romney, Camilla Eyring was born December 7, 1894, in Colonia
Juarez, Chihuahua, Mexico. As a child she loved to read; she had an
insatiable appetite for books and read everything she could. She read
in bed under the covers at night, and often propped a book on her
music stand when practicing the organ. The more she read, the more
questions about truth surfaced. "I always had an enquiring mind. I am
not satisfied just to accept things," she said. "I like to follow through
and study things out."

It was her father who taught Camilla that there is a difference between theory and truth. She learned early that the gospel was absolute truth, whereas theories come and go. She developed a philosophy in her youth that served her well through the years: "When things troubled her, she put them on the shelf; later when she looked at them again, some were answered, some looked no longer important, and some needed to go back on the shelf for another time."[2]

Just before her sixteenth birthday, a political rebellion in Chihuahua forced her family to flee from Mexico to Texas. Camilla lamented that her family of thirteen was limited to one trunk of clothing. "I wanted so much to put in my doll and some other treasures, but there was no room," recalled Camilla. "I had always been a great collector and had kept all my school papers, letters, toys—everything I had ever owned; now I had to leave them all, never to see them again."[3]

Several years later as Camilla was making plans to marry Spencer Kimball—a young man she met on the bus as she commuted six miles from her home to teach home economics at Gila Academy—she went to her principal to get time off to travel to Utah for the wedding. Camilla was given permission to marry only "so long as it didn't interfere with [her] job." Camilla and Spencer were married civilly on November 16, 1917. When Camilla's obligation to the academy ended, Camilla and Spencer were sealed on June 7, 1918, in the Salt Lake Temple. The sealing took place just before her first child was born. "I felt quite self-conscious because of my condition and the way I looked," recalled Camilla. "Of course, I was unduly sensitive. One woman tactlessly said to me, 'You surely are not going through for your own endowment, are you?' I started to cry and said, 'Yes, but I have been married a long time.' But the discomfort I felt was far overshadowed by the satisfaction of knowing that Spencer and I were now husband and wife for all eternity."[4]

Camilla was a quiet woman, the result of personal discipline. She enjoyed daily reading as well as having greenhouse plants in her home—her way of not submitting to winter. One of her favorite activities was playing bridge with friends; she played at least once or twice a week, and played well enough to win prizes offered at bridge parties. In 1936 when Elder Melvin J. Ballard visited her stake, he admonished members to give up playing bridge. "This hit hard and distressed Camilla," wrote her son Edward. "She could see no harm in bridge." But upon "considering the source of the advice, she and her friends resolved to make the sacrifice and conform."[5] Camilla's children learned from her example. Though she never compelled them to choose the right, her strong example helped them "work things out for themselves."

Edward said that his "friends set their standards by those of the Kimballs. If the Kimball children were going to a party or a movie, their friends could go; if not, then the friends could not go either."[6] In this way, Camilla's commitment to sacrifice spiritually damaging pleasures had a great influence not only on the lives of her children, but also on the lives of their friends.

Camilla enjoyed her friends and life in Arizona with Spencer and her children. But when Spencer's call came to serve in the Quorum of the Twelve Apostles on October 7, 1943, Camilla willingly packed up their possessions and moved to Salt Lake City. There she tried to fill her home with peace, believing this would benefit Spencer. She was a hostess to many and a friend to all, although she shunned the spotlight on most occasions. When Spencer died on September 5, 1985, Camilla remained in Salt Lake City. Family, friends, reading, gardening, and Church work filled her days until her own death on September 20, 1987.

When people asked Camilla how she felt about being married to a prophet, she liked to say, "I didn't marry a prophet, I married a returned missionary." Of her husband, she said, "He was always completely dedicated to the Church and it has been that way in our married life since the beginning. He would be just as devoted if he were a ward clerk." As for her, sacrifice of self was viewed as an opportunity.

"I feel that fulfilling obligations is the most direct opportunity to grow—the very best way," said Camilla. "Any woman should be alive to opportunities—alive to public interest, to her family, to growth from Church service. Life is so interesting, it worries me that I can't get it all done."[7]

1   Lavina Fielding, "Camilla Kimball: Lady of Constant Learning," *Ensign,* October 1975, 61.
2   Caroline Eyring Miner and Edward L. Kimball, *Camilla: A Biography of Camilla Eyring Kimball* (Salt Lake City: Deseret Book, 1980), 110.
3   *Journal of Camilla Eyring Kimball* as cited in Miner and Kimball, 1, 28, 34.
4   *Journal of Camilla Eyring Kimball* as cited in Miner and Kimball, 64, 70–71.
5   Miner and Kimball, 96.
6   Miner and Kimball, 109.
7   Fielding, 61.

SARAH GRANGER KIMBALL
Faithfulness

In 1842 when Sarah Granger Kimball and her seamstress Miss Cook began to sew shirts for the workers on the Nauvoo Temple, little did either woman realize that something great and long lasting would come of their efforts. Sarah had shown discontent upon seeing one or two temple workers with new shirts when so many were in need. She believed that an organized charitable ladies' society was needed to look after the poor; other women in Nauvoo agreed and expressed an interest in joining Sarah's society.

Wanting to ensure that the organization was founded on a firm base, Sarah asked Eliza R. Snow to create a constitution and bylaws for the society. In the course of writing the constitution, Eliza showed her efforts to the Prophet Joseph Smith. He told Eliza to "tell the sisters their offering is accepted of the Lord, and He has something better for them than a written constitution." On March 17, 1842, Joseph organized the Female Relief Society of Nauvoo—and today the Relief Society has become one of the largest women's organizations in the world.

Daughter of Oliver and Lydia Granger, Sarah was born December 29, 1818, in Phelps, New York.[1] Her father was the first in her family to embrace Mormonism. Baptisms of other family members soon followed, as did the gathering of the family to Kirtland, Ohio. By age fifteen, Sarah was living in Kirtland and was closely associated with the Prophet Joseph Smith; her father served as his fiscal agent for several years. When the Saints moved to Missouri and then Illinois, her family stayed in Ohio. [2]

On a visit to Commerce, Illinois, twenty-one-year-old Sarah attracted the attention of thirty-four-year-old Hiram S. Kimball, one of the wealthiest men in town. On September 22, 1840, they married.[3] Sarah and Hiram enjoyed each other's company, but not a common religious faith. For example, three days after Sarah gave birth to her firstborn son, she asked Hiram, "What is the boy worth?" He replied, "O, I don't know, he is worth a great deal." Sarah said, "Is he worth a thousand dollars?" Hiram replied, "Yes more than that if he lives and does well." Sarah said, "Half of him is mine, it is not?" "Yes, I suppose so," said Hiram. "Then I have something to help on the Temple," she replied. "You have?" asked Hiram. "Yes and I think of turning my share right in as tithing," Sarah said. "Well, I'll see about that," replied Hiram.

A few days later, Hiram was walking along the streets of Nauvoo when he saw Joseph Smith and shared with him what he considered a humorous incident. To his surprise, Joseph said, "You now have the privilege of paying $500 and retaining possession [of your son] or receiving $500 and giving possession." Hiram asked if city property was good currency. Joseph assured him the property would be accepted. To Sarah, Joseph said, "You have consecrated your first born son, for this you are blessed of the Lord."[4]

Sarah was faithful. Her goodness and kindness to Hiram led to his baptism on July 20, 1843. His faithfulness has been questioned, for when Sarah fled from persecution and mobs in Nauvoo to the safety of Iowa, Hiram was not by her side—but in truth, he was on an extended business trip to New York City at that time. Not waiting for him to return to the main body of the Saints, Sarah, her two sons (Hiram W. and Oliver), and her widowed mother journeyed to the Salt Lake Valley in 1851. Hiram joined them the next year, financially ruined.

To support her family, Sarah taught school in the Salt Lake 14th Ward. Unfortunately, she taught under difficult circumstances. At this juncture, she was convinced there needed to be some improvement for women working outside of the home. When Hiram recouped his financial standing in 1857, Sarah left the classroom, never to return. In that year, she was named president of the Salt Lake 15th Ward Relief Society.[5] She served in that capacity for a decade, long after the death of her husband and the rearing of her children.

With more spare time than previously anticipated, the last years of Sarah's life were more public than private. When seated in a railway carriage with people on one side discussing fashions, and those on the other discussing politics, she would turn to the discussion of politics. In 1882 she was an active participant in the Utah Constitutional Convention. In 1891 she was a leader in the Utah Woman Suffrage Association. As such, she petitioned the Congress of the United States for help to stop outrages inflicted by federal deputies upon Utah women. In 1895 she was named an honorary vice-president of the National American Woman's Suffrage Association.

Sarah was perhaps best known, however, for her speeches. As one biographer wrote, "As a public speaker she was concise and always to the point, never made long speeches, but said what she felt forcibly and always with effect." Sarah died on December 1, 1898, in Salt Lake City at age seventy-nine.[6]

In remembrance of her contribution to the women of the Church, her first home in Nauvoo was restored and opened to the public on March 17, 1982, 140 years after the organization of the Relief Society.

---

1   Barbara B. Smith and Blythe Darlyn Thatcher, "Sarah Has Got a Little the Advantage," *Heroines of the Restoration* (Salt Lake City: Bookcraft, 1997), 103–114; Andrew Jenson, *LDS Biographical Encyclopedia* (Salt Lake City: Western Epics, 1971), 2:372.
2   Smith and Thatcher, 104.
3   Ibid., 105.
4   Ibid., 106.
5   See "Fifteenth Ward, Riverside Stake, Relief Society Minutes," Church History Library; Jenson 2:373.
6   See Jenson 2:374.

KING SISTERS

Loyalty

Courtesy of the Church History Library, The Church
of Jesus Christ of Latter-day Saints.

The King Sisters—Donna, Yvonne, Louise, and Alyce—were the dynamic, swinging sisters of the Big Band era. Their billing as the most technically accomplished vocal group was not hyperbole. Their "unfailing sense of rhythm, perfect intonation and bubbly personalities" won the heart of America.[1] What Americans did not know was that family came before show business in their lives.

The story of the King Sisters begins with their father, William King Driggs, who worked as a professor of music and a voice teacher in Colorado. He loved his work and brought it home, where he taught his children—six girls and two boys—how to sing. To supplement his income, he accepted invitations on behalf of his children to perform for any and all gatherings throughout the western states. As it turned out, they were a happy traveling family until hard times caught up with them. More than once, the children awoke to find the family car repossessed. Hoping to better his options, William Driggs relocated his family to Oakland in 1924.[2]

It was not until 1931 that the King Sisters, then known as the Driggs Sisters, made a broadcast debut on Oakland radio station KLX.

They were an instant hit with the up-and-coming generation. Money earned from their broadcasts ($25 a week) supported the entire family. In 1932, when the family moved to Salt Lake City, the girls performed on KSL. They were paid $10 for each fifteen-minute show, and again their wages supported the family.[3]

By 1935 the sisters took their father's middle name, King, and formed the King Sisters. That year, they accepted their first on-the-road employment with bandleader Horace Heidt. "Heidt was hard to please, very strict," recalled Donna. "He would get upset about something you did and then, the next thing you knew he wouldn't speak to you."[4] Due to Heidt's uneven temperament, the King Sisters left his band and joined legendary guitarist Alvino Rey and his orchestra. In 1939 they broadcast performances on KHJ in Los Angeles and signed a seven-year recording contract with RCA Victor Records.

Their first smash hit was a vocal version of the Glenn Miller hit "In the Mood." This was followed by a concert at the Pasadena Civic Auditorium, where more than four thousand fans came to cheer for them. "That's when we realized just how many people were listening to our KHJ broadcasts," said Donna. The broadcasts had made them radio stars. Over the airwaves, their lively personalities were almost as important as the songs they sang. To most fans, the King Sisters had a unique sound: Donna and Alyce sang low harmonies in the male range. Each of the sisters was an excellent sight reader and, according to their biographer, "could run through a new arrangement once, then record the song usually in the first take."[5]

In 1939 the King Sisters were asked to join the Glenn Miller Orchestra. The temptation to ditch Alvino Rey was real, but loyalty was at stake: by this time, Rey had married one of the King Sisters. Ever true to family, the opportunity was declined. Most critics say that this decision was not in their best interest.[6]

It was nearly four years before the Alvino Rey Orchestra and the King Sisters were playing at top venues and making good money.

Wherever they performed, in concert or on the radio, their act always closed with "Nighty-Night" sung by Yvonne. At a tribute dinner honoring the King Sisters in 1977, Frank Devol said, "Every GI in World War II heard that song on Armed Forces Radio, just before going to bed. It was even played by Tokyo Rose. . . . It was her sign-off to the men. She'd play it and then ask the men in the South Pacific Theater of Operations, 'Don't you wish you were home, fellas?'"[7] Yvonne enjoyed joking with concert audiences that she personally sang every American soldier to sleep.

When World War II broke out in the Pacific, the Alvino Rey Orchestra split up. Band members, including Rey, either voluntarily joined the military or were drafted. The King Sisters continued singing, touring countless military bases and appearing on the wartime radio programs *G. I. Journal* and *Mailcall.* From 1941 to 1945, thirteen of their recordings made the top 30 hit list. The King Sisters signed a seven-year contract with MGM and appeared in such B movies as *Cross Your Fingers, Sing Your Worries Away,* and *Cuban Pete.*[8]

When the war ended, the popularity of the King Sisters dramatically declined; they were out of the public eye by the 1950s, when their time and talent were spent raising families. Then, almost as a fluke, Yvonne organized a series of benefit concerts for Brigham Young University in 1964. She invited the entire King family to join in the concerts. Audience response was so positive that one concert was videotaped and shown to the head of ABC. With this, a new chapter opened for the King Sisters. The weekly *King Family Show* debuted on television in January 1965. Although the variety show was dismissed by critics, the public loved it. The show provided wholesome, family entertainment at a time of social and political turmoil.[9]

When ABC dropped the *King Family Show* in 1969, more than 200,000 letters of protest were sent to the network—the largest protest of a canceled program in television history up to that time. To compensate, ABC presented a series of one-hour specials staring the

King family. This was followed by performances at Disneyland, Knott's Berry Farm, state fairs, trade shows, and as featured entertainers at the 1985 inauguration ball of President Ronald Reagan.

As time passed, the sisters eased into retirement. They occasionally organized musical functions for their wards and at schools, but little more.

"We had lots of opportunities to make major career moves that definitely would've made the King Sisters more successful, but we always followed our hearts and did what we thought was right for our families," said Donna. "I wouldn't trade what we have now for anything in the world, which is all our family who support and really care about each other."[10]

---

1   Dana Countryman, "The King Sister Biography: Solid Sisters of Swing," The King Sisters Official Fan Page, http://danacountryman.com/kingsisterswebpage.

2   Ibid.

3   Ibid.

4   Ibid.

5   Ibid.

6   Ibid.

7   Ibid.

8   Ibid.

9   Ibid.

10   Ibid.

HANNAH TAPFIELD KING

Intelligence

Biographer Maureen Ursenbach Beecher wrote of Hannah Tapfield King, "Gregarious, elitist, but no longer wealthy—her husband had used their last money to pay fifty dollars to the Perpetual Emigration fund and to buy a small house—Hannah King learned to cope with poor furnishing and food shortages."[1] Though she may have dealt with these limitations, she never learned to cope with her fellow Mormon pioneer women. In her diary, Hannah wrote, "Silly women! They only expose their ignorance and ill manners, and what do they know of the English, or English society?"[2] Few pioneer women could understand or relate to Hannah. But while isolated, too often by her own choice, Hannah reached out to society through poetry and prose.

Daughter of Peter Tapfield and Mary Lawson, Hannah Dorcas Tapfield was born March 16, 1808, in Sawston, Cambridgeshire, England. She grew up in Cambridge—and the world center of learning had a definite impact on Hannah. She began in her youth to ask introspective and philosophical questions. In an attempt to explain her intellectual pursuits, she wrote, "I was reared among its classic shades and bowers. . . . The home and haunts of childhood and youth, leave

on every mind indelible impressions and when brought to focus upon the past as at the present moment, 'The distant spires and antique towers rise up before me in all their vividness as by the power of that most wonderful faculty, memory.'"³

Hannah's parents, devoted members of the Church of England, encouraged her literary flair. When her father was away from home, he expected Hannah to write him profound letters. He also encouraged her to write a thought-provoking journal. Hannah needed little encouragement, for she was incessantly writing short essays and prose and sending her literary works to local newspapers.

On April 6, 1824, Hannah married Thomas Owen King. They became the parents of ten children, four surviving to adulthood—Georgiana, Louisa, Bertha Mary, and Thomas Owen, Jr. In 1827, just three years after her marriage, Hannah published her first two books: *The Toilet* and *Three Eras*. These books were "patronized by the aristocracy of England."⁴ Thomas became a very successful farmer and proprietor of Dernford Dale, about seven miles south of Cambridge. He hired fourteen laborers to help him cultivate three hundred and fifty acres. Hannah had twenty-two-year-old Ann Newling, a personal dressmaker and seamstress, at her beck and call. By anyone's standards Thomas and Hannah were in the upper middle class of English society.

A change came in 1849 when Ann Newling shared with Hannah her newfound religion, Mormonism. Hannah and her daughter Georgiana were baptized members of the LDS Church on November 4, 1850, by Joseph W. Johnson. Thomas refused baptism, but did not discourage his wife from her religious persuasions. Three years later, on January 24, 1853, the entire family emigrated from Liverpool to New Orleans on the sailing vessel *Golconda*. They then took passage on a steamer up the Mississippi River to Keokuk, Iowa, a trailhead for Mormon emigrants. Hannah crossed the Mississippi from Keokuk to Nauvoo to meet the mother of the Prophet Joseph Smith, Lucy Mack Smith. In remembrance of their meeting, Hannah wrote a poem honoring Mother Smith:

Mother of Joseph! Yes, I've seen thy face,
And felt thy kiss imprinted on my cheek;
And, furthermore, (with thy peculiar grace),
Thou blessed me with the blessings that I seek.

Lady! Mother! Priestess! I rejoice
That thou didst bless the pilgrim on her way;
That I have seen thy face and heard thy voice,
And that I live in this, the Gospel day. . . . .

No queen, no royalty, that e'er I'd seen,
Impress'd my soul as did that aged Saint!
No earthly grandeur, with its pomp and sheen,
Or beauties that a Raphael or a Guido paint.[5]

With the help of Horace Eldredge and Hector C. Haight, Hannah and her family acquired teams and wagons in Iowa for their journey to the Salt Lake Valley. They arrived in the valley on September 19, 1853.

In the valley, Thomas supported his family as a farmer, this time with no money to hire laborers. Hannah struggled to find her place in the pioneer West. She viewed herself educated and cultured and her neighbors as lacking refinement. Fortunately, she found a friend in Eliza R. Snow and enjoyed exchanging poetry and prose with her. In 1861 Hannah wrote to Eliza:

My Spirit bends instinctively to thine:
And at thy feet I fain would sit and learn
Like Paul of old before Gamaliel.[6]

Hannah published an epic poem of some 1,800 lines in remembrance of the Prophet Joseph Smith. This poem and others reflect her personal

response to people and events of the Restoration.

Hannah participated in the Polysophical Society, an intellectual LDS society composed of men and women impressed with "things of the mind" that met every other week at Lorenzo Snow's home in Salt Lake City. During their meetings, members recited original poetry, performed on instruments, and occasionally sang in tongues. It was not until Jedediah M. Grant, a member of the First Presidency, spoke of the Polysophical Society as a "stink in his nostrils" that attendance at their meetings declined. In less than two years after the society began, it ended.[7]

When Thomas died on November 16, 1875, Hannah's world collapsed. She remembered Cambridge and their lives together at Dernford Dale with fondness, but didn't regret immigrating to the United States. "For the last thirty years America has been my adopted country," she wrote. "I love her with a loyal and devoted appreciation."[8] Hannah died on September 25, 1886, at the home of her daughter Louisa in Salt Lake City.[9]

Hannah was an anomaly in pioneer Utah. She disdained anti-intellectuals, especially women who saw no need for intellectual pursuits. For Hannah, "the active mind will have its life, often beyond or despite the requirements of practicality."[10] Hannah never became caught up in the day-to-day cares of living in frontier Salt Lake City, but valued the quest for culture, refinement, and expansion of the mind.

1   Maureen Ursenbach, "Three Women and the Life of the Mind," *Utah Historical Quarterly*, Vol. 43, no. 1, Winter 1975, 27.
2   Ursenbach, 27.
3   Kate B. Carter, "My Story—Hannah T. King," *Treasures of Pioneer History* (Salt Lake City: Daughters of the Utah Pioneers, 1954), 3:43–45.
4   Kenneth L. Holmes, ed., "My Journal: Hannah Tapfield King," *Covered Wagon Women: Diaries & Letters from the Western Trails, 1840–1890* (Glendale, California: The Arthur H. Clark Company, 1986), 4:184.
5   Hannah Tapfield King, *Songs of the Heart* (Salt Lake City: Star Book and Job Publishing, 1879), 34–36.
6   Hannah Tapfield King, "Lines, Affectionately addressed to Sister Eliza," as cited in Ursenbach, 27.
7   Ursenbach, 32.
8   Hannah Tapfield King, "My Journal," in Holmes, 4:183.
9   Ibid., 4:187.
10 Ursenbach, 40.

GLADYS KNIGHT

Gratitude

Courtesy of the Church History Library, The Church
of Jesus Christ of Latter-day Saints.

"I sang through two marriages and two divorces. I sang through
three pregnancies and one terrifying miscarriage," says soul singer
Gladys Knight. "I sang through love affairs and abusive relationships,
through addiction and recovery (both mine and others'), through
bare-floored poverty and marble-tiled affluence. Carrying my dolls,
my homework, or my babies, I sang in country churches and national
cathedrals. I sang in gospel choirs . . . and the White House."[1]

Daughter of Merald and Sarah Knight, Gladys was born May 28,
1944, in Atlanta, Georgia. As a child she became a guest soloist with
the Mount Moriah Baptist Church choir; her father believed that
her "voice was God's gift and that it should be used only in God's
service." Her mother disagreed—and put Gladys on stage at every
opportunity.

When Gladys was eight, her mother took her on a train to New
York City to be a contestant on the national television show *Ted Mack
Original Amateur Hour.* Gladys won the contest singing her rendition
of Brahms's "Lullaby" and Nat King Cole's "Too Young." Little did she
or her mother realize the impact that win would have.

Soon after Gladys and her mother returned to Atlanta, Gladys Knight and the Pips was formed. "The Pips"—named after her cousin, James "Pip" Woods—was a family musical group consisting of her brother, sister, and two cousins. By the time Gladys was eleven, Gladys Knight and the Pips were traveling the country as an opening act for performers like Sam Cooke and Jackie Wilson.

Gladys had known something of racial prejudice in Atlanta. On one occasion she saw signs over two water fountains that read *White* and *Colored,* and she asked her mother, "Momma, what color is water?" Yet nothing prepared her for the prejudice she encountered on the road. "Often we had to go to the back door to be served food at restaurants, and most hotels and motels put out the NO ROOMS sign when we pulled into the parking lot." When she told Governor Bill Clinton of being run out of Little Rock, he said, "Gladys, it wasn't me; I didn't do it." Years later, they danced together at the White House. She says, "He and I, and the country, too, had come a long way."[2]

By the time Gladys was in her teens, Tina Turner was giving her tips on makeup, Sammy Davis, Jr. was tutoring her on audience-reading, and she was signing her first recording contract. Yet this was not the life she wanted: "My dreams weren't of gold records or Grammys. I wanted a house and a family. The whole white-picket-fence package." But it was an elusive goal; her singing talent repeatedly pushed her back to the road, which too often meant sleazy motels and smoke-filled bars. The atmosphere took its toll: "Although I have certainly lost my way from time to time—sometimes for long and painful stretches—I've always sought to follow God's way, to do the right thing, and to be a good person" despite the surroundings.[3]

By 1964 Gladys Knight and the Pips were covering nearly 80,000 miles a year. Their big break came in 1966 when they joined the Motown roster and toured as the opening act for Diana Ross and the Supremes. Being second fiddle did not suit them well, however, and in 1973 they left Motown. "I've heard it said that when you close one door in your life, another always opens," says Gladys. "When we closed the door on Motown, doors opened all over the place." So did the Grammies, with such hits as "Midnight Train to Georgia" and "I Heard It through the Grapevine."[4]

In 1989 Gladys launched a solo career with a premier at Bally's in Las Vegas. "When I saw the waiters and waitresses stop to listen, I knew I was reaching them," Gladys said. Her solo debut was followed by an HBO television special. In 1995 a star was placed on the Hollywood Walk of Fame in her honor, and in 1996 she was inducted into the Rock and Roll Hall of Fame. Yet fame and fortune did not bring her happiness: "I have known loneliness in front of a crowd of thousands, and I have known fulfillment in a night spent alone with a good book."[5] The good book she wanted was one that brought her closer to God.

When family and friends ask *Why the Mormons?*, she simply responds that she was reared to love Christ and His gospel—and that she would never believe something that doesn't testify of Him. In 1997 Gladys was baptized a member of The Church of Jesus Christ of Latter-day Saints. She enjoyed teasing President Gordon B. Hinckley that his flock needed to inject some "pep" into their music. Since then she has led and still occasionally directs the Saints Unified Voices, a multicultural choir of Latter-day Saints who sing an African-American heritage style of music. Their *One Voice* CD won a Grammy. As to the effect of Church membership on the rest of her life, Gladys says, "Since I joined the Church, I desire to be more and more obedient to God."[6]

In her autobiography—*Between Each Line of Pain and Glory: My Life Story*—Gladys writes, "I am extremely grateful for the gift [of singing] I have been given and the opportunities that it has created for me."[7] She also expresses confidence that in spite of missteps, the Lord has guided her life: "He is with me even when things don't turn out as I envisioned." As to the good and bad that have come her way, Gladys says, "Bring on the pain. Bring on the glory. I will be in this fight to share my gifts, to enjoy my blessings."[8] She will sing and in so doing,

she says, "First and foremost, I give honor to the Lord for giving me my life and His infinite blessings."[9]

1   Gladys Knight, *Between Each Line of Pain and Glory: My Life Story* (New York: Hyperion, 1997), 4.
2   Ibid., 27, 72–73, 75.
3   Ibid., 10, 107.
4   Ibid., 211.
5   Ibid., 9, 271.
6   "Gladys Knight: Renowned Singer and Entertainer," blacklds.org (accessed September 21, 2010); Dana King, "Gladys Knight and the Saints Unified Voices Choir in St. Louis, Missouri," STLtoday.com (accessed September 21, 2008).
7   Knight, 259.
8   Ibid., 270–271.
9   Ibid., vii.

LUCY JANE (JENNIE) BRIMHALL KNIGHT
Missionary Work

Photo courtesy of D.V. Groberg family.

Although Lucy Jane (Jennie) Brimhall Knight was not among the Saints who crossed the plains with the Mormon pioneers, she was a pioneer in her own right—one of the first two Latter-day Saint women to fulfill a proselyting mission. She and her companion, Amanda Inez Knight, served in England with such competence and devotion that George Q. Cannon, a member of the First Presidency, extended a call for other "wise and prudent women" to serve missions.[1]

Daughter of George H. Brimhall and Alsina E. Wilkins, Lucy Jane (Jennie) was born December 13, 1875, in Utah. She spent her early childhood in Spanish Fork, where her father worked as a school principal. When Jennie was eleven, she and her family moved to Provo when her father found employment as a professor at the Brigham Young Academy. Jennie graduated from the BY Academy in the class of 1895 and then taught school for a term in Bluff City, Utah, before returning to the academy in fall 1896 to teach third- and fourth-grade classes.[2]

After a brief stint in the classroom, Jennie, now twenty-three and engaged to missionary J. William Knight, wanted to travel to Europe before settling down to become a wife and a mother. She shared her

thoughts with a former classmate and soon-to-be sister-in-law, Amanda Inez Knight, age twenty-two, who had just returned to Provo after a season of genealogical research in St. George.[3] Inez liked the idea of travel, and the two friends began to make formal plans for a European vacation. When Jennie's bishop, J. B. Keeler, heard of their travel plans, he asked if the two young women would consider going to Europe as missionaries for the LDS Church instead of going to Europe for a vacation.

Such a thought had never occurred to Jennie or Inez. Single sisters had never been called to serve proselyting missions.[4] Both young women replied without hesitation that they would be willing to serve a mission if formally called. Bishop Keeler wrote to President Wilford Woodruff, asking if the two young friends could be called as proselyting missionaries. After careful consideration of the matter, the First Presidency of the Church authorized President Edward Partridge of the Utah Stake to set Jennie and Inez apart to serve in Great Britain as the first single LDS sisters to be proselyting missionaries.[5]

The two young women were set apart on April 1, 1898. The next day they departed for England, traveling by train to Philadelphia and from there by ship to the port city of Liverpool. They arrived on English shores on April 22, 1898. The next day Jennie spoke to a gathering in a crowded hall in Liverpool. To at least one observer, the crowd listened "with rapt attention" as she delivered her message with "intelligence and sincerity" to an audience unfamiliar with "Utah and her people."[6]

Jennie and Inez were then assigned to labor in the Chiltenham Conference "doing all things required of male missionaries." For a time they served in Oldham in northwest England. Inez wrote that "Oldham is a large manufacturing city and on the Sat. night the streets were thronged with people." She then told of their nightly proselyting efforts: "We formed a circle, sang a hymn, one offered prayer then we sang again. A large crowd stopped to listen." From Oldham the two sisters were assigned to labor in Bristol. Inez reported that in the month of August 1898 in Bristol that she and Jennie "distributed 523 tracts, visited 295 houses in tracting, visited 14 homes by invitation, had 22 gospel conversations, and distributed two books."[7] Of their missionary labors, Jennie especially enjoyed times when she had the opportunity to share her testimony. Inez wrote, "So effective was her testimony that after twenty years an unbeliever who listened to her speak wrote, saying he could never forget her sincere, guileless expression and was led further to investigate and receive the blessings of membership."[8]

Jennie was honorably released in November 1898 due to health issues after six months of missionary service. Liza Chipman was called to take her place as the companion to Inez. Jennie traveled home with returning missionaries, including J. William Knight, whom she married two months later in the Salt Lake Temple.[9]

After their marriage, Jennie and "Will" moved to Raymond, Alberta, Canada, where Jennie became the mother of two sons. She presided over the Taylor Stake Young Ladies MIA (YLMIA) in Alberta before returning to Provo with her family. In Provo, Jennie served for eight years in the Utah Stake YLMIA. From 1921 to 1928 she was the first counselor to Clarissa Williams, the Relief Society general president. Jennie was also involved in the Red Cross and the Utah Women's Council of Defense. In 1925 she attended the International Council of Women Conference in Washington, DC.

Much like her pioneer predecessors who made great sacrifices to gather to the Salt Lake Valley, Jennie and her friend Inez were pioneers in the missionary work of the LDS Church. Orson F. Whitney wrote, "The novel spectacle of two young and innocent girls—whose appearance alone betokened modesty and virtue, as their utterances shared intelligence and sincerity—declaring in words of soberness that Mormonism was divine" was sufficient to extend the call to other single sisters to share the gospel of Jesus Christ.[10]

1   Diane L. Mangum, "The First Sister Missionaries," *Ensign,* July 1980, 38.

2   Orson F. Whitney, *History of Utah,* 4 vols. (Salt Lake City: George Q. Cannon & Sons Co., 1904), 4:613–614; and Inez Knight Allen, "Jennie Brimhall Knight," *The Relief Society Magazine* 15 (1928), 645646.

3   Whitney, 4:613–614.

4   Diane L. Mangum, "Heroes and Heroines: Called to Serve," *The Friend,* July 1980, 38.

5   Whitney, 614.

6   Ibid.

7   Mangum, 64.

8   Allen, 646.

9   Mangum, 62.

10   Ibid.

ETTIE LEE

Generosity

A well-known educator, philanthropist, and social service worker in southern California, Ettie Lee was a "mother" and counselor as well as benefactor to thousands of disadvantaged young boys. For her persistent compassion to the youth in the greater Los Angeles area, she received a prestigious plaque from the governor of California. In the ceremony that followed, one speaker said, "[Ettie] may well be the nation's foremost enemy of delinquency, because of the pattern she has set."[1] In response to this accolade and others, she said, "My work with misguided boys was set up from the beginning to bring joy to them; to give them love and guidance and to teach them responsibility and self-reliance. The extra bonus is that it has brought me joy untold."[2]

Ettie was born November 2, 1885, in Luna Valley, New Mexico. Her mother died when she was a baby. Her goal in life was to emulate her father's innate ability to search out and help the less fortunate. He never offered the vague prayer, "Bless the poor, the needy, the sick, and the afflicted." Instead, he prayed, "Lord, the oldest Quentin girl is needing shoes; and one of the Durfee boys will have to have a warmer coat. Please hold off the storms until we can get these needs taken care of."[3]

When Ettie was fifteen, her father moved his family to Thatcher, Arizona, where Ettie enrolled in the Gila Academy to learn how to make her contributions to the world. Her father told her, "It isn't enough just to take what life offers. Somebody has to put something back."[4]

After completing her education at Gila, she began a career as a schoolteacher. "If ever a girl was born to teach, it was Ettie Lee," wrote her biographer.[5] At age seventeen, she was a first-year teacher in a small pineboard schoolhouse in southwest Arizona. At Christmastime, it was expected that she would host a party for her students. Just as her party was getting underway, children rushed to tell her, "Miss Lee, Charles is outside." Charles was a young boy who had been expelled the year before. "Tell him to come in," Ettie said. "I am glad that he would come to our party. I will tie another orange on the tree." At this, the wife of a school trustee loudly announced, "That boy has been expelled." Ettie replied, "That was last year's mistake. . . . This is my party . . . and it is my privilege to invite the boy." When Charles came through the door, the woman "grabbed the tea kettle from the stove and dashed the boiling water over the bewildered boy."[6] Ettie turned to the woman and said, "I'm going to the trustees—I'll go to Phoenix—I'll go to the governor of the territory if I have to. I'm going to get that boy back into circulation." And to everyone's surprise, she did just that.[7]

After three years of teaching in southwest Arizona, she enrolled in the Northern Arizona Normal School. After graduation from Normal School, she began teaching at the Gila Academy. One of her students was Spencer W. Kimball. Of Ettie, Spencer said, "I love Ettie Lee. . . . I have loved her for half a century. . . . This lady taught us reading, writing, and arithmetic."

By 1914 Ettie was in Los Angeles seeking a degree in English and sociology from the University of Southern California (USC); in 1917 she graduated. Out of the 3,500 students who took an examination to teach in Los Angeles, she scored the highest. She accepted a teaching position at San Pedro High School and later at a local junior high. Back in the classroom, she once again found many young boys struggling to meet the challenges of life with confidence. "Someone must go out of the beaten path and take these children by the hand—by the heart—and lead them back," she said.[8] Hoping to help minority youth, she wrote English textbooks that were adopted first by the Los Angeles School District and then in ever-widening circles. She was invited to speak at USC, UCLA, and other teaching institutions across the nation. But for her, it was not enough.

She wished that all children could have been reared in a home like hers. She didn't agree with the way these boys were treated by the courts and unsuccessfully tried to convince the California legislature that a change was needed. "So," Ettie said, "I decided to be like the little red hen and do it myself."[9] She made plans to establish "good homes, where boys could come, problems and all, and where they could ripen naturally, under the sunshine of love."[10]

To achieve her goals, she needed money—lots of money. She went to a library and checked out the book *How to Make Millions in Real Estate.* She then began saving $100 a month from her $200 monthly salary to buy and repair buildings, then sell them for additional investments. By 1950, sixty-five-year-old Ettie had enough money for a down payment to purchase her first home for neglected, delinquent boys. Through consistent, sound financial investing, Ettie was able to purchase ten homes for "her boys." In one year alone, more than three hundred "abused, abandoned, neglected, and delinquent boys" received shelter, love, and instruction in the Ettie Lee Homes.[11]

At the dedication of an Ettie Lee Home in Mapleton, Utah, President Spencer W. Kimball said, "I should like to add my word of appreciation to her, commendation for the great work that she has done. . . . She may not live forever in mortality; but her work will live on forever into eternity and through eternity, for boys and their offspring will praise her name forever and ever and ever, for the good that she has done."[12]

1   Ora Pate Stewart, *Tender Apples: A Biography of Ettie Lee* (Salt Lake City: Deseret Book, 1965), 330.
2   Ibid., 331.
3   Ibid., 226.
4   Ibid., 157.
5   Ibid., 175.
6   Ibid., 177–179.
7   Ibid., 182.
8   Ibid., 236.
9   "California Utah Women Philanthropy Ettie Lee Homes for Youth," in author's possession.
10   Stewart, 249.
11   See "California Utah Women Philanthropy."
12   Stewart, 326.

MARY ELIZABETH ROLLINS LIGHTNER

Courage

Knowing that Queen Esther had a chance to save the Jewish people, Mordecai said to her, "Who knoweth whether thou art come to the kingdom for such a time as this?"[1] These same words could have been spoken to Mary Elizabeth Rollins Lightner, who risked her life to save the words of God.

When Mary was two years old, her father died in a shipwreck on Lake Ontario. Following his death, she and her mother and siblings moved into the home of Uncle Algernon Sidney Gilbert in Ohio. In 1828 the extended family moved to Kirtland. It was in Kirtland that Mary first heard of the Book of Mormon. In October 1830, news of the book was confirmed by Oliver Cowdery and other missionaries. "Quite a number of the residents of Kirtland were baptized, among them, mother and myself," penned twelve-year-old Mary.[2]

Upon learning that Kirtland resident Isaac Morley had a copy of the Book of Mormon, Mary went to his house to see the book. "I felt such a great desire to read it that I could not refrain from asking [Brother Morley] to let me take it home and read it." Morley said, "My child I have not read one chapter in it myself and the Brethren will want to

see it tonight at the meeting." But upon seeing her disappointment, Morley said, "Well if you will bring it back early or before breakfast tomorrow morning you may take it." Mary said, "If anyone was ever perfectly happy I was." She ran home. Upon entering the house, she said, "Oh Uncle I have the Golden Bible."[3] That night she and her family stayed up late to read the book.

"As soon as it was daylight I was up and learned the first paragraph by heart," she wrote. Mary then took the book back to Brother Morley. "Well you are early, I guess you did not read much of it," he said. "I showed him how far we had read, he was more surprised and said: 'I don't believe you can tell me a word of it.' I then repeated what I had learned and gave an outline of the history of Nephi. He gazed at me in surprise and said, 'Child you take this back and finish it, I can wait.'"[4]

Just before Mary finished the last chapter, the Prophet Joseph Smith arrived in Kirtland. Upon seeing that copy of the Book of Mormon in Gilbert's home, he asked about Mary. "He came and put his hands on my head," she recalled, "and gave me a great blessing, the first I had ever received, then he made me a present of the book saying he would give Brother Morley another copy."[5]

With such love of the scriptures, is it any wonder that Mary would be willing to risk her life to save another scripture: the Book of Commandments?

In autumn of 1831 Mary and her family moved to Independence, Missouri, where her Uncle Gilbert opened a dry goods and grocery store. Their circumstances were prosperous for a time, but then tensions between Mormons and the old settlers erupted. "One night a great many men got together and stoned our house, part of which was hewed logs and the other part or front was brick. After breaking all the windows they started tearing off the roof on the brick part, amidst awful oaths and yells that were terrible to hear," she wrote. More extreme difficulties followed. "I saw Bishop Partridge tarred and feathered, and also Brother Charles Allen," wrote Mary. "My sister saw them cover them with tar, then empty a pillow of feathers over them. Oh what a sight, our hearts ached for them." [6]

But for Mary, it was on the night that the "mob renewed their work again by tearing down the printing office" that she risked her life to save the word of God. Recalling the circumstances, she penned, "My sister Caroline and I were in a corner of the fence trembling watching them." But Mary knew what she had to do when the sisters saw mobbers bring out a pile of large sheets of paper and heard them say, "Here are the damned Mormon Commandments." Mary determined to save some of the papers even though it would put her life in grave danger. Her sister Caroline agreed to help her, but said, "They will kill us." The sisters waited until the mob turned to pry "out the gable end of the [printing] building." They then "ran and got our arms full and were turning away when some of the mob saw us and called for us to stop," recalled Mary. "But we ran as fast as we could into a large cornfield, laid the papers on the ground and then we laid flat over them."[7]

The corn was about five or six feet tall and extremely dense. The mobbers "hunted quite a while for us, coming very near and making our hearts beat faster but finally left," Mary penned. After the sisters were satisfied that the men were gone, they came out of the cornfield and ran to safety. The pages that they saved were later "bound in small books." Of the book given her, Mary wrote, "I prized it highly."[8]

Although Mary later married, became a mother, journeyed west, and did much good in her life, the most remembered vignette will always be her determination to save the words of God even when to do so put her own life in jeopardy. Her actions fulfilled the promise given to Joseph Smith: "[The scriptures] shall be preserved in safety."[9]

---

1   Esther 4:14.
2   "Autobiography of Mary E. R. Lightner," 1, Mss. 363, Fd. 5, L. Tom Perry Special Collections, Harold B. Lee Library, Brigham Young University, Provo, Utah. (See also Marlene Bateman Sullivan, *Latter-day Saint Heroes and Heroines: Stories of Courageous Saints Around the World* [Springville Utah: Cedar Fort, Inc., 2007], 69–71.)

3   "Autobiography," 1.
4   Ibid.
5   Ibid., 2.
6   Ibid., 4.
7   Ibid.
8   Ibid.
9   D&C 42:56.

Amy Brown Lyman

Problem Solving

"The hardest problem," remarked Amy Brown Lyman, "[is] getting people to realize there [is] a problem."[1] When problems are acknowledged, Amy believed, people could move forward and deal with life's trials. As she recognized and confronted her own problems, she developed a pattern of confidence to face life and move forward.

While attending Brigham Young Academy, Amy met Richard R. Lyman, son of Elder Francis M. Lyman. As their friendship blossomed, Richard pressed for marriage. Amy hesitated to accept his proposal. "I want to see and hear a few more things," she wrote, "before I sink into oblivion."[2] She eventually consented to marriage, and on September 9, 1896, Richard and Amy were married in the Salt Lake Temple by President Joseph F. Smith. At the time of their marriage, Richard was a professor of civil engineering at the University of Utah, and she a graduate of the Brigham Young Academy Normal School.

For many years, marriage for Amy was the opposite of what she had once feared it would be. Richard encouraged her to take advantage of opportunities to hone her talents; as one example, in 1901, when Richard enrolled at the University of Chicago, he supported Amy's desire

to follow suit by enrolling in a course on the new science of sociology.[3] While completing her coursework, she concluded that organized relief should replace indiscriminate giving and that "old fashioned charity" should be "replaced by modern welfare which calls for getting to the very roots of the trouble."[4] These simple truths became her hallmark for the next sixty years.

In October 1909, when Amy was invited to become a member of the Relief Society general board, she had many opportunities to speak about these truths. Those opportunities increased as she served on the Relief Society general board for the next three decades, eventually becoming the Relief Society general president. Her position gave her many opportunities to speak about giving greater and more meaningful service.[5] From policy and procedures to personalities involved in the Child Placing Agency of the Relief Society, Amy's contribution was seen in the lives of birth mothers, babies, and adoptive parents.

As her circle of influence increased, Amy became a delegate to the National Conference of Social Work and the National Council of Women. Believing that there was yet more for her to do, in 1922 she was nominated for a seat in the Utah State Legislature. As a legislator, she worked to secure federal aid to state agencies for maternity, child health, and welfare programs. Some claimed that "infancy and maternal mortality rates in the state decreased markedly" as a direct result of her efforts.[6] When opponents argued that women belonged in the home and were not suited for a role in government, Amy countered that the virtues traditionally ascribed to women because of their experience as mothers and homemakers "endowed them with a special knowledge of human needs and humanistic rights."[7]

At the very time she was being extolled as a woman of extraordinary talents and energy, her world toppled. On November 11, 1943, her husband, Richard, an Apostle for nearly twenty-five years, was excommunicated from the Church through his own confession and the action of the First Presidency "for violation of the Christian Law of

Chastity."[8] When mettlesome friends "advised [Amy] to get a divorce and move to California and make a fresh start," she refused.[9] It went against her love for Richard and her long-held belief that difficulties must be faced.

To resolve problems at home, she resigned her presidency of the Relief Society on April 6, 1945. after serving thirty-six years on the general board through the Great Depression and two world wars. But in the years that followed, Amy was no recluse; she was often present at Relief Society functions and Daughters of Utah Pioneers meetings.[10] As for Richard, he was rebaptized and died in full fellowship at age ninety-three.

In many respects, the triumphs for Amy Brown Lyman came at great personal cost. It was only when she moved beyond pain to renew and rebuild a life of service that she again found her life. Her philosophy—a determination to recognize problems and seek for solutions—blessed her life and the lives of generations of Latter-day Saint women. Although her sphere of influence dimmed in later years, Amy said, "I honor beyond my power of expression this great sisterhood of service."[11]

1   David Roy Hall, "Amy Brown Lyman and Social Service Work in the Relief Society," Master's Thesis (Provo, Utah: Brigham Young University, 1992), 168.
2   Amy Brown to Will Hayes, February 24, 1895, holograph in possession of David Hall, as cited in Hall, 32.
3   Jill Mulvay Derr, "A History of Social Services in the Church of Jesus Christ of Latter-day Saints, 1916–1984" (n.p. 1988), 15; in possession of Jill Mulvay Derr, Provo, Utah.
4   Janet Peterson and La Rene Gaunt, *Elect Ladies* (Deseret Book: Salt Lake City, 1990), 135–136.
5   See Amy Brown Lyman, "The Development of Spirituality through the Social Service Department," *Relief Society Magazine* 23, November 1936, 699–700.
6   Hall, 83.
7   Brown, 82–83.
8   *Deseret News,* November 13, 1943, 1.
9   Hall, 168.
10 See "Amy Brown Lyman Papers," L. Tom Perry Special Collections, Harold B. Lee Library, Brigham Young University, Provo, Utah.
11 Peterson and Gaunt, 142.

Ann N. Madsen

Tolerance

Asi, asi paco—a Samoan phrase meaning "ducks are different"—was used by Ann's father, who served a mission in the Samoan Islands, when differences arose between Ann and her brother. Her father's reminder of the uniqueness of each person helped Ann realize that differences between people always exist, but differences should be respected and prized. That attitude helped Ann build strong relationships with a variety of people. Drawing upon the scriptures, Ann defines *tolerance* as allowing all men the same privilege and refusing to be a "respecter of persons." She resonates to the saying, "All are alike unto God."[1]

Daughter of Barnard J. Nicholls, Ann Nicholls was born in 1932 in Salt Lake City, where she grew to womanhood. Following her graduation from East High School, Ann enrolled at the University of Utah, where she met graduate student Truman G. Madsen. Ann graduated from the U of U with a degree in elementary education; Truman's graduate studies led to a degree in philosophy and further schooling.

Soon after Ann and Truman were married in 1953, they moved to Cambridge, Massachusetts, where Truman pursued academic training at Harvard. Ann found the many cultures represented in Cambridge delightful. She recalls that while attending her first Relief Society meeting in the Cambridge Ward, she heard Elizabeth Hinckley say, "Now don't you Utah girls come here and hold your noses for four years wishing you were back in the only true West where things are done right! Absorb this wonderful culture. Learn New England cookery, get to know your Yankee neighbors; that may take some patience, but it's well worth it."[2] Taking her advice, Ann embraced the New England culture and fell in love with the people of Boston. "I learned that tolerance can lead to love," she said.[3]

In 1962, only a few years after leaving Harvard, Truman was called at the age of thirty-five to be president of the New England Mission. Ann, now a mother of three children, returned with enthusiasm to Boston in hopes of sharing the culture she loved with her children. Her attitude of embracing differences helped her to be effective as a mission president's wife and to share the gospel of Jesus Christ with a variety of people. She successfully taught many who willingly entered baptismal waters.

After completing the mission in New England, the Madsen family settled in Provo, Utah, where they became foster parents to their fourth child—a nine-year-old Navajo son. "What a blessing it was to open our arms and home forever to this fine young Navajo," Ann says.

Also while in Provo, Ann pursued a master's degree in ancient studies at Brigham Young University. She then accepted employment as a part-time instructor in religious education. Her favorite course to teach is Isaiah.

She became a gifted and inspiring teacher. In 1987 she taught Bible classes at BYU's Jerusalem Center for Near Eastern Studies. From 1991 to 1993, Ann again taught Bible classes there while Truman was the director of the center. Living in Jerusalem among Israelis and Palestinians for the better part of five years tested Ann's openness to cultural differences. Grappling with two cultures—Israeli and Palestinian—that dealt in retaliation after an attack, she wrote *Making*

Their Own Peace: Twelve Women of Jerusalem.[4] In her book, she tells of women in Jerusalem on both sides of the conflict who were able to accept differences and enjoy an inner peace.

Looking back on a lifetime of openness and tolerance, Ann is grateful to have an ever-widening circle of friends "in every different walk of life, in every different religious persuasion, every different nationality."[5] Recently Ann wrote the poem "Love Closes the Distance," expressing her belief in tolerance:

Dear Lord, Thank you.
You've helped us
See Your world.
Touch it,
Hold it
In our hands
And stand
Humbled
By the grandness
Of it all.

You've pushed it
So close
That we could
Scarcely breathe
Without
Fogging the glasses
Of the man
Beside us.

You knew
That this familiarity
Would breed in us

A burgeoning
Love.
It is the same with You.
Love closes the distance
Between us.

1   Ann N. Madsen, "Differences . . . 'Allow All Men the Same Privilege,'" July 20, 1982, Brigham Young University Devotional, Provo, Utah; interview with Ann N. Madsen, January 11, 2010, Provo, Utah.

2   Madsen.

3   Ibid.

4   Ann N. Madsen, Making *Their Own Peace, 12 women of Jerusalem* (Brooklyn, New York: Lantern Books, 2003).

5   Ann Madsen, Interview with Wendy Vardeman, January 12, 2010, Provo, Utah; transcription in author's possession.

ELIZABETH ANN CLARIDGE McCUNE

Friendship

Anyone exploring the downtown area of Salt Lake City will surely discover an intriguing mansion located at 200 North Main Street. The McCune Mansion stands as a regal symbol of an era of entrepreneurs and elegance—the era of Elizabeth Ann Claridge McCune.[1] In her early years Elizabeth Ann knew all too well the effects of extreme poverty of a family—but in her later years, she was surrounded with opulence. Her close friend Elizabeth Snow Ivins observed, "The one thing which most impressed me in her life was, that when wealth came to her, when her every wish that money could purchase was at her command, when her home was a palace, she remained the same simple, lovable woman, with the same friendships, the same hopes and aspirations which characterized her in adversity."[2]

Daughter of Samuel and Charlotte Joy Claridge, Elizabeth Ann was born February 19, 1852, in Hemel Hempstead, England; shortly after her birth, her parents joined The Church of Jesus Christ of Latter-day Saints. When Elizabeth was just eleven months old, the Claridge family emigrated from England to America with the help of the Perpetual Emigration Fund.

The family settled in Nephi, Utah, until accepting a call from LDS Church leaders to settle in the Muddy Mission in Nevada's Moapa Valley, about fifty miles northeast of Las Vegas.[3] In 1867, when Elizabeth Ann was fifteen, the Claridge family left Nephi bound for the Muddy. As they neared their destination, their wagon rolled and plunged over a precipice. Everything they owned scattered across the desert, including flour and Elizabeth Ann's clothes. Her father calmly turned to Elizabeth Ann and said, "My daughter, I prophesy that the day will come when you will have much better clothes than those to wear."[4]

Life in the Muddy proved difficult for the Claridge family. The climate was hot and dry, shelter was made of willows, and food was poor. Coarse bran was used to make bread, and roots were added to food staples to stretch supplies.[5]

Due to harsh conditions and high Nevada taxes, the Claridges and other LDS families were asked by Church leadership to abandon the Muddy Mission, and the Claridges returned to Nephi. In Nephi, Elizabeth Ann met Alfred McCune; they were married in 1872 in the Endowment House. A successful railroad contractor, Alfred was said to have the Midas touch in all financial dealings. Whether contracting for railroads, establishing lumber businesses, working with livestock, mining for metals,[6] or converting Salt Lake's trolley car system from mule power to electric power, everything he did succeeded.[7]

Alfred's ever-widening circle of influence included the wealthy and prestigious. As for Elizabeth Ann, her friends were not chosen for position or prestige but for qualities she recognized in them; she, in return, was loyal and true to her friends. For her, a wonderful life meant being surrounded by her family of nine children and friends from her childhood.

Elizabeth Ann enjoyed frontier living until one day when the men were a mile or two away cutting lumber and she was at home baking bread. A band of twelve starving Indians covered with war paint broke in to her home. Instead of screaming, Elizabeth Ann took the hot bread she was baking and gave it to the angry Indians; they shook Elizabeth Ann's hand and left peacefully.[8] In spite of a peaceful interchange, Elizabeth Ann now looked forward to living in a larger city away from Indian attacks.

The McCunes soon moved to northern Utah, where from 1905 to 1910 Elizabeth Ann was a trustee of the Agricultural College in Logan, the last two years acting as vice-president of the board—the first woman in the United States to occupy such a position. She was also instrumental in establishing the Domestic Science and Domestic Art departments. Through her influence, Alfred contributed liberally to the building of the Salt Lake Temple and the *Young Women's Journal.* With each donation Elizabeth Ann made two requests—anonymity and use of the money where it would do the most good.[9]

Elizabeth Ann served in many prominent LDS Church positions, including as a member of the YLMIA (Young Ladies Mutual Improvement Association) and the Relief Society general boards. In her capacity as a leader among women, she visited LDS missions in Europe, Canada, Mexico, and the Sandwich Islands. Before beginning these visits, President Lorenzo Snow promised her, "Thy mind shall be as clear as an angel's when explaining the principles of the gospel." The promise was literally fulfilled.

Elizabeth Ann was also an active supporter of women's rights and was an avid supporter of temple work. President Heber J. Grant said that he knew "of no one connected with our temple work and the genealogical work, who has given more devoted service."[10]

During the many years of her service, Alfred and Elizabeth Ann constructed what became known as the McCune Mansion. Sparing no expense, they sent their architect, S. C. Dallas, to study design in Europe for two years. Upon his return, he created their home of San Domingo mahogany, English oak, Dutch red roof tiles, German mirrors, and Russian leather. The home was completed in 1901 at a cost of more than $1 million ($22.5 million in 2011 dollars). It was the grandest home west of the Mississippi.[11] In 1920 Elizabeth and Alfred gave their mansion to the LDS Church with the stipulation that general authorities decide how it would be best used. [12]

The McCunes then traveled to Los Angeles and elsewhere. In the spring of 1924, they went on their last trip together to Bermuda, where Elizabeth Ann became ill. They returned home to Salt Lake immediately. Her children were present when she died on August 1, 1924.[13] In her will she left $100,000 each to forty-six relatives and friends and the Genealogical Society of Utah.[14] Though Elizabeth Ann had been entertained in a Queen's court and lived in all the opulence her era had to offer, she remained a true friend and supporter of the Church to which her impoverished parents had converted when she was a baby.

1   Carol Ann S. Van Wagoner, "Elizabeth Ann Claridge McCune: At Home on the Hill," in Collen Whitley, ed., *Worth Their Salt, Notable but Often Unnoted Women of Utah* (Logan, Utah: Utah State University Press, 1996), 90.

2   Susa Young Gates, *Memorial to Elizabeth Claridge McCune: Missionary, Philanthropist, Architect* (Salt Lake City: n.p., 1924), 87.

3   "Muddy Mission Settled a 'Forbidding, Lonely' Area," *LDS Church News,* January 12, 1991.

4   Gates, 21–22.

5   Leon R. Hartshorn, comp., *Remarkable Stories from the Lives of Latter-day Saint Women,* 2 vols. (Salt Lake City: Deseret Book, 1973), 1:118.

6   Gates, 11.

7   Van Wagoner, 95.

8   Gates, 25.

9   Ibid., 73.

10 Ibid., 60.

11 McCune Mansion, toured August 10, 2010.

12 Gates, 45.

13 Van Wagoner, 96–97.

14 Gates, 57.

EMMA RAY RIGGS McKAY

Being a Helpmeet

When Emma Ray Riggs informed her father that she was contemplating marriage to David O. McKay, her father advised, "Now my darling daughter I want to impress upon you the fact that it is not any more difficult to get a man's love than it is to hold it—after you have it. There are so many little things that a man appreciates in a woman, that some women never think of. . . . When a true man sees his wife doing every thing she can for his pleasure will he not do likewise for his wife? Surely he will, then there is mutual compensation & mutual happiness."[1] On January 2, 1901, Emma and David were the first couple married in the twentieth century in the Salt Lake Temple. Following her father's advice, Emma became a role model of a wife for many generations of Latter-day Saint women.

Emma Ray was born June 23, 1877, in Salt Lake City. Her father viewed her as a "ray of sunshine" as she joined a family of four boys. It was her father who named her "Ray."

From the beginning of her marriage, Emma Ray tried to put her husband's needs before her own. After just four months of marriage, when she was gone from home for a day, David wrote to her, "I want my comforting Ray. This isn't home without you. When I came from school tonight I missed you; as I walked to meeting I wanted you by my side; and since coming home I have longed for you."[2] Emma Ray returned home quickly.

When she learned that David liked coconut custard pie, she made the best pie in town. She tinted the custard pink and toasted the coconut before adding a creamy topping. Once when she and her son David Lawrence were eating at a restaurant, her son suggested that she order coconut custard pie for herself. Emma Ray remarked, "I don't like coconut custard pie." Her son queried, "You don't like it! But you've made it all these years!" Emma Ray said, "It was your father's favorite, and I made it, but I never ate it."[3]

Trying to be a supportive wife was not always easy for Emma Ray. She recalled the first night the nurse left her alone with her newborn infant. When she saw David put on his hat and coat, Emma Ray thought, *Surely you aren't going to a meeting tonight.* As if reading her thoughts, David looked at her for a moment and said, "Have you forgotten that it is Sunday School board meeting tonight?" There was no warmth in her kiss as she bade him goodbye. The closing door awoke the baby. Emma Ray went to the rocking chair and rocked the crying baby while tears of frustration and hurt rolled down her cheeks. That night she determined that if possible she would go with David to his meetings. Many nights she packed the baby in a heavy shawl and rode in a buggy with him as he traveled to visit the Saints.[4]

As Emma Ray watched her husband fulfill his Church responsibilities, she found him to be inspired of God. For example, David would often tell Emma Ray what would happen that day before he left home to complete his Church assignments. When he returned in the evening, Emma Ray would ask, "Well, did it happen like you said it would, David?" He would reply, "Just exactly."[5]

Neither David nor Emma Ray anticipated David's call to the Quorum of the Twelve Apostles. When Emma Ray heard his name read off in the Salt Lake Tabernacle, she thought she had heard incorrectly. But when she looked at David, she could tell by the look on his face that she had heard correctly, and burst into tears. Now he will never be home, she thought.[6] She heard someone behind her say, "There's the wife of one of them. See, she's crying."[7] Through his years in the quorum David was seldom home. The most taxing of their many separations was his world tour from 1921 to 1922. Fortunately, some of his assignments were shared with Emma Ray. They served together in the European Mission, and when Emma Ray was set apart for that assignment, President Heber J. Grant assured her that if she would depend on the Lord, He would give her "the necessary strength to discharge every responsibility."[8] This blessing was fulfilled as she served the Saints in Europe.

Emma Ray praised David publicly for his love, and David reciprocated; he pictured heaven to be a continuation of his home.[9] He was speaking of Emma Ray when he said, "Pure hearts in a pure home are always in whispering distance of heaven."[10]

In her nineties Emma Ray insisted that her hair be combed, makeup applied, and a lovely dress be put on before she saw her husband.[11] It was touching for those who watched President McKay say goodbye to Emma Ray as he left their home to attend meetings. He would pull his wheelchair alongside her wheelchair and give her a kiss. Then he'd say, "All right, I'm ready to go."[12] In his later years, he wrote poetic expressions of endearment to Emma Ray called "Heart Petals." He shared these beautiful sentiments from the tabernacle pulpit and in the *Deseret News* on their anniversary, holidays, and other occasions. On President McKay's ninetieth birthday in 1963, he wrote of Emma Ray:

> Family cares came heavy but not a complaint
> Forty-four children now crown her a saint;
> Companion, counselor, advisor alway
> My wife for eternity, my own Emma Ray.[13]

Emma Ray and David died within ten months of each other in 1970. They had lived together as husband and wife for nearly seventy years. During those years Emma Ray heeded her father's advice to "study the likes and dislikes of her husband and try hard to do everything to accord with his likes." [14] To an entire Church, it appeared she succeeded—for Emma Ray and David lived after the manner of happiness and mutual love.

1   Obadiah H. Riggs to Emma Ray Riggs, December 13, 1900, David O. McKay transcripts, University of Utah Manuscript Collection, Mss. 668, Box 1, Fd. 2, J. Willard Marriott Library, University of Utah, Salt Lake City.

2   David Lawrence McKay, *My Father, David O. McKay* (Salt Lake City: Deseret Book, 1989), 10; David O. McKay to Emma Ray Riggs McKay, April 23, 1901, David O. McKay transcripts, University of Utah Manuscript Collection, Mss. 668, Box 1, Fd. 2.

3   McKay, 11–12.

4   Zella Farr Smith, "A Romantic Story from the Life of President and Sister McKay," McKay Scrapbook, no. 131, Church History Library, as cited in Mary Jane Woodger, *Beloved Prophet* (American Fork: Covenant Communications, 2004), 72; and Emma Ray Riggs McKay, September 8, 1957, Wells Stake Conference, Granite Stake Tabernacle, Salt Lake City, McKay Scrapbook, no. 39.

5   Emma Ray Riggs McKay.

6   Woodger, 82.

7   David Lawrence McKay, 40.

8   Blessing given to Emma Ray Riggs McKay, McKay Scrapbook, no. 188.

9   David O. McKay, *Gospel Ideals* (Salt Lake City: Improvement Era, 1953), 490.

10   David O. McKay, as cited in Harold B. Lee, *Stand Ye in Holy Places* (Salt Lake City: Deseret Book, 1974), 176.

11   Woodger, 263.

12   Thomas S. Monson, interview for David O. McKay School of Education, October 7, 1996, Salt Lake City; video in author's possession.

13   Lee, 178.

14   Obadiah H. Riggs to Emma Ray Riggs.

STEPHENIE MEYER

Imagination

Photo from http://blog.newsok.com/bamsblog/

Stephenie Meyer is the closest thing to a rock star in the book world since J. K. Rowling wrote the Harry Potter series—and she is the world's most popular vampire novelist since Anne Rice. Does she get her creative ideas by reading horror novels? "I just know I'm too much of a wuss for Stephen King's books," says Stephenie. "I'm waaay *[sic]* too chicken to read horror."[1] But she is never too chicken to stand up for her beliefs as a member of The Church of Jesus Christ of Latter-day Saints.

 Daughter of Stephen Morgan, Stephenie was born December 24, 1973, in Hartford, Connecticut. When she was four her family moved to Phoenix, Arizona, and she considers herself a native Arizonan. Days after the move, Stephenie met Christian "Pancho" Meyer, another four-year-old, who would later become her husband. "We were never anywhere close to being childhood sweethearts," she laments. "In fact, though we saw each other at least weekly through church activities, I can't recall a single instance when we so much as greeted each other with a friendly wave, let alone exchanged actual words."[2]

 Stephenie grew up in a faithful LDS home and community. "I grew up in a community where it was not the exception to be a good girl.

It was expected," she says. "And all of my friends were good girls too, and my boyfriends were good boys."[3] To Stephenie and her friends, it was "about keeping yourself free of addictions." They believed then and now that "free will is a huge gift from God."[4]

Stephenie attended Chapparral High School in Scottsdale, "the kind of place where every fall a few girls would come back to school with new noses and there were Porsches in the student lot. For the record, I have my original nose, and never had a car until after I was in my twenties. Our football team was renowned statewide—for having the highest GPA average."[5] It was a time in her life when holding hands at age sixteen "was just—wow."[6]

Stephenie was awarded a National Merit Scholarship, which she used to pay her way through Brigham Young University—where she majored in English literature. She said, "I didn't consider reading books as work (as long as I was going to be doing something anyway, I might as well get course credit for it, right?)." During her college years, there were jokes about English majors ending up in the food service industry. "To all the people who made those jokes," she "now says, 'Ha, ha.'"[7]

When she was twenty, Stephenie again met Christian "Pancho" Meyer. "It only took nine months from the first 'hello' to the wedding in 1994. Of course, we were able to skip over a lot of the getting to know you parts," she says. "Many of our conversations would go something like this: 'This one time, when I was ten, I broke my hand at a party when—' 'Yeah, I know what happened. I was there, remember?'"[8] Stephenie and Pancho are now the parents of three sons—Gabe, Seth, and Eli. They live in Cave Creek, a small town outside Phoenix.

Once Stephenie held baby Gabe in her arms, she just wanted to be his mom. "Then what's a nice Mormon girl like you doing writing about vampires?" she is often asked. She explains that she enjoyed being a full-time mother, occasionally working on scrapbooks and making elaborate Halloween costumes, until June 2, 2003. On that date, she dreamed of an ordinary girl sitting next to a sparkling vampire in a sunlit meadow. They were in love, and he was telling her how hard it was for him to keep from killing her.[9] When she awoke, Stephenie began to write like a "woman struck by lightning, barely sleeping, typing one-handed with a baby in her lap."[10] Three months later she finished a five-hundred-page manuscript titled *Twilight*.

Little, Brown and Company agreed to publish the manuscript, unaware that they had acquired the publishing rights to a new phenomenon. *Twilight* hit the bookstores in October 2005. By November, *Twilight* was number five on the *New York Times* bestseller list for young adult chapter books. For the next 142 weeks *Twilight* and its two sequels remained on the *New York Times* bestseller list.[11] By 2009 the *Twilight* series had sold more than 25 million copies worldwide and had been printed in thirty-seven different languages.[12]

Stephenie was named the bestselling author in 2008 by *USA Today*. Lev Grossman of *Time* magazine wrote, "Maybe Americans aren't ready for a Mormon presidential nominee yet [a reference to Mitt Romney's unsuccessful 2008 bid for the U.S. presidency]. But they're more than ready to anoint a Mormon as the best-selling novelist of the year."[13] Her books have since been adapted for film. To Stephenie, the "queen of fantasy," writing *Twilight* and watching its success "has been a crazy, rollercoaster-sans-seatbelts experience from the very beginning."[14]

That rollercoaster ride now includes millions of fans. "My fans count on me to be a fast writer, once-a-year release schedule, which you know, isn't entirely fair," she says.[15] In the meantime, they dress up like her characters, write their own stories and plots about her characters, and post their efforts on the Internet. Some fans have even formed *Twilight*-themed rock bands. The small town of Forks on the Olympic Peninsula in Washington state, the setting of the *Twilight* series, celebrates "Stephenie Meyer Day."

As to her future, Stephanie says that she is just beginning to write: "I have a file of novel ideas just waiting for me. . . . I've got mysteries and adventures and all things in my files."[16] What of the Church in her life and her writings? She says that being a Mormon "has a huge influence on who I am and my perspective on the world, and therefore what I write."[17] Amid fame and fortune, she maintains a strong faith in God and His restored Church.

1   Gregory Kirshling, "The Q&A: Stephenie Meyer's 'Twilight' Zone," August 5, 2008, *Entertainment Weekly*, http://www.ew.com/ew/article/0.,20049578.00.html (accessed September 2, 2010).

2   Unofficial Bio of Stephenie Meyer, www.stepheniemeyer.com/bio_unofficial.html (accessed August 28, 2010).

3   Kirshling.

4   Lev Grossman, "Stephenie Meyer: A New J. K. Rowling," *Time,* April 24, 2008.

5   Unofficial Bio.

6   Grossman.

7   Unofficial Bio.

8   Ibid.

9   Grossman.

10   Ibid.

11   Carma Wadley, "Meyer on Fire with Books," *Mormon Times,* May 16, 2008.

12   Claudia Parsons, "'Twilight,' Publisher see Film Boosting Book Sales," Rueters, November 21, 2008.

13   Grossman.

14   Unofficial Bio.

15   Kirshling.

16   Ibid.

17   Unofficial Bio.

MARIE OSMOND

Hope

Singer Marie Osmond's faith does not come from her parents; she insists, "I am a member of my Mormon faith because I want to be."[1] Her faith in God and His restored Church is her anchor amid the storms that threaten her sense of peace. In 2010, after attending the funeral of a son who committed suicide, Marie said, "Little did I know I would be relying on my faith, especially as much as I did this past week." With faith in the eternal nature of life and a promise of a "forever family," Marie, like so many times before, returned to the stage at the Flamingo Hotel in Las Vegas, where she was performing with her brother Donny. She told a standing-room-only crowd, "The way Osmonds survive is we keep singing and that's what we want to do tonight."[2]

Daughter of George and Olive Osmond, Marie was born October 13, 1959, in Ogden, Utah. She and her eight brothers were raised on Mormonism and show business. It was in show business that Marie became a legend. At age three, she debuted as part of her brothers' act on *The Andy Williams Show*. With Marie seated on Williams's lap, Andy introduced her as "the youngest Osmond Brother."

Marie did her first show when she was four, and she worked overseas at six and seven. Yet she laments that success cheated her "of a normal, happy childhood." For her, there was always one more performance. "I had to sacrifice a lot. I grew up in a suitcase—I never did the things normal girls do." Her parents told her that "show business wouldn't be easy." She concludes, "They were right."[3]

"I didn't like show business at first," Marie confesses. "I decided I wanted to be a secretary. I took shorthand and typing."[4] But as her life unfolded, she realized, "I love crowds. It's nice to be in front of a television camera or to be in a studio and record."[5]

Marie made a name for herself at age thirteen by recording "Paper Roses." The recording reached number one on the country hit charts. She was named the Best Female Country Vocal Performer and Best New Artist. She then booked her first concert performance at Madison Square Garden to a sold-out crowd. The title song of her next album, *Who's Sorry Now,* climbed to number twenty a month after its release. "You know, in the recording business it was all men, television was all men," said Marie of the 1970s. But she knew then and now, "I'm one of the exceptions to the rule."[6]

At age fourteen, Marie and Donny hosted the ABC television variety show *Donny & Marie.* "I'm a little bit country," Marie announced at the beginning of each show. Donny answered, "I'm a little bit rock and roll." Together the "toothy duo" performed comedy sketches and musical moments. By the time the show was cancelled in 1979, Donny and Marie had endeared themselves to an international audience. They were celebrities and confronted with all the problems associated with fame. Through it all Marie and Donny maintained their Mormon standards. Marie turned down the lead role as Sandy in *Grease* due to the script's lack of moral content. She carefully selected which roles to take in television movies and serials, like *Ripley's Believe It or Not,* and which children cartoon voice-overs met her criteria. In 1985 Marie and Dan Seals's duet "Meet Me in Montana" was named the number-one country hit of the year. In 1986 Marie and Paul Davis sang, "You're Still New to Me," which also reached number one in the country hits.

Since then Marie has been in great demand for television performances, Broadway musicals, films, concert tours, and authoring. She is president and CEO of Marie Osmond Collector Dolls. In 1991 her first sculpture, a toddler doll named "Olive May" after her mother, set a collectible record on QVC. She is also cofounder of the Children's Miracle Network, a project that has raised in excess of $3.4 billion since 1983 for children's hospitals throughout the United States and Canada.

But domestic life is difficult for the showgirl who once said, "Showbiz isn't for eternity. Marriage is."[7] She has been married and divorced twice. She is the mother of eight children—five adopted—from these marriages. One biographer wrote, "So joyfully has Marie taken to adoptive motherhood that she insists she doesn't know which child is of her flesh." As to eternal marriage, she insists, "I have had many good examples of what marriage can be, and I see all the happiness in my parents' lives, in my brothers' lives, and I want the same. There are scars, however, and you just need to work through them and get on with life and learn to trust again."[8]

In 1999 Marie revealed that she suffered from severe postpartum depression. She coauthored the book *Behind the Smile* that chronicles her experience with depression. "I guess God never gives us anything we can't handle," she writes, "and through all of it, I keep saying there's got to be a reason you go though it. . . . When you feel like hope is gone, look inside you and be strong, and you finally see the truth that a hero lies in you."[9] Since the book's release, Marie has starred in an exercise video, published a beauty book, and designed a line of clothing. In 2006 she launched a machine-embroidery line with Bernina and promoted the Nutri-system brand of weight loss. In August 2007 Marie danced on ABC Network's *Dancing with the Stars*. She joked, "There are worse habits I could take up going through a mid-life crisis."[10]

What's next? For this legend in the entertainment industry, happiness is the hope. She and her family were recognized as one of the most prolific entertainment families in the world when a star was placed in their honor on the Hollywood Walk of Fame. At that time, the Osmonds had forty-seven gold and platinum records and had sold more than a hundred million records worldwide. Yet Marie hopes for something more. Amid her ups and downs, she believes that her faith in God will bring her the happiness that she desires.

1   Fred Robbins, "Marie Osmond: Doing What I Want Now," *McCalls,* July 1988, 14.
2   Oskar Garcia, "Marie Osmond: My Mormon Faith Got Me Through Son's Death," *The Huffington Post,* May 12, 2010.
3   "Marie Osmond: about my family that TV didn't tell," *Star,* May 4, 1982.
4   Ibid.
5   Robbins, 14.
6   Larry King Live: Marie Osmond Discusses Her Battle with Depression and Her Work with Children, May 30, 2000. http://archives.cnn.com/TRANSCRIPTS/0005/30/lkl.00.html (Viewed July 2, 2010).
7   "Marie Osmond Biography," http://www.biography.com/articles/Marie-Osmond-342934 (viewed July 2, 2010).
8   Robbins, 12.
9   Larry King Live.
10 "Marie Osmond Biography."

ROMANIA PRATT PENROSE

Ambition

"It is a trite but true saying that 'There is no excellence without great labor,'" wrote Romania Pratt Penrose.[1] The first LDS woman to leave Utah to enter a medical college in the East, she exemplifies putting forth great labor to obtain an education. Sometimes studying sixteen hours a day, she graduated with high honors and returned to Utah to bless thousands of mothers and their newborns in the Intermountain West over several generations.

Daughter of Luther and Esther Bunnell, Romania was born August 8, 1839, in Washington, Indiana.[2] While boarding at the Female Seminary in Crawfordsville, Indiana, she studied music, painting, and German—but her "very finished education" ended when, as she put it, "my blooming womanhood began to draw around me admirers which warned my mother to flee from Babylon before I became fastened by Gentile bonds." Her concerned LDS mother purchased an ox and a wagon and in 1855 joined the John Hindley Company on their journey to the Salt Lake Valley.

In the valley, sixteen-year-old Romania was hired as a teacher at the private school Brigham Young established for his children. She also taught music lessons in her home.

On February 23, 1859, Romania married Parley P. Pratt, Jr., son of the LDS Apostle. She became the mother of seven children, five living to adulthood. The loss of two children—Luther, a few days after his birth, and Corinne, just before age two—caused her much sorrow. Believing that other mothers should never suffer as she had, Romania considered enrolling in medical school to learn how to alleviate infant mortality, but she was married and had five sons, ages nine months to fourteen years. Such consideration seemed impossible until Romania saw a close friend die: "I saw her lying on her bed, her life slowly ebbing away, and no one near knew how to ease her pain or prevent her death. Oh, how I longed to know something to do, and at that moment I solemnly vowed to myself never to be found in such a position again."[3]

Her ambition mapped onto Brigham Young's advice: "We believe that women are useful not only to sweep houses, wash dishes, make beds, and raise babies, but that they should [study] law or [medicine], . . . and this to enlarge their sphere of usefulness for the benefit of society at large."[4] Romania wanted to answer the call to be a woman of "nerve, energy and ambition" to go east and become a medical doctor.[5]

Leaving home to attend medical school was not without its sacrifice. Romania's mother agreed to care for the children; the piano, home, and farm were sold to pay for traveling and tuition expenses. Thirty-four-year-old Romania and her husband boarded a train bound for New York City on December 3, 1873, where Romania helped Parley edit and proofread the *Autobiography of Parley P. Pratt* before enrolling in classes at the Woman's Medical College in Philadelphia.

At medical school, Romania described herself as "a stranger in a strange land, besides being almost a 'hiss and a byword' on account of my religion." She found comfort in attending an LDS branch in Williamsburg "each Sunday to partake of the sacrament for I felt it gave me more strength and power to perform my daily duties."[6] She struggled to keep up with her financial obligations; becoming aware of her situation, Brigham Young encouraged Eliza R. Snow to raise the needed funds from the Relief Society sisters, saying, "We need her here, and her talents will be of great use to this people."[7]

Romania proved a diligent student. "During the summer vacation, while [other medical students] were recreating, sea bathing and visiting with friends, I daily plodded studiously up the rugged hill of knowledge," she wrote.[8] Romania graduated with high honors in March 1877; she then enrolled in classes at the Wills' Hospital and Philadelphia Dispensary and later the New York Eye and Ear Infirmary. After finishing these studies, she returned to her family in Utah.

Romania opened her medical practice at the Constitutional Building on Main Street in Salt Lake City. She also taught free midwifery classes to Relief Society sisters, hoping to repay their kindness to her. *The Woman's Exponent* advertised her obstetrics courses, and stated that "the brethren of the highest authority have extended their approval and expressed their desire that the people take advantage of the opportunity."[9] In addition to obstetrics, Romania specialized in diseases of the eye and has been credited with performing the first cataract surgery in Utah.

During this most busy time, Romania divorced her husband Parley in 1881. This left her a single parent with a large medical practice and a heavy teaching load. Adding to her responsibilities, in 1882 she was asked to help open the first LDS hospital in the Utah Territory.[10] She served on the board of directors of the hospital, as a visiting physician, and later as a resident physician.

On March 11, 1886, Romania married Charles W. Penrose, editor-in-chief of the *Deseret News*. Due to the high-profile position of her second husband and severe persecution against polygamist marriages, their marriage was not publicly announced until 1903. In letters that passed between Charles and Romania during the seventeen-year interim, Romania was referred to as "the Doctor." When their marriage was finally announced, Romania moved her medical office and increased her practice, but she closed it in 1905 when Charles was called to be an

Apostle. She wanted time to prepare herself to accompany Charles to Europe, where he was to preside over the European Mission.

When she returned to Utah, Romania opened her medical practice once again but retired in 1912, too busy to keep up with medical advances. At the end of her life, Romania lost her eyesight. She died on November 9, 1932, at the age of ninety-three.

The life of Romania Pratt Penrose was a life of learning and giving. She not only healed her own patients of afflictions and disease, but passed her knowledge on to others. As a result of her labors, mothers survived childbirth, infants lived, and the infirm found relief. Through her lifetime of service, Romania epitomized her most quoted statement, "There is no excellence without great labor."[11]

---

1   Romania Pratt Penrose, *Memoir of Romania B. Pratt, M.D.*

2   Marie W. Mackey, "Romania Pratt Penrose: 'Up the Rugged Hill of Knowledge,'" in Barbara B. Smith and Blythe Darlyn Thatcher, *Heroines of the Restoration* (Salt Lake City: Bookcraft, 1997), 203–219.

3   *Woman's Exponent,* September 1, 1888, 49.

4   *Discourses of Brigham Young,* 216–17.

5   Lori L. Nickerson, *Women of Nerve, Energy, and Ambition: The Relief Society's Commitment to Frontier Health Care* (Provo, Utah: Women's Research Institute, Brigham Young University, 1992), 1.

6   Penrose.

7   Susa Young Gates, *Young Woman's Journal* (September 1891): 534.

8   Penrose, 11–12, 15.

9   *Woman's Exponent,* September 15, 1880, 59.

10   *History of the Relief Society 1824-1966* (Salt Lake City: General Board of the Relief Society, 1966), 33.

11   Penrose, 7.

ANNE PERRY

Repentance

Recognized as one of the best living mystery writers in the world, Anne Perry was drawn to Mormonism by the doctrine of the Church "like iron filings to a magnet." After attending sacrament meeting and Relief Society with her neighbors many times over a period of months, she prayed to know if the Church was true. The next morning when she awoke "it was as if the room was full of the sun," she said. She believed that the light was an answer and requested baptism.[1] Anne's conversion to the Church helped her discover that others believed the same things she had come to believe, helping her to become a strong, immovable member of the Church.[2]

Anne was born October 28, 1938, in London, England. At the age of six she contracted double pneumonia and bronchitis; her physician expressed little hope for her recovery and told her mother that he would be back the next morning to sign a death certificate. Anne survived, but missed three full years of school due to lingering illness and constant moves. Fortunately, her mother continued her education at home during this difficult period in her life.[3]

When Anne was ten her family moved from the British Isles to

New Zealand, where her father became rector of the University of Canterbury. Anne continued to struggle with health issues on the secluded island.[4] Despite several hospitalizations she was able to attend several different schools and did well. Anne eventually left school at age thirteen and was self-educated after that due to serious illness.

During this time, Anne became close friends with another girl, and the two of them planned to become writers. They got into some serious trouble as teenagers, and their association ended. In her twenties, Anne worked many different jobs, including working as a flight attendant.[5]

In 1967 Anne moved to California, where she worked as a domestic housekeeper and met Raymond Barnes and his wife, Chlo, who were members of the Church. "I knew from the start that my neighbors were something special," she said. "Their spirit was great and beautiful. I knew they were good, so I asked to learn more about their religion."[6] As Anne learned about their religious beliefs, she discovered for herself a moral compass for her life. Anne had previously spent some time determining what she believed, and she felt the Church taught what she also believed to be true.[7]

At this same time, Anne was drawn to writing historical stories, which she had a hard time getting published. Over a ten-year period, in which she worked at odd jobs, she submitted many manuscripts and received many rejections. She then found herself "totally absorbed by what happens to people under the pressure of investigation." When she started writing about this in mystery stories she succeeded in getting one published. In 1979 her first mystery novel, *Cater Street Hangman,* was accepted by St. Martin's Press in New York.[8]

Today Anne has published nearly sixty mystery novels—most translated into fourteen different languages. "The violence in my books takes place off stage," she says. Although readers seldom view the violence directly, she hopes that "they are left with a sense of a horror of it. To write about ugly things and make them seem right and commonplace is ultimately a betrayal."[9] One reporter observed, "If all her novels seem to reek of modern social consciousness, it's because ethics, whether modern or Victorian, are at the core of Perry's thinking. A Mormon, she has made religion a very important part of her life and has tried to infuse her characters with a strong sense of morals."[10]

Of her own writing, Anne shares, "I have written my religious and philosophical beliefs, and therefore I care about them [her characters] in a unique way. They have caused people to ask if I am a member of The Church of Jesus Christ of Latter-day Saints—yes, I am, and have been for about forty years."[11]

Anne received the 2001 Edgar Award for Best Short Story and has more than 25 million books in print worldwide. Her books have appeared on bestseller lists in a number of countries, and the *London Times* selected her as one of the "100 Masters of Crime" in the twentieth century.[12]

She lives as a committed Latter-day Saint, teaching Sunday School in her LDS branch in Invergordon, Scotland. Anne does not separate her beliefs from her mystery novels and says, "Even when you are writing a story, you must be loyal to the truth within you. If that doesn't affect you, you've blown it somewhere."[13] She has also shared, "How much does it behoove us to do all we can, as well as we can? If we make anything, build it, write it, or in any other way create it, let it reflect the best in ourselves, in our dreams and our beliefs, so that those who come after us may catch a glimpse of our trust and our gratitude and our love, a heritage from Him who made the whole world."[14]

Recently Anne said, "We all need faith in a purpose, a meaning to life. We need to believe that this journey has a destination that is beautiful and makes the travelling worthwhile however easy or hard it may be. We need to be able to trust that it is there for everyone, without exception, not just a chosen few. We need to know that slipping and falling is not the end. There is no failure that getting up and trying again will not cure."[15]

Anne Perry's journey seems an improbable story. To change from a young teenager involved in serious trouble to a champion of moral right was not an easy journey for her. Perhaps her mystery books are her way of infusing morality into the troubled world she has known. Through it all, she has become an example of how trying to live the gospel, repentance, and conversion can change a life for the better.

1   Richard R. Robertson, "Anne Perry: LDS British Novelist with 'a Commitment to Morality,'" *Ensign,* January 1984, 47.
2   Telephone conversation with Anne Perry by Mary Jane Woodger, November 15, 2010.
3   Robertson, 46; Anne Perry, "About Anne Perry," 2007, www.anneperry.net/aboutanne.
4   Anne Perry, http://www.goodreads.com/author/show/633/Anne_perry, [accessed 25 October 2010]; Anne Perry, "About Anne Perry."
5   Anne Perry, http://www.goodreads.com/author/show/633/Anne_perry.
6   Robertson, 47.
7   Telephone conversation.
8   Robertson, 47; Anne Perry, "About Anne Perry."
9   Robertson, 47.
10 Jane Widerman, *Globe and Mail,* September 11, 1982; Robertson, 47.
11 Anne Perry, "About Anne Perry."
12 Ibid.
13 "Anne Perry: An Heir of Mystery," *Meridian Magazine,* February 22, 2001; Robertson, 47.
14 Anne Perry, "Letters from the Highlands: What Novels Can Teach Us," *Meridian Magazine,* April 27, 2009, http://www.meridianmagazine.com/article/248?ac=1 (accessed November 15, 2010).
15 Anne Perry, "Needing to Believe This Journey has a Destination, Letters from the Highlands—January 2010," *Meridian Magazine,* February 22, 2010.

JANICE KAPP PERRY

Finding Comfort

Janice Kapp Perry is the first to say that she never expected to become one of the premier songwriters in the LDS community—and insists that in her case, extraordinary events arose from a very ordinary life.

Daughter of Jacob Kapp and Ruth Saunders, Janice was born in Ogden, Utah, at the end of the Great Depression. A child prodigy, she played "tunes by ear on the piano when [she] was two years old." When she was eight, her family moved from Utah to Vale, Oregon, where the Kapps thrived spiritually, but not financially. In spite of financial woes, her childhood home was "always filled with happy music."[1] She grew up playing the piano and organ for LDS Church services and the tympani and snare drum in the high school band. But for at least the first forty years of her life, her heart was in sports—softball, volleyball, basketball, and even football.

After graduating from high school in Vale, Janice moved back to Ogden to live with her grandparents and work as a secretary and organist at her uncle's mortuary. In Ogden she fell in love and became engaged. When she brought the young man to Vale to meet her family, her father sought guidance of the Holy Spirit as to whether this was the right decision for her. While praying in the irrigation fields, Jacob Kapp "received an undeniable revelation from the Spirit that it was not right for [Janice] to marry the man to whom [she] was engaged." He told Janice and her fiancé about the revelation and suggested they break off the engagement. "It was a difficult thing for him to ask of me," Janice says, "and an even more difficult thing for me to accept, but the trust that had grown between us through the years prevailed and I knew I must follow his counsel."[2] The engagement was broken.

Janice entered Brigham Young University, where on the first day of classes in her sophomore year she met Douglas Colton Perry—who shared her love of music and sports. They were married a year later on September 24, 1958, in the Logan Temple.

The newlyweds moved around the country often during their first years of marriage due to Doug's military obligation. But in the 1970s Janice and her family settled in Provo, Utah, where she participated in city softball leagues and on Church sports teams. A broken ankle Janice sustained during a one-on-one basketball game with her nephew brought a change to her life; it was then that Janice was asked to write a roadshow for her ward. She hesitated, claiming that she had not written any music since being at BYU. "I wasn't sure I could do it, but something inside me whispered that I probably could and it might even be fun," she said. [3]

After the success of her roadshow, *The Cat That Quacked,* Janice wrote popular music, but discovered that walking the line between popularity and her own standards was not where she wanted to be. After a heartfelt prayer at her piano bench, she wrote her first gospel song, "I'll Follow Jesus," in 1976. Seeing the tears in Doug's eyes as she played it for him was the encouragement she needed to compose other gospel-centered hymns.

Songs came quickly. After several successful sheet music publications, Janice recorded her first album, *Where Is Heaven.* Janice has since produced an astounding volume of work—more than twelve hundred songs, two musicals, and eight cantatas as well as recording more than seventy-five albums, several in Spanish, Japanese, Portuguese, and Korean.[4] The songs that have touched others most are the songs about her own experiences—songs from her heart.[5]

Some of Janice's most treasured memories have been when her music touches the lives of others. For instance, she wrote the Primary song "I'm Trying to Be Like Jesus" at the request of local Primary leaders for a regional conference and felt prompted to teach children that they should strive to become like "the kindest man that ever lived, our Savior Jesus Christ." Several years after its publication, Janice was invited to attend a seminary graduation of handicapped children at the American Fork Training School. As a chorus made up of these children performed her song, she felt "humbled in their presence." She said, "If only the whole world could express love as freely and naturally as they did." Janice received a special witness that those children were truly like Jesus.[6]

Janice feels that her experiences are often not complete until she writes about them in verse. As her cousin and longtime collaborator, Joy Saunders Lundberg, observes:

> A choice thing about her songwriting is that each was written for a purpose beyond herself. Many were written at the request of Church leaders wanting a song for a specific theme. Some were written simply to give comfort to someone who was suffering. Others were written to give guidance to children and youth that they might seek for goodness in their lives and for women and men who needed to feel the loving touch of the Savior through music. . . . She did it all with only two years of college musical training, a disabled left hand, and a constant reliance upon the Lord for guidance."[7]

Every song Janice composes is preceded by scripture study of the topic, prayers for guidance, and temple attendance to renew her covenants and personal commitment to the Lord. She strives to keep herself worthy of the Spirit so that she can compose music that is uplifting to others. "When I get letters back from [people] telling me how my music has helped them through a hard time—that means everything to me," says Janice. That, she says, is why she writes.[8]

1   Janice Kapp Perry, *Songs from My Heart: The Stories Behind the Songs* (Sandy, Utah: Sounds of Zion, Inc., 2000), 1.
2   Janice Kapp Perry, "My Father's Faith," *Meridian Magazine,* June 18, 2010.
3   Perry, *Songs from My Heart,* 10, 12.
4   John Perry, *Janice Kapp Perry,* n. p., 2010. Transcription in author's possession.
5   Interview with Janice Kapp Perry.
6   Perry, *Songs from My Heart,* 36–37.
7   Joy Saunders Lundberg, "Foreword," in *Songs from My Heart,* x–xi.
8   Interview with Janice Kapp Perry.

ANNE OSBORN POELMAN

Discovering Truth

"I believe that every one of us has a real purpose and mission in life," wrote Anne Osborn Poelman in her book, *The Simeon Solution.* "Each of us is truly special, with a unique and important role to fill."[1] For Anne, there has always been more than one role to fill. For her, everything begins and continues with an inquisitive mind.

As a child, she had many questions: "Why are we all here, and what is the purpose of our existence? Why am I here? Is there a God? And if there really is, will He answer the prayers of a curious child?" She pestered local ministers for answers, but found few.[2] It was in science that her inquisitive mind found answers to some of life's important questions. "Among my fellow NSF students brains were admired, not scorned," she recalled. "Good grades were a mark of achievement. Achievement was valued, not denigrated."[3] Anne excelled so well in the world of science that Stanford University beckoned—not only on the undergraduate level, but for medical school as well.

Anne was a top student at the university, yet there was always a void. Questions of spirituality lingered. She attended various churches, but none seemed to answer her questions. As for The Church of Jesus

Christ of Latter-day Saints, her first impression came from a self-guided tour of Temple Square. From the tour, she concluded that Mormons worshiped seagulls and "some guy named Joseph Smith." With this belief, she was surprised to find that a respected professor in Stanford's medical school was a member of the Church.

"I thought it was really weird that a guy of his stature would worship seagulls. But then I said to myself, 'Well, this is California and people do all sorts of strange things.'" Despite her first impressions, she decided to attend an LDS Sunday service. The service "was a real eye-opener, unlike anything else I'd ever seen," she wrote. "The informality and warm, friendly chaos was stunning. So was the church itself. No cross, altar, or candles. No priest or minister in robes. Just a bunch of ordinary people doing quite extraordinary things."[4]

It was not long before Anne agreed to have lessons presented by LDS missionaries. "I took the missionary lessons, studied the gospel, and recognized what I'd been looking for all my life. It wasn't a sense of discovery as much as a feeling of recognition. I'd come home," Anne wrote.[5] "Do I know all the answers to all my questions? Certainly not! But that really doesn't concern me. I refuse to be distracted by peripheral issues and the doctrinal sidebars that some would use to weaken our testimonies of the gospel."[6]

Anne completed her medical training amid "a blur of tireless study, sleepless nights, and endless examinations."[7] After graduation, she accepted a faculty position at the University of Utah School of Medicine. It is not surprising that she rose to the top in her career. She became a University Distinguished Professor and Presidential Endowed Chairholder at the University of Utah School of Medicine. She was also the first woman to be president of the American Society of Neuroradiology (ASNR) and cocreator of the first comprehensive point-of-care electronic imaging reference system. She has received gold medals and honorary memberships in numerous international radiology professional organizations.

She became one of the world's most prominent neuroradiologists and has authored the definitive reference books in her field. She has given many invited lectures in Asia, Australia, India, South Africa, and the Middle East and has been a visiting professor at Harvard, Stanford, and John Hopkins.

Yet with all her accomplishments, she felt alone. "If I heard it once, I heard it a thousand times. In fact, it got to be downright annoying. . . . 'Sister Osborn, why aren't you married yet?'" Anne confessed, "The truth of the matter [was], I worried about it myself. Trying to remain gospel-centered and sane while being single in an avowedly married church isn't an easy job."[8]

Yet she did remain active in the Church. As the years passed, Anne was called to serve on the Sunday School General Board and then the Relief Society General Board. After years of service, Anne met Elder Ronald Poelman of the First Quorum of the Seventy. Of this, she wrote, "There's a bit of the miraculous in most people's lives."[9] At age thirty-eight, she married Elder Poelman.

Anne set a high standard for the discovery of truth, refusing to settle for the mere truths found in science or medicine. She pressed forward to find truth in the spiritual realm, and concludes, "The most precious blessings of my life have come directly through the gospel of Jesus Christ."[10]

1   Anne Osborn Poelman, *The Simeon Solution* (Salt Lake City: Deseret Book, 1995), 7.
2   "Anne Osborn Poelman," in *Why I Believe* (Salt Lake City: Bookcraft, 2002), 255.
3   Poelman, 37.
4   *Why I Believe,* 255–257; and Poelman, 41.
5   *Why I Believe,* 257.
6   Poelman, 23.
7   Ibid., 93.
8   Ibid., 89.
9   Ibid., 112.
10   Ibid., 151.

LOUISA BARNES PRATT

Devotion

While Louisa Barnes Pratt and her husband, Addison Pratt, were living in San Bernardino, Brigham Young asked all Church members in California to return to Utah due to military threats against the Saints. Addison refused, but Louisa left her husband and moved to Utah— hoping that Addison would recognize his loss and soon follow. Although he never joined her, Louisa stood by her decision to follow a prophet of God.[1] Throughout her days, her example of obedience to the gospel of Jesus Christ and to Church leadership was an inspiration to other faithful women.

Daughter of Willard and Dolly Barnes, Louisa was born November 10, 1802, in Warwick, Massachusetts. She attended school at a young age. Although a timid student who hated being reprimanded by teachers and parents alike, Louisa excelled in her studies. Yet obedience did not come easy. She wrote:

> Going to a neighboring house on an errand, I had leave to stay half an hour, but told the lady two hours were permitted me. She was suspicious, and dispatched her little girl to inquire into

the truth of my statements. I was called home and reprimanded severely, and felt the greatest contrition of heart, while mother painted my crime in its strongest colors, and rehearsed the threatenings of scripture. . . . My age then did not exceed five years.[2]

Because of this, Louisa was sent twelve miles away to live with an aunt, who took an immediate liking to Louisa. Like her parents, her aunt was a devoted member of the Church of England, and Louisa was a religious child. She remained under her aunt's care until her father sold his farm and took the family, including Louisa, to Canada in July 1810.

At age fourteen, Louisa was baptized a member of the Episcopal Church. Soon thereafter, she left home again to live with a sister-in-law who taught her the art of tailoring. Louisa eventually accepted employment as a teacher in Winchester, New Hampshire. There she became friends with Rebekah J. Pratt and learned about her adventurous brother, Addison, who sailed the high seas. More than a little curious about the whaler, Louisa wrote Addison Pratt a few letters. When he sailed into the Boston Harbor, the letters gave him reason enough to go looking for Louisa; they were married April 3, 1831.[3]

The Pratts built a home near Lake Erie at Ripley, New York, where several of their children were born. In 1838, when Louisa's sister Caroline and her husband, Jonathan Crosby, came for a visit, the Pratts learned about The Church of Jesus Christ of Latter-day Saints, founded eight years earlier. Addison and Louisa soon converted to Mormonism and made plans to gather with the Saints in Missouri. Due to religious persecution, however, they journeyed on to Nauvoo,[4] where they hoped to enjoy the fellowship of the Saints for years to come.

For Addison, this was not to be. He was called to serve a mission to the Society Islands, today known as French Polynesia and Tahiti. He accepted the call even though it meant that he would not be with Louisa and their four daughters for several years. Of this separation and others that followed, Louisa wrote, "More than half the years of my married life I have stood alone. Created the means to sustain myself and children: and although I had kind friends around me I had no one immediately interested to supply my daily wants. My cares often weighed heavily upon me, yet for the most part I have been cheerful."[5]

During her remaining days in Nauvoo, Louisa nursed her children through measles, trained her own horse, started a school, and offered her services as a tailor to paying customers.[6] She then brought her children across the plains to the Salt Lake Valley.

Extended time away from her husband led Louisa to become more self-sufficient than most of her female contemporaries. Louisa became an example, if not standard, to women seeking independence and strength, yet inwardly she struggled with hidden sorrows.[7]

Louisa and Addison were reunited in Salt Lake City in 1848 after five years of being separated, but within a short time Addison was called once again to serve a mission in Tahiti. This time Louisa and her daughters joined him. Their mission was cut short when the French Protectorate government enforced a law forbidding foreign missionaries to live and work among the Tahitians.[8] After leaving Tahiti, the Pratt family settled first in San Francisco and then in San Bernardino, a newly established LDS colony.

Addison, who was used to presiding over Church matters in the islands, found it difficult to accept LDS leaders in San Bernardino. He also had trouble at home. He liked his independence and often left home to hunt and fish, neglecting household matters.

Addison was called back to Tahiti in 1854 and again in 1856. But the government refused to lift its negative policy toward foreign missionaries, and Addison returned to San Bernardino, disappointed with his last two missions. He united with Louisa, but not for long. When Brigham Young asked Latter-day Saints living in California to move to Utah, Addison refused while Louisa moved with two of her daughters to Beaver, Utah, where she was a corresponding writer for the *Woman's Exponent.* Though Louisa and Addison did not want their separation to be permanent, Addison died in California on October 14, 1872,[9] and Louisa died of pneumonia on September 8, 1880, in Beaver, Utah.

In spite of the difficult times Louisa endured, she remained a strong and obedient member of the Church. For example, when sisters of the Church were invited to pay fifty cents toward buying nails and glass, Louisa said, "If I have no more than a crust of bread each day for a week, I will pay this money into the treasury."[10] Although she was tried and tested through many marital separations, her faith never wavered. She was always a stalwart—a woman of persistent obedience.

1   Louisa Barnes Pratt, *The History of Louisa Barnes Pratt: The Autobiography of A Mormon Missionary Widow and Pioneer,* ed. S. George Ellsworth (Logan, Utah: Utah State University Press, 1998), xvi.

2   Ibid., 5.

3   Ibid., 8, 16–18, 25, 28–29, 35.

4   Ibid., xv.

5   Ibid., xv, xxi.

6   Lavina Fielding Anderson, "They Came to Nauvoo," *Ensign,* September 1979, 22.

7   Pratt, xxi–xxii.

8   Pratt, xv–xvi.

9   Pratt, xvii.

10   Anderson, 22.

IVY BAKER PRIEST
Talent

Tall and trim Ivy Baker Priest—the thirtieth treasurer of the United States—was asked by President Dwight D. Eisenhower how she liked her new job. Ivy responded, "I'm enjoying it immensely, Mr. President . . . but at the moment I'm just so overwhelmed to be here. . . . I never expected to get anywhere near the White House." Eisenhower replied, "I know just how you feel. Neither did I."[1]

The oldest daughter of Orange Decatur Baker and Clara Fearnley, Ivy Maude Baker was born September 7, 1905, in Kimberly, Piute County, Utah. Her birthplace was symbolic: "The future treasurer of the world's richest country, being born atop a gold-silver-lead-copper mine was wonderfully symbolic."[2] Ivy's father was a miner who frequently moved the family; due to a series of mishaps and injuries, he was often unemployed. To pay the bills, Ivy's mother opened a boarding house for miners. Between twenty and thirty miners came to board at her home on any given day. The mess their muddy shoes left on the floor led in a roundabout way to Ivy's lifelong political career.

Ivy's mother decided that wooden sidewalks would solve her problem; she found a sympathetic mayoral candidate who agreed with her. With ten-year-old Ivy by her side, her mother was very influential in rounding up foreign-born residents and getting them registered if they agreed to vote for her candidate. When the candidate won, Ivy "felt as elated as a kingmaker" and determined to enter politics and make a difference in the world.[3]

Believing politicians needed more education, Ivy made plans to enroll at the University of Utah, but poverty interferred. Instead of becoming a famous politician and an attorney, Ivy took a position selling tickets at a movie theater to help support her family.

In 1924 Ivy married Harry Howard Hicks, a North Carolina traveling salesman, but there were problems in the marriage. They divorced in 1929, just as the Great Depression was starting to grip the nation. Ivy knew that despite poverty she must "sink or swim on my own." She returned to her family in Utah.[4]

Once in Utah, Ivy learned that her father had sustained a fractured skull when hit by a car; his medical bills deepened the family's poverty. The LDS Church provided welfare to keep the family afloat, and Ivy became a long-distance telephone operator and then a sales clerk in downtown Salt Lake City to help out.

In 1932, attractive Ivy Baker cast aside feelings of inadequacy brought on by continuing poverty and launched her political career as a delegate to the GOP state convention. She also went on a blind date with Roy Fletcher Priest, a short, balding man twenty-one years her senior. His smile, which Ivy claimed "just warmed up the room," attracted her to him. During most of their three-year courtship, Ivy served as president of the Utah Young Republicans and ran for the Utah State Legislature on the Republican ticket. Roy said, "I didn't know whether I was supposed to be winning a bride or an election."[5]

After Ivy lost the election, she and Roy married on December 7, 1935. Eventually settling in Bountiful, Roy provided a comfortable living for the family, and they became the parents of four—Patricia Ann, Peggy Louise, Nancy Ellen, and Roy Baker. Ivy enjoyed her roles as mother and homemaker until fifteen-month-old Peggy Louise died of a congenital heart condition. Ivy became despondent and withdrawn. Her mother's advice to remember her God-given talents propelled Ivy back into politics.

Ivy entered the political realm, serving as chairwoman of the Young Republicans for eleven western states and as Utah's Republican National Committee chair. She ran on the Republican ticket for Congress in 1950 and lost. It was not until 1952 that her political world changed for the better when she met Dwight D. Eisenhower. "I felt as if I'd known him all my life, and a sense of confidence and optimism swept through me," she said.[6]

When Eisenhower ran for president in 1952, Ivy was the assistant chairwoman of the Republican National Committee in charge of women's interests. She was credited with increasing the Republican women's vote by 40 percent in 1952. Eisenhower garnered 52 percent of the women's vote, much to the credit of Ivy.

In appreciation and recognition of her talents, President Eisenhower appointed Ivy treasurer of the United States—only the second woman to hold the position.[7] She served for two terms, 1953 to 1961. Despite a hectic schedule, she wrote her own speeches, emphasizing the importance of a sound dollar and the need to reduce taxes.[8] Ivy received many honorary degrees for her work and became a celebrity in Utah. A *Salt Lake Tribune* editorial stated, "All Utahns will read with pride and pleasure the signature 'Ivy Baker Priest' on their paper money."[9]

In 1954 Ivy's husband Roy retired due to a debilitating stroke; he died of a heart attack four years later at seventy-five. With her personal world thrown asunder, fifty-four-year-old Ivy Priest resigned as U.S. treasurer and moved to California. On June 20, 1961, she married Sidney Williams Stevens, a Beverly Hills real estate developer, and was elected to two terms as the California state treasurer. To keep the press interested in her agenda, Ivy used such gimmicks as wearing a hat spiked with $1 bills and attempting to throw a silver dollar across the

Sacramento River. When the coin sunk in the river, she said, "A dollar doesn't go very far these days."[10]

As her health deteriorated in the 1970s, Ivy moved from the public arena to her home in Santa Monica, where she died of cancer on June 23, 1975.[11]

From an early age, politics was her passion. Poverty and a failed marriage would have thwarted most women from achieving a political goal. Not Ivy! Recognizing that few get ahead in this world without overcoming obstacles, Norman Vincent Peale asked her the greatest obstacle she had overcome. Without hesitation Ivy said, "Poverty." Peale laughed and said, "And now you are in charge of all that money." She quipped, "We women don't care too much about getting our pictures on money as long as we can get our hands on it."[12]

1   Ivy Baker Priest, *Green Grows Ivy* (New York: McGraw-Hill, 1958); "Biographical Clippings" in Utah State Historical Society Library; Ivy Baker Priest Papers, University of Utah; W. Paul Reeve, "Ivy Baker Priest: A Bingham High Coed Rose to the Post of U.S. Treasurer," *History Blazer,* June 1995, 1.

2   Stanford J. Layton, "Ivy Baker Priest: Treasurer of the United States," in Colleen Whitley, ed., *Worth Their Salt: Notable But Often Unnoted Women of Utah* (Logan, Utah: Utah State University Press, 1996), 220.

3   Reeve; Layton, 221.

4   Ibid.

5   Ibid., 222.

6   Ibid., 223.

7   See *Deseret News,* 20 April 1953.

8   See *Salt Lake Tribune,* June 4, 1965, as cited in Whitley, 224.

9   Reeve, 1.

10   *Ogden Standard-Examiner,* December 5, 1965, as cited in Whitley, 226.

11   Obituary Notice, *Salt Lake Tribune,* June 25, 1975, as cited in Whitley, 227.

12   Reeve, 1.

ROSE MARIE REID

Modesty

Rose Marie Reid exemplified being a strong and devout member of The Church of Jesus Christ of Latter-day Saints despite the glamour of Hollywood and celebrity life. As a result, she succeeded in the fashion world without straying from her beliefs about modesty.

The daughter of Elvie and Marie Yancey, Rose Marie Reid was born September 12, 1906, in Cardston, Alberta, Canada.[1] Rose Marie learned many of her designing and sewing skills from her mother. She said, "At first she [Mother] would sew and I tended the children. Then I began to sew beside her."[2] When the family moved to Weiser, Idaho, in 1916, Rose Marie worked on the family farm and entered a beauty pageant to win money to help support her brother's mission fund.[3]

In September 1925, Marie purchased a beauty salon in Baker City, Oregon, and Rose Marie worked with her mother in the salon while her brothers set up a painting studio next door. Her brothers began taking painting lessons from traveling artist Gareth Rhynhart, whom they had known in Cardston, but after two weeks Rhynhart refused to continue to teach them unless he could marry Rose Marie. Even though she was not interested, she agreed to the marriage because she wanted

her brothers to continue with their art lessons—an arrangement Rose Marie's family did not know about until many years later. The marriage did not last long; Rose Marie divorced Rhynhart in 1935.[4]

After her divorce, Rose Marie moved to Vancouver, British Columbia, and began taking swimming lessons from Jack C. Reid; she soon fell in love with him, and they planned to marry. Rose Marie's family was not so keen on the union. They did not like the idea that Reid was not a member of the Church, but Rose Marie assured them that he would join the Church. He did exactly that, and the two were married soon afterwards.[5]

Jack, who spent many hours at the swimming pool, was not happy with the swimsuits of the day. They were made of wool, and when soaked in water became heavy and uncomfortable. Rose Marie decided to make a new swimsuit for Jack; she cut a pair of swim trunks from an old duck-fabric coat and laced the sides for a snug fit. Jack loved the suit, and wanted Rose Marie to design similar suits for the Hudson Bay Department Store to sell. Leery of selling swimsuits, Rose Marie turned to the Lord, kneeling in prayer and asking if God wanted her to make bathing suits. The day after she received an affirmative answer, Rose Marie found some beautiful fabric with which to make a woman's swimsuit with laces up the sides. Seeing the design, the Hudson Bay buyers ordered ten dozen men's and six dozen ladies' suits—and Reid Holiday Togs, Ltd., began.[6]

Rose Marie's suits became very popular because they were the first to include brassieres, tummy-tuck panels, stay-down legs, and laces.[7] During the company's first year, it featured only six styles. In later years, more than a hundred styles were shown in one season. In 1946, Rose Marie decided to take her company from Canada to the United States. Triumphing over other swimsuit companies in the U. S., by 1958 the company had $14 million in sales.[8] In 1959, production went up to 10,000 suits a day, and worldwide distribution reached into 46 countries, making Reid the largest manufacturer of swimsuits

worldwide. She was also named one of the *Los Angeles Times* Ten
Women of the Year in 1955, and in 1958 she was awarded Designer
of the Year.[9]

Rose Marie's popularity grew immensely after the introduction of
her swimsuit in the United States. Joan Crawford, Jane Russell, Rhonda
Fleming, Marilyn Monroe, and Rita Hayworth all wore Reid swimsuits
in their respective movies or pinup pictures. Marilyn Monroe gave
Rose Marie "almost as much credit as Mother Nature for her pinup
popularity."[10]

While Rose Marie achieved success in the business world, she
faced trials in her personal life. Though Jack had expressed no desire to
have children, Rose Marie had three children with him. As time went
on, Jack became abusive to Rose Marie and their children. She also
began to feel that her husband had joined the Church without any real
commitment or testimony. Their marriage ended in 1946.[11]

In the 1960s, Rose Marie's business started to decline with the
popularity of the bikini. She refused to design a bikini, advocating
modest one-piece swimsuits. She left her company in 1962, claiming
that the bikini was its "ultimate demise."[12]

After leaving her company to other designers, Rose Marie was asked
by President David O. McKay—through Belle Spafford, the general
president of the Relief Society—to redesign the temple garments so
women would feel more comfortable and beautiful while wearing
them. Rose Marie discovered while working on the garments that she
was related to Elizabeth Warner Allred, who helped design the very
first garments in this dispensation. Rose Marie wondered if the Lord
"[kept] that privilege in our family."[13]

Rose Marie died on November 18, 1978, in Provo, Utah.[14] Due to
her faith and perseverance, she showed others that you can be strong in
your beliefs and not change those standards for celebrity life.

1   Donald Q. Cannon, Richard O. Cowan, and Arnold K. Garr, "Rose Marie Reid," in *Encyclopedia of Mormonism* (Salt Lake City: Deseret Book Company, 2000), 991.

2   Carole Reid Burr and Roger K. Petersen, *Rose Marie Reid: An Extraordinary Life Story* (American Fork, Utah: Covenant Communications, Inc., 1995), 13–14.

3   Ibid., 6–7, 21–23.

4   Ibid., 25–26, 28.

5   Ibid., 31

6   Ibid., 32–33.

7   Ibid., 35

8   April Ainsworth, "Introducing Great Designers," www.vintagevizen.com/articlesDesigners/vintageRoseMarieReid.asp (accessed November 17, 2010).

9   Cannon, Cowan, and Garr, 991.

10   Burr and Petersen, 94.

11   Burr and Petersen, 39–40, 45–47.

12   Ainsworth.

13   Burr and Petersen, 201.

14   Cannon, Cowan, and Garr, 991.

ALICE LOUISE REYNOLDS
Teaching

"[Alice Louise Reynolds] had no inclination nor talent for handwork, such as sewing, knitting, crocheting, or mending," wrote biographer Amy Lyman. Her world was books. "Aside from her supreme joy in reading, she loved to be surrounded by books, to touch and handle them and above all, to own them, or to present them as gifts to dear friends."[1]

George Reynolds recognized his daughter's deep and abiding interest in books when she was very young. When Alice was four, he insisted that she be enrolled in a school setting. Although neighbors and school officials scoffed, Alice took her place in the classroom and soon led classmates in academic pursuits. By age twelve, she was living in the Legion Hotel in Orem, Utah, and attending Brigham Young Academy,[2] where she was privileged to be a student of Karl G. Maeser. "He had the ability to inspire as few have inspired," Alice wrote. "He made his students feel the worth of life; he told us that the Lord had sent each of us to do some special work, and that the proper preparation was necessary for that mission."[3] She graduated from the Normal School at Brigham Young Academy in 1890.

After graduation, Alice taught school for a year at the Salt Lake 14th Ward Seminary and another year at the Juab Stake Academy in Nephi. By then, she was eighteen. Upon learning that the LDS Church offered loans for educational pursuits, she applied for a student loan. She was awarded $500, which enabled her to attend the University of Michigan.[4] Her studies in English literature at Michigan opened other educational opportunities to her.

At age twenty-one, she joined the faculty at Brigham Young Academy. At the time, English coursework at the academy consisted of high school courses such as grammar, rhetoric, and composition. Alice was the first faculty member to introduce college literary courses. By so doing, she became the first woman at the academy to teach classes other than needlework, cooking, and music.

She was a favorite instructor to more than five thousand students in her forty-four-year career at the academy. Student Ralph A. Britsch said of her, "She clearly believed that the chief functions of a teacher of literature are to illuminate and to stimulate—to imbue her students with a thirst for reading and to help them to explore, to understand, and (in the best sense) to enjoy."[5] A poem written in her honor describes her impact in the classroom:

> She is a lighter of lamps—
> And whether they are beacons
> Or only candle flame,
> The bearers of a radiant light
> Shall hail the teacher's name!
> —Vesta P. Crawford[6]

Alice was the first woman at the academy to become a full professor—and was a professor of English literature. Yet she always considered herself a student. She took advantage of summer holidays to study at the University of Chicago, Cornell, and Berkeley. She spent three years in graduate studies, two in Europe and one at Columbia University in New York.

Amid all her studies, her passion remained books—especially new books in the library. For nineteen years, she served as chair of the Library Committee of what became Brigham Young University.[7] In 1932 former students established the Alice Louise Reynolds Club in her honor.[8] This book club quickly expanded to seventeen chapters. When asked which chapters she liked best, Alice replied, "What mother wouldn't love all her children."[9] Her own poem reveals the philosophy she hoped club members would adopt:

> Lord, help me live from day to day
> In such a self forgetful way
> That even when I kneel to pray
> My prayer may be of others.
>
> Others, Lord, yes others
> Let this my motto be
> Help me to live for others
> That I might live for Thee.[10]

Alice made time to also serve in Church and civic organizations. She served on the board of directors of the Utah Education Association, the general board of the Relief Society, and the editorial board of the *Relief Society Magazine*. In each assignment, she championed reading for women. "If you are in a community where you have not a single volume of Longfellow or Lowell or Holmes or Whittier," penned Alice, "find some way to relieve the situation." Her bottom line for women was "get hold of books," even if it means borrowing them "from your children."[11]

As her health waned in December 1938, she said, "I am not afraid to die. I have lived the best I could, and I am sure no girl or

woman ever had a more wonderful life, with more opportunities, more privileges, and more friends. I have been most fortunate, and for all these blessings I am sincerely grateful."[12] Her parting advice for women was, "My prayer is that the Spirit of the Lord may be with us, that that contribution which it is ours to give may become greater and mightier as the days roll on."[13]

The contribution of Alice Louise Reynolds was in the world of academics. She excelled in inspiring students, especially female students, to become better by surrounding themselves with good books.

1   Amy Brown Lyman, *A Lighter of Lamps: The Life Story of Alice Louise Reynolds* (Provo, Utah: Alice Louise Reynolds Club, 1947), 30, 67. (See Alice Reynolds [1873–1938], "Journals of Alice Louise Reynolds" 11 vols., Church History Library, Salt Lake City.)

2   When Alice enrolled in 1886, the Brigham Young Academy was only ten years old. (See Ernest L. Wilkinson, ed., et. al., *Brigham Young University: The First One Hundred Years*, 4 vols. [Provo, Utah: Brigham Young University Press, 1976], 1:51–76.)

3   Jean Anne Waterstradt, *They Gladly Taught: Ten BYU Professors* (Provo, Utah: Brigham Young University and the Emeritus Club, 1988), 3:132, as cited in Jeff McLellan, "A Lingering Influence: Top 10 BYU Professors," *BYU Magazine*, Winter 1999.

4   At the time of her enrollment, it had been only twenty-two years since the University of Michigan had opened its doors to women.

5   Waterstradt, 3:142, as cited in McLellan.

6   Lyman, ix.

7   Dr. Albert E. Winship, editor of the *Journal of Education* (Boston), in writing to the BYU president, penned, "It is not too much to say that no woman has done so much for the library of any institution as she has done for your library." Winship, as cited in Lyman, Life 30.

8   The organization had its official beginning on February 19, 1933, after a constitution and bylaws were adopted by a central committee of the Alice Louise Reynolds Club. (See Lyman, 58.)

9   Lyman, 58–59.

10   Lyman, 63.

11   *Relief Society Magazine* 10, no. 12, December 1923, 610. (See *The Relief Society Magazine: A Legacy Remembered,* 1914–1970 [Salt Lake City: Deseret Book, 1982]; Patricia Ann Mann, "A History of the Relief Society Magazine 1914–1970," Master's Thesis, Brigham Young University, 1971), 56.

12   Lyman, 72.

13   *Relief Society Magazine* 9, no. 12, December 1922, 636.

LOUISA "LULA" GREENE RICHARDS

Ingenuity

The earliest preserved text of Louisa Greene Richards is a poetic dialogue written when she was fourteen, in which a fictional mountain queen pleads with a beautiful princess to help her gain freedom from the wicked king.[1] Although the dialogue is fanciful and a far cry from her more serious writings, it reveals her early interest in written stories.

As time passed, Louisa had many opportunities to tell stories of a greater magnitude as editor of the *Woman's Exponent,* the first magazine owned and managed by Latter-day Saint women. The *Exponent* was intended to address "every subject interesting and valuable to women," including news, household tips, educational matters, health, fashion, and miscellaneous readings. As editor, Louisa was expected to be an authority on many subjects and to write with clarity and efficiency. Her words filled the *Exponent* for four years, although few are attributed to her—Louisa used pen names or omitted her name altogether.[2]

Daughter of Evan M. Greene and Susan Kent, Louisa was born April 8, 1849, in Kanesville, Iowa. Early converts to Mormonism, her parents followed the Prophet Joseph Smith from New York to Kirtland, Ohio. Louisa's father taught Joseph grammar and was called by him to be a clerk. The family moved on to Missouri and then to Illinois before joining the Mormon exodus to the Salt Lake Valley.[3] By the time Louisa was three, she and her family were living in Cache Valley, Utah, where Louisa grew to womanhood.[4]

When Louisa was twenty, she was called to be the editor of the *Smithfield Sunday School Gazette,* a weekly handwritten paper distributed after Sunday School to "those who had paid the subscription price." [5] In the *Gazette,* Louisa wrote about blessings, good manners, and the Book of Mormon as well as the importance of paying attention in Sunday School.

Wanting more publication opportunities, Louisa ventured from Cache Valley to Salt Lake City. In the larger community her first published work was "Tired Out," a poem printed in the *Salt Lake Daily Herald.* Shortly after the poem was published, Louisa wanted to travel home, but did not have the funds. Believing that the editor of the *Herald,* Edward L. Sloan, might help, Louisa stayed up all night writing poetry. The next day she handed Sloan her work. To her surprise, she not only received money for her poetry, she was offered a chance to begin a magazine devoted exclusively to women.[6]

Feeling insecure about her qualifications to begin such a magazine, Louisa sought out Eliza R. Snow, Relief Society general president. When Louisa shared with Eliza her belief that she should be working on marriage rather than a magazine, Eliza said, "To be sure, while unmarried, one cannot be fulfilling the requisition of maternity; but let me ask 'Is it not as important that those already born should be cultivated and prepared for use in the Kingdom of God as that others should be born?'"[7] Louisa then went to see President Brigham Young. She asked him to call her to perform the duties associated with the *Exponent;* President Young granted her request. Louisa then established *The Woman's Exponent,* the first magazine owned and edited by Latter-day Saint women.[8]

In 1873, shortly after establishing *The Woman's Exponent,* Louisa married Levi W. Richards. Like his bride, Levi had a heritage of faithful service in the LDS Church.[9] Levi continued the family tradition through his service as secretary of the Deseret Sunday School General Board, temple ordinance worker, ward clerk, president of stake priesthood quorums, and patriarch.[10]

Although Louisa was married to a wonderful man, she faced much heartache during her first years of marriage when her first two daughters died in infancy. Louisa concluded that her work as editor was too taxing under the heavy emotional load she now carried. Although she enjoyed writing and associating with leading LDS women, her greatest desire was to raise a family. She asked Brigham Young for a release from the *Exponent* so that she could pursue the "higher and holier mission" of motherhood. Emmeline B. Wells, whose children were grown, took over the editorship until the *Exponent* was discontinued in 1914.[11] As for Louisa, she bore seven children.

As the years passed, Louisa enjoyed motherhood but always kept a hand in the publishing field. She wrote for the *Exponent,* the *Relief Society Magazine,* the *Children's Friend,* the *Improvement Era,* and the *Young Woman's Journal.* In addition, she was called by President George Q. Cannon to write a column for children, "Our Little Folks," in The *Juvenile Instructor.*[12] In 1905 Louisa won first prize in a Church-wide contest for writing the best poem honoring Joseph Smith on the one hundredth anniversary of his birth, a poem that was set to music by composer Evan Stephens.[13] In 1905 she published a collection of her writings in *Branches That Run over the Wall.* The book, illustrated by her son Levi, contains a Book of Mormon epic as well as poems, essays, songs, and dialogues for children.[14]

Besides writing, Louisa served in other meaningful ways. She was an ordinance worker in the Salt Lake Temple, a member of the general boards of the Primary and Sunday School, and a much sought-after speaker. She represented the Church at various conventions and met with young LDS women in Mexico and Canada. In 1944 she died in Salt Lake City at age ninety-five.[15]

Lessons from the life of Louisa Richards are many, but perhaps none more so than the lesson that rearing children comes before sharing talents with a broader community. Yet Louisa taught by example that talents should not be neglected. By organizing and prioritizing her life, she was able to enjoy both the blessings of motherhood and the joy that comes from building on God-given gifts. *The Woman's Exponent,* hymns, poetry, and a host of essays attest to her willingness to share her literary talents.

1   Louisa Richards to Rhoda Bullock, March 13, 1874., as cited in Sherilyn Cox Bennion, "Lula Greene Richards: Utah's First Woman Editor," *BYU Studies* 21, no. 2, Spring 1981, 156.
2   Bennion, 161–162.
3   Bennion, 156.
4   Leonard J. Arrington, "Louisa Lulu Greene Richards: Woman Journalist of the Early West," *Improvement Era,* May 1969, 29–30.
5   Arrington, 28.
6   Thomas C. Romney, "Louisa Lula Greene Richards," *The Instructor* 8, September 1950, 262.
7   Arrington, 30.
8   Bennion, 160–162.
9   D. Michael Quinn, "They Served: The Richards Legacy in the Church," *Ensign,* January 1980, 25.
10 Andrew Jenson, *Latter-day Saint Biographical Encyclopedia,* 4 vols. (Salt Lake City: Andrew Jenson History Company, 1901–1936), 3:703–706; Smith, *History of the Church,* 6:366.
11 Richards to Brigham Young, June 16, 1877, as cited in Bennion, 166.
12 Arrington, 32.
13 Bennion, 168.
14 Bennion, 171–173.
15 Arrington, 32.

CHELSEA S. RIPPY
Standing for Beliefs

Like other home industries with humble beginnings in cramped basements, From the Attic—an interior decorating and design company owned by Chelsea Rippy—closed its doors without providing its founder with anticipated profits. But Shade Clothing, a popular clothing company founded by Chelsea, is another story. Shade has beaten all odds on any business scale. Beyond learning about the volatile nature of business ventures, Chelsea's entrepreneurial experiences have taught her that persistence and finding a place in the commercial market is personally fulfilling.

Wife of Tyler J. Rippy, Chelsea Ruth Stenson was born in August 1974. She grew up in Wyoming and Oregon before beginning her university studies at Ricks College in Rexburg, Idaho, in 1993. In 1999 she finished her educational pursuits at Brigham Young University, earning a bachelor's degree in health science education but never thinking that one day she would make millions in the clothing industry.

Five years later Chelsea was a frustrated twenty-nine-year-old mother of two children residing in American Fork, Utah. Her frustration stemmed from shopping for clothes: She wanted to buy

cute and trendy fashions, but it was very important to her to dress in modest clothing. Being "surrounded by low-rise jeans and short shirts" only more firmly reminded her of her standards. She said, "I didn't feel cute in anything." She grew "tired of going shopping and coming back empty-handed." [1]

One day her shopping experience was exceptionally frustrating. At that point, Chelsea said, "I just thought . . . 'If I create an undershirt that covered me in all the right places, I could really wear anything that I wanted to." She added, "If I need the shirt, so does every other woman in my position."[2]

Instead of recognizing that she had a good idea but then discarding the idea, Chelsea determined to resolve the "hip-but-modest dilemma."[3] With the help of a fellow mother and BYU graduate whose background was in health science, Chelsea launched Shade Clothing in October 2004. She began selling undershirts with higher necklines and a longer cut that could be worn to cover midriffs and shoulders left bare by trendy sheer and cropped tops.

Chelsea's modest designs were an instant hit. Sales quickly proved that she had been right—there *were* other women in her position. In its first year, Shade Clothing sold more than $2 million in undershirts to women looking for modest clothing options.[4]

Such immediate success came as a complete surprise. To Chelsea the biggest shock came when she found her clothing appealed to a wider audience than just Latter-day Saint women. She had hoped that LDS women were going to love—and buy—her new brand of modest apparel, but she didn't think that her "ultimate undershirt" would appeal to women of other faiths. But upon sending her shirts to several non-LDS friends, Chelsea discovered her concerns about modesty were shared by women of other religious backgrounds who also wanted to look cute but covered.[5]

Perhaps this explains the rapid proliferation of businesses like Chelsea's in recent years and the shift "back to refinement" in many department stores that cater to customers wanting more modest options.[6] The growing popularity of Chelsea's undershirts and the explosion of businesses like Shade Clothing have prompted some to speculate that this is merely a passing trend. Chelsea agrees with her critics that modest styles may not be long lasting, yet she insists that there will always be those, like her, who opt for modesty: "I think in a few years the [businesses] that are there for a short ride—quick money—will be gone," she says.[7] But to Chelsea, "Modesty is not a trend. It's a lifestyle."[8] Although she maintains her modesty in dress, the Shade Clothing brand was recently sold to a large retailer, and Chelsea is preparing for her next exciting venture.

1   Kimberly Palmer, "Anti-Britney: The New Look," *U.S. News and World Report,* April 2007, 50.

2   Sara Israelson, "Modesty is Fashion Statement," *Deseret News,* October 8, 2005.

3   Rob Walker, "Cover Brand," *The New York Times,* October 8, 2006.

4   Goff, "Au-Courant but Covered; Girls and Women Weary of Suggestive Clothing Demand, Get Alternatives," *Washington Times,* November 6, 2005.

5   Walker.

6   Palmer, 50.

7   Israelson.

8   Palmer, 50.

LOUISE YATES ROBISON

Compassion

Courtesy of the Church History Library, The Church
of Jesus Christ of Latter-day Saints.

"Sister Robison stressed the volunteer compassionate services, 'Go where you're needed; do what you can.' That was her theme," said Belle Spafford, who served on the Relief Society General Board with Louise Yates Robison.[1] Louise spent much of her life helping those who were poor and uneducated, since she too suffered from meager wealth and lack of education.

The daughter of Thomas Yates and Elizabeth Francis, Louise was born May 27, 1866, in Scipio, Utah. Louise thought of her childhood as "happy and her parents as 'splendid, . . . refined, spiritual, and loving.'" She spent much of her childhood undergoing pioneer experiences. From her mother—who served as a ward Relief Society president for three years and as a stake Relief Society president for twenty-five years—Louise learned "to know what service in Relief Society entails."[2]

At a young age Louise also realized the importance of education. She attended home school and then classes in the Scipio town hall. At fourteen, Louise went to Brigham Young Academy in Provo, Utah, for a year. Because her parents wanted her to gain some vocational training, Louise then moved to Salt Lake City to take a course in dressmaking.[3]

Louise's education was cut short when she married Joseph L. Robison on October 11, 1883. They would become the parents of six children, two sons and four daughters. Motherhood did not stop Louise's desire to learn; when she took her children to school, she studied their lessons. When her children were grown, she enrolled in university extension courses while she was gainfully employed. She woke up at 4 A.M. every day and worked two hours on her university courses; she then did her housekeeping and worked in the garden between 6 and 7:30 A.M. before working seven or eight hours a day in the burial clothes department of the Relief Society, and worked again on her university courses for several hours in the evening. It was a schedule she maintained for several years.[4]

In 1921, Louise was called to be second counselor in the general Relief Society presidency under President Clarissa Smith Williams. She was a bit surprised by the call. "I had never heard of her but I voted for her," Louise said of sustaining herself in sacrament meeting. "When I realized it was myself, I was so upset."[5] Her daughter Gladys recalled her mother being set apart by President Heber J. Grant:

When Mother went to President Grant's office to be set apart, she felt sure he had been misinformed about her abilities, so she told him she'd be happy to do her best in whatever he asked her to do, but she wanted him to know that she had a limited education, and very little money and social position, and she was afraid she wouldn't be the example that the women of the Relief Society would expect in a leader. She finished by saying, "I'm just a humble woman!" President Grant answered, "Sister Louizy, 85% of the women of our church are humble women. We are calling you to be the leader of them." Mother never forgot what she felt was a special call, and throughout her administration, her main concern was for those who were underprivileged because of lack of money or opportunity for education.[6]

During her service as second counselor, she worked with the Maternity Welfare Program, placing wheat accounts in a central fund in the Presiding Bishop's office. Interest on the entire wheat trust fund was then used for maternity and child-welfare work until 1939.[7]

In 1928, Louise was called to be the seventh general president of the Relief Society. During the Great Depression, she spent much time focusing on sisters who lacked formal education and material wealth, feeling she was in similar circumstances and wanted to help those also suffering.[8] She claimed, "For ninety-three years Relief Society has been saying that we take care of our needy ones. There are still some needy church members in every community who are trying to get along without federal aid, because they have the spirit of the pioneers." She continued, "Encourage your Ward Presidents to see that these people are not allowed to suffer and are not forced to ask for Federal help if you can help them."[9]

During Louise's tenure, the Relief Society Service Department strengthened employment, adoption, and foster care services and continued to care for Latter-day Saint families referred by bishops.[10] The Relief Society also played an integral role in the Church Security Plan, with "all policies relating to the administration of relief, sewing centers, social welfare, family budgets, conservation of family resources, and contacts with other relief agencies."[11]

Louise was the first general Relief Society president to visit Church branches of the Church in England and Europe. She also visited Hawaii and Paris as a member of the National and International Councils of Women.[12]

Louise was released from her calling as general Relief Society president in December 1939. Her impact on the welfare programs of the Church and Relief Society were great—she truly loved those she served. Louise died just six years later on March 30, 1946. As Belle Spafford said, "I think Sister Robison was greatly loved. In fact, I've heard board members who were with her say there will never be a president more beloved by the women than was Sister Robison. . . . Sister Robison was a humanitarian . . . and stressed the volunteer compassionate services."[13]

1 Oral History Interviews—Belle S. Spafford, 40.
2 *History of Relief Society 1842–1966,* 15.
3 Janet Peterson and LaRene Gaunt, *Elect Ladies: Presidents of the Relief Society* (Salt Lake City: Deseret Book, 1990), 114–115.
4 Peterson and Gaunt, 118–119.
5 Ibid., 120–121.
6 Family scrapbook compiled by Gladys Robison Winter, LDS Church Archives.
7 *History of Relief Society,* 42.
8 Peterson and Gaunt, 121.
9 Jill Mulvay Derr, Janath Russell Cannon, and Maureen Ursenbach Beecher, *Women of Covenant* (Salt Lake City: Deseret Book, 1992), 254–255; *The Relief Society Magazine,* May 1935, 272.
10 Derr, Cannon, and Beecher, 254–255; *The Relief Society Magazine,* 255–256.
11 Derr, Cannon, and Beecher, 254–255; *The Relief Society Magazine,* 257; Message from the First Presidency, April 7, 1936.
12 Peterson and Gaunt, 124.
13 Oral History Interviews—Belle S. Spafford.

AURELIA SPENCER ROGERS

Service

"I reflected seriously upon the necessity of more strict discipline for our little boys," Aurelia Spencer Rogers wrote. It seemed strange to her that Latter-day Saint children "should be allowed to indulge in anything approaching rowdyism" in her LDS settlement. She questioned, "Why should anything be allowed to come before the most sacred duty of parentage, that of looking after the spiritual welfare of the children?" It was while pondering this question that she heard a voice say to her that there was an auxiliary organization for all ages except the children.[1] Aurelia not only listened, but acted on the divine inspiration she received, becoming the impetus for what is today the Primary organization.

As a child, Aurelia enjoyed playing school with "sticks of wood for my scholars." She recalled, "I think my forte would be to teach children, if I could have been educated for it." But a formal education was never to be hers. When she was twelve, her mother died at Indian Creek—near Keosaqua, Iowa—following the forced Mormon exodus from Nauvoo. Aurelia contended that her mother "fell a victim to the cares and hardships of persecution."[2] A few months after her death, Aurelia's father was called to edit the *Millennial Star* in Liverpool, England. He accepted the call even though it meant leaving his young children without adult supervision in the temporary encampment at Winter Quarters, Nebraska. Letters from him encouraged Aurelia and her older sister to be mothers to their siblings: "My oldest daughters; on you is rolled a great responsibility, seemingly beyond your years. Be womanly, kind and patient, act the part of mother to the younger children."[3]

In May 1848, Aurelia and her siblings began their journey across the plains in the Brigham Young company. "There were many ups and downs in our travels," she wrote. "When the weather was pleasant we enjoyed ourselves very much, although having to walk over the roughest part of the road, as the wagons were heavily loaded."[4] She added, "Many a night I have gone to bed without supper having to wait until I was hungry enough to eat our poor fare."[5]

After arriving in the Salt Lake Valley, Aurelia earned money "by taking in sewing and making bracelets and necklaces out of hair, some of which I sold for a trifle." When her father returned from his British mission in September 1849, she wrote: "Oh! What a joyful time, to see the only parent we had, after so long [three years] an absence."[6]

At age seventeen, Aurelia married Tom Rogers, a young man she had met on the westward trek. They settled in Farmington, a small community sixteen miles north of Salt Lake City. "I remember how lovely and romantic the place looked," Aurelia recalled in speaking of Farmington, "with high mountains on the east and the Great Salt Lake on the west."[7] She bore Tom twelve children, five of whom died in infancy.

By the time Aurelia was in her early forties, nearly all of her children were raised. At this time, she turned her attention to the rowdy behavior of the young boys in town.[8] She shared her concerns with Eliza R. Snow and other leaders of the Relief Society General Board. She said to them, "What will our girls do for good husbands, if this state of things continues?"[9]

Eliza was responsive to Aurelia's concerns. She spoke with the First Presidency of the Church of the need for a children's organization.

Eliza proposed that the organization be called Primary. The First Presidency felt positive about starting such an organization, and Eliza was authorized to write to Bishop John W. Hess of Farmington, inviting him to start a Primary for the young boys in his ward. When Aurelia learned of Eliza's invitation to Bishop Hess, she wrote to Eliza asking if little girls could also take part in Primary. On August 4, 1878, Eliza penned, "My dear sister Rogers: The spirit and contents of your letter pleased me much. I feel assured that the inspiration of heaven is directing you. . . . President John Taylor fully approbates it."[10]

Bishop Hess asked Aurelia if she would preside over an organization of the children in the ward. Aurelia "felt willing, but very incompetent." Nevertheless, on August 25, 1878, under her guidance, the first Primary meeting in the Church, with 115 of the 224 enrolled present, was held. For the next seven years, Aurelia served as the Farmington Ward Primary president.[11] Of the young children in her ward, she wrote:

> Our children are our jewels; we have counted well the cost;
> May their angels ever guard them, and not one child be lost.[12]

In 1880 Primary was instituted Churchwide as the organization for children in the Church. Eliza R. Snow organized most of the Primaries throughout the LDS settlements. By 1897 there were 484 primary associations, 2,767 officers, and 33,659 children enrolled. In that year, children throughout the Church were asked to give money to Aurelia so that she could publish *Life Sketches of Orson Spencer and Others, and History of Primary Work.* She dedicated her published book to "her children and all the children of the Latter-day Saints."

Aurelia was honored to serve on the Primary General Board from 1893 to 1922. During those years, she continued to show great love and concern for little children:

Little children how I love them,
Pure bright spirits from above;
What would Heaven be without them?
Or this world, without their love?

Yet these little angel spirits,
Sometimes have been heard to say
Naughty words, use impure language,
While in anger at their play.

Then dear children be ye always
Pure and holy day by day;
Ask the Lord to guard and keep you
In the straight and narrow way.

Never grieve your Heavenly Watchers
By a coarse or impure word;
Nor forget to pray for loved ones,
For the children's prayers are heard.[13]

1 Aurelia Spencer Rogers, *Life Sketches of Orson Spencer and Others, and History of Primary Work* (Salt Lake City: George Q. Cannon and Sons, 1898), 205–207.
2 Ibid., 18, 35–40.
3 Ibid., 71.
4 Ibid., 76.
5 Ibid., 51.
6 Ibid., 81, 121.
7 Ibid., 123.
8 See Michaelene P. Grassli and Dwan J. Young, "All That Is Wanting Is Faith Sufficient: Aurelia Spencer Rogers (1832–1922)," in *Heroines of the Restoration,* Barbara B. Smith and Blythe Darlyn Thatcher, eds. (Salt Lake City: Bookcraft, 1997), 181–191.
9 Rogers, Life Sketches, 208.
10 Ibid., 209–210.
11 Ibid., 209, 230.
12 Ibid., iii.
13 Ibid., 282–283.

ANN ROMNEY

Involvement

"We urge Latter-day Saints everywhere to become actively engaged in worthy causes to improve our communities, to make them more wholesome places in which to live and raise a family," said President Spencer W. Kimball.[1] That prophetic advice was taken seriously by Mitt and Ann Romney—and in many ways, it was advice that defined the life of Ann Romney.

Ann first noticed Mitt in elementary school; she was attending the private all-girls Kingswood School in Bloomfield Hill, and Mitt was attending the all-boys Cranbrook School. They were reintroduced in high school and began dating in March 1965. "We fell in love when we were young, very young," recalled Mitt. "Genuinely, fundamentally, we cared for the other more than we cared for ourselves. Perhaps that was the test of true love, that the other's happiness dwarfed our concerns about ourselves."[2] They informally agreed to marry after his senior prom in June 1965—but before they married, there was Stanford University and an LDS mission to France for Mitt.

During his absence, although her parents were against organized religion, Ann joined The Church of Jesus Christ of Latter-day Saints and began attending Brigham Young University. She and Mitt were married on March 21, 1969. After Mitt graduated from BYU, they moved to Boston, where he attended Harvard Business School and Harvard Law School. Ann finished her undergraduate work by taking night courses at Harvard Extension School.

While Mitt went on to be CEO of Bain Capital (a private investment holding company with $13 billion of capital under management) and CEO of Bain & Company, Inc. (a leading international management consulting firm with more than 2,500 employees worldwide), Ann was a stay-at-home mom raising five boys. "I had not planned to choose motherhood as a career," she said. "The all-girl's high school I had attended set high academic expectations: like my friends, I assumed I would use what I had learned to pursue a professional career." Explaining her former goals, she said, "Not having grown up in the LDS faith, I hadn't given much thought to becoming a mother. When our tiny son was placed in our arms, however, I took on the work of the ages." Of motherhood, she said, "There is so much routine in being a mother— you feed, you wash, you clean, and then you do it again and again. But between the routines were defining moments." She concluded, "For me there could be no more fulfilling and exhilarating career."[3]

Believing "no service in the Church or in the community transcends that given in the home,"[4] Ann felt that an extension of her home was standing by her husband as he pushed forward his career—first in business, then as president and CEO of the Salt Lake Organizing Committee for the 2002 Olympic Winter Games, and then in politics. As he moved into ever-widening societal circles, so did she—serving on the Massachusetts General Hospital Women's Cancer Advisory Board and becoming an active voice in campaigns to prevent teen pregnancy. She also served as the liaison for the governor of Massachusetts to the White House Office of Faith-Based and Community Initiatives; helped develop Faith in Action, a program of the United Way of America; and served as a board member for the United Way of America. She was also involved in a number of children's charities, including director of the inner-city-oriented Best Friends. For her philanthropic work with children, she was awarded the 2006 Lifetime Achievement Award from Salt Lake City-based Operation Kids.

When Ann was diagnosed with multiple sclerosis (MS) in 1998, some wondered if she would retreat from the public arena. "As [she and Mitt] cried together, holding each other, in the doctor's office, we acknowledged that any problem would be okay as long as we could be together and not be separated by death."[5] She said, concluding, "You learn the most from tough lessons in life, and MS has been my toughest teacher. It has taught me a lot. It has taught me how to appreciate the good days. It's taught me how to pace myself better. Most importantly, it's taught me to recognize that nobody gets through life unscathed. Everyone is dealing with their own MS in one way or another."[6]

Although MS is a difficult challenge, Ann determined to stay in the public sector. She became a board member for the New England chapter of the National Multiple Sclerosis Society and was awarded the MS Society's Annual Hope Award.

After serving as the first lady of Massachusetts from 2003 to 2007 during her husband's gubernatorial service, she crossed the nation giving numerous speeches to forward the 2008 presidential bid of her husband. When asked, "What prepared you for the intensity of it all?" she replied, "Giving church talks. I've been Relief Society president, stake Young Women president. I've learned to run things and plan events and speak on a moment's notice."[7]

Her "Olympic-sized businessman" may still have a political future, but as for Ann, she has returned to a regular life "of horse training, making homemade granola, and leaving Mitt in the car while she runs in to the grocery store." She laughs, "It's either that or have him put a paper bag on his head so that it doesn't take so long to go anywhere."[8] As for her continuing role in the public life, she is ever ready to follow the prophetic advice to "become actively engaged in worthy causes to improve our communities."[9]

1   Spencer W. Kimball, "News of the Church: First Presidency Issues Statement on Election Year Concerns," *Ensign,* June 1976, 85.

2   "Mitt and Ann Romney," *Why I Believe* (Salt Lake City: Bookcraft, 2002), 280.

3   "Mitt and Ann Romney," 281–282.

4   Boyd K. Packer, "Called to Serve," *Ensign,* November 1997, 6.

5   "Mitt and Ann Romney," 280–281.

6   Jeanette Bennett, "Would-be First Lady is a First-Rate Lady," *Utah Valley Magazine,* July/August 2008, 27.

7   Ibid., 30–31.

8   Ibid., 24.

9   Kimball, 85.

PATTY BARTLETT SESSIONS

Service

Courtesy of the Church History Library, The Church
of Jesus Christ of Latter-day Saints.

Little is known of the first fifty years in the life of Patty Bartlett
Sessions. She was born February 4, 1795, in the small township of
Bethel, Maine; at age seventeen Patty married David Sessions in the
Methodist church in Newry, Maine. Of the eight children born to their
union, five died as infants from epidemics and three lived to adulthood.

Patty's life might have been lost to future generations had she not
accepted a simple gift—a small notebook. The first inscription in the
notebook reads, "I am now fifty-one years, six days old. February 10,
1846, City of Joseph, Hancock County, Illinois."[1]

Never realizing that her words would one day be an inspiration to
women around the world, Patty's daily notations disclose her thoughts
and actions on the westward Mormon trek and her medical assistance to
the needy in the Salt Lake Valley. She told later readers about an enduring
faith in Jesus Christ and His holy prophets; an abiding happiness in the
face of difficult, even insurmountable, challenges; and a willingness to be
inconvenienced to provide medical assistance to the needy.

Of her willingness to be a follower of Christ, Patty penned, "I
desire to do right and live my religion that I may enjoy the light to

see as I am seen and know as I am known. O my Father, help me to live my religion, this is my greatest desire."[2] Her later entries reveal that she did live her religion. On February 25, 1862, she wrote of giving Brigham Young "$175 cash." The money was deposited in the Perpetual Emigration Fund to help convey the poor to the Salt Lake Valley. Subsequent entries give other examples of her donations.

By centering her life on Jesus Christ, Patty found abiding happiness. "I am happy all the time," she penned.[3] Even when her happiness was tested as she traversed the hills of Iowa, she was able to pen, "I have been in the cold and in the mud. There is no food for our teams. I never have felt so bad as now, but I am not discouraged yet . . . although alone by myself I am happy."[4]

Her happiness increased as she gave Christlike service when such service required her utmost effort to reach the sick. On the trek west, she wrote, "About six o'clock in the morning I was called for to go back two miles. It then snowed. I rode behind the men through mud and water, some of the way belly deep to the horse. I found the sister that I was called to see in an old log cabin."[5] In her journal entry of March 6, 1846, she penned, "I go back ten miles this morning to see Sarah Ann. She is sick. Sent for me. I rode horseback."[6] She later recorded, "Was sent for to go back two miles to a sick woman, Sister Stewart. I asked her [for] no pay."[7] She also wrote of her medical skills helping men who complained of blistered feet, ague, and muscle cramps on the trek.

There is no hint of self-pity or resentment for the time spent in the service of others. Nor is there a single negative comment about those she served.

Of her continuing medical service, none is more acclaimed than her service as the foremost pioneer midwife in Utah, which began when she was called on to assist in the birth of a son to Harriet Page Young two days after reaching the valley. She believed that caring for mother and son was the fulfillment of a prophetic promise given in Nauvoo "that my hands should be the first to handle the first-born son in the place of rest for the Saints, even in the City of God." She recorded, "I have come more than one thousand miles to do it since it was spoken."[8]

Patty is credited with delivering fourteen babies in the Salt Lake Fort that first winter. Near the end of the year, Thomas Bullock reported, "'Mother Sessions' has had a harvest of 248 little cherubs since living in the valley. Many cases of twins; in a row of seven houses joining each other, eight births in one week."[9] Most of her 3,977 deliveries were successful in saving both mother and child. Instances of death, however, were a painful reminder to Patty of her limited medical knowledge.

Although her medical talents were always in demand, she also served in other ways. She founded the Patty Sessions Academy to provide children with an education at no cost. She pursued her talents as a seamstress—from the basics of carding, spinning, and weaving to the more sophisticated process of creating clothes, rugs, and comforters. She spent time reading: "I take 3 papers: Deseret News, Juvenile Instructor and Woman's Exponent. I read them all."[10] Of her reading, none brought her more joy than the hours spent reading her daybook: "I am here alone. I have been reading my journal and I feel to thank the Lord that I have passed through what I have. I have gained an experience I could not have gained no other way."[11] On December 18, 1892, diarist Patty Sessions died at age ninety-seven. The *Deseret Evening News* recorded, "She has gone to her grave, ripe in years, loved and respected by all who knew her."[12]

By her daily entries, Patty revealed that seemingly insignificant notations about a life of faith and service can change an ordinary, too easily forgotten life into a saga of grand proportions. As she lived true principles, she taught her later readers that the campfire hymn, "Come, Come, Ye Saints," was not merely a pleasing refrain—it was her way of life. She also taught that the pains of loneliness, whether at age fifty-one or age ninety-seven, can be lessened through service and quiet moments of reading and meditation.

1 Patty Bartlett Sessions, daybook, as quoted in Claire Augusta Wilcox Noall, *Guardians of the Hearth: Utah's Pioneer Midwives and Women Doctors* (Bountiful, Utah: Horizon Publishers, 1974), 22.

2 Sessions, as quoted in Elizabeth Willis, "Voice in the Wilderness: The Diaries of Patty Sessions," *Journal of American Folklore* (Boston: Houghton Mifflin, 1988), 45.

3 Sessions, as quoted in Noall, 37.

4 Ibid., 26, 44.

5 Ibid., 25.

6 Ibid., 23.

7 Ibid., 26–27.

8 Ibid., Guardians 40.

9 Ibid., 42.

10 Ada Sessions Eddins, "Life Sketch of David and Patty Bartlett Sessions," 32.

11 Sessions, as quoted in Willis, 43.

12 *Deseret Evening News,* December 22, 1892, 1.

ELLIS REYNOLDS SHIPP

Desire to Learn

Courtesy of the Church History Library, The Church
of Jesus Christ of Latter-day Saints.

In a dramatization of the life of Ellis Reynolds Shipp, ten-year-old Ellis tells her grandfather of wanting to become a medical doctor when she grows up. He replies in a shocked but gentle tone, "Ellis, being a doctor is a man's job!"[1] Despite his proclamantion, Ellis was one of the early pioneers in the practice and teaching of obstetric medicine in the Territory of Utah.

Oldest child of William Fletcher Reynolds and Anna Hawley, Ellis was born January 20, 1847. As an infant, she had a brush with death. A biographer relates, "A doctor who had been called to treat [Ellis] for some slight ailment administered an overdose of paregoric." With the help of her grandfather, a medical physician himself, she survived the incident in spite of a grim prognosis. This story, often related in her childhood, became the foundation for a powerful bond with her grandfather.[2]

Ellis grew to maturity in Pleasant Grove, Utah, where she showed an early interest in reading. Aside from being well-read, Ellis was a very attractive young girl. By age twelve, she had several eager suitors. But Ellis's youth was hardly ideal. Her younger brother died of smallpox, and her mother died shortly after Ellis turned fourteen.[3] Ellis was then given responsibility for the management of the home for nearly a year until her father remarried. Incompatibility with her stepmother led Ellis to move in with her grandparents.[4]

At age nineteen, Ellis married Milford Shipp, who had previously lost one wife to death and another to divorce. They were married May 5, 1866, in the Salt Lake Temple. Ellis and Milford lived in Fillmore until economic woes led to Milford's business failure. They then returned to Salt Lake City, where Ellis devoted much of her time to sewing, knitting, reading, and creative writing.[5] Milford entered the law of plural marriage with Margaret Curtis in 1868, Elizabeth Hilstead in 1871, and later Mary Smith. Ellis gave birth to ten children, four dying in infancy.[6]

Distraught by the death of her infants, Ellis studied medical books, hoping to learn enough about medicine so that she would not lose another child to a curable health condition. She arose each morning to read for at least one hour before her family awakened, and then she attended to daily chores.[7] Although Ellis loved serving her family, she longed for intellectual growth. Milford encouraged her to press forward. Ellis wrote in her journal, "He encourages me to cultivate my talents to study, write, and improve every moment of time, and he says he thinks I will be enabled to do good in the world."[8]

About this same time Eliza R. Snow, Relief Society general president, began to point to the lack of medical care as the cause of death among mothers and their infants. Eliza advocated medical opportunities for LDS sisters, believing that properly trained women could provide necessary care for mothers and newborns and curb the high mortality rate.

By 1873 Brigham Young was echoing her sentiments. "The time has come for women to come forth as doctors in these valleys of the mountains," he said.[9] On October 4, 1875, Milford's second wife, Maggie, left the Salt Lake Valley to attend medical school in

Philadelphia, leaving a nine-month-old baby in the care of Ellis.[10] Maggie returned within four weeks, unable to cope with loneliness. Ellis, while remaining supportive of Maggie, perceived an opportunity for her own dreams to be met in the situation. She determined that if she could find the courage, sufficient funding, and the strength to leave her children with her sister-wives, she could become a doctor.

With encouragement from Milford and Brigham Young, Ellis left the Salt Lake Valley on November 10, 1875, to attend the Women's Medical College in Pennsylvania. She progressed quickly in her studies, focusing on obstetrics. "I think there could be no greater accomplishment in the medical line than to be able to treat these conditions and diseases [in newborns and mothers] successfully," she penned in her journal.[11] She spent extra hours and even holidays doing laboratory work to ensure her success.

About a year into her studies Ellis developed a heart condition that forced her to return to Utah. Her concern at that time was not for herself, but for others. She recorded in her journal, "So many of my sisters are dying when they have their babies. Someone must be trained to try to save them."[12] After months of convalescing, she returned to Philadelphia to complete her degree. On March 14, 1878, Ellis graduated from the Women's Medical College of Pennsylvania at age thirty-one.

Ellis delivered more than 5,000 babies and helped found the School of Nursing and Obstetrics in Salt Lake City in 1879, and trained nearly five hundred women to become licensed midwives. She pursued graduate work at the University of Michigan Medical School in 1897. Her medical career lasted more than fifty years; Ellis was still teaching obstetrics courses well into her eighties.

Ellis was also a devoted member of the LDS Church, serving on the general boards of the Young Ladies' MIA and the Relief Society. She was president of the Utah Women's Press Club and a delegate to the National Council of Women. She also wrote poetry. Ellis died January 31, 1939, in Salt Lake City at age ninety-two.[13]

Ellis Reynolds Shipp knew at an early age that she wanted to be a medical doctor like her grandfather. Although there were many twists and turns in her life, she eventually reached her goal. Her medical education blessed untold thousands as she extended loving expertise to mothers and their infants in the Territory of Utah.

1   Orson Scott Card, *Great Mormon Women: Ellis Reynolds Shipp*, audiotape, part 6, side 1.

2   Susan Evans McCloud, *Not In Vain* (Salt Lake City: Bookcraft, 1984), 1, 3–4.

3   McCloud, 4, 23, 29.

4   Ibid., 32–33.

5   Ibid., 64–66.

6   Ibid., 71–72, 75–76, 88, 94–95, 97, 129–131, 139, 143–144, 150.

7   Ibid., 84–85.

8   Ellis Reynolds Shipp, "Early Autobiography and Diary," 47–48, 66, 77.

9   Brigham Young, October 1873 General Conference Address, as cited in Claire Noall, *Guardians of the Hearth; Utah's Pioneer Midwives and Woman Doctors* (Bountiful, Utah: Horizon Publishers, 1974), 105.

10   McCloud, 102.

11   Shipp, 176.

12   McCloud, 117.

13   See Gail Farr Casterline, "Ellis R. Shipp," in Vicky Burgess-Olsen, *Sister Saints* (Provo, Utah: Brigham Young University Press, 1978); Ellis Reynolds Shipp, *While Others Slept: Autobiography and Journal of Ellis Reynolds Shipp, M.D.* (Salt Lake City: Bookcraft, 1985).

AMANDA BARNES SMITH

Heroism

"My husband and son murdered, another little son seemingly mortally wounded, and perhaps before the dreadful night should pass the murderers would return and complete their work! But I could not weep then," wrote Amanda Barnes Smith.[1] She needed to pray. "O, Thou who hearest the prayers of the widow and fatherless, what shall I do? Thou knowest my inexperience. Thou seest my poor wounded boy, what shall I do? Heavenly Father, direct me!"[2] The Lord did direct her. In following the answer given, Amanda was able to preserve the life of her son—and in so doing, she became a heroine of Mormonism.

Daughter of Ezekiel and Fannie Barnes, Amanda was born February 22, 1809, in Becket, Massachusetts,[3] but grew to womanhood in Ohio. At age eighteen, Amanda married Warren Smith, a fellow believer in the Campbellite faith. On April 1, 1831, Amanda and Warren were converted to the gospel of Jesus Christ. Soon after their baptisms, they moved their family to Kirtland, Ohio, where they assisted in building the Kirtland Temple.

In 1838, they journeyed to Missouri in hopes of uniting with other Latter-day Saints. Upon entering Caldwell County, Missouri, they were "stopped by a mob of armed men who told us if we went another step they would kill us all."[4] The mob informed them that they anticipated killing every Mormon in the state within ten days. Warren and Amanda and their children were held hostage for three days. During this time, they witnessed a mob loot their wagon, taking "every bit of ammunition and every weapon we had."[5]

When they were finally allowed to leave, they hurried on to the LDS community of Haun's Mill. On the morning of October 30, Warren pitched a tent next to the blacksmith's shop, not knowing that a mob of some 240 men were marching toward Haun's Mill. About 4 P.M. Amanda saw the men that had taken away their weapons and ran to the blacksmith shop to warn the men inside. But as balls began to pierce the air, she was too late. She grasped the hands of her daughters and ran towards the woods. "I ran down the bank and crossed the mill pond on a wood plank, ran up the hill on the other side into the bushes; and bullets whistled by me like hailstones and cut down the bushes on all sides of me," she wrote.[6] Although bullets passed through her clothing, she was not harmed. For two hours, she and her daughters hid from the mob.

When the mob opened fire on the blacksmith shop, her young sons Sardius and Alma crawled under the bellows for protection. Sardius survived the first attack on the shop, but during the second attack, one of the mobbers put a rifle to his head and fired, killing him instantly. Her husband, Warren, was shot in the initial attack and dragged across the floor by a man trying to yank off his new boots. He died a few minutes later.

When gunfire ceased, Amanda—unaware of the horrific events—went back to Haun's Mill in search of her three sons and her husband. When she saw her oldest son, Willard, come out of the blacksmith shop carrying the body of his six-year-old brother, Amanda cried, "Oh, my Alma is dead!" Her son exclaimed, "No mother; I think Alma is not dead. But father and brother Sardius are killed!"[7]

Alma's hip joint had been shot away. Amanda prayed for guidance and heard a voice tell her to go to the smoldering fire, make a lye from the warm ashes, pour the lye into a cloth, and put the cloth on the boy's wound. In faith, Amanda prepared the cloth and pressed it repeatedly into the wound until it was clean.

"Having done this, [I] prayed again to the Lord to be instructed further and was answered as distinctly as though a physician had been standing by speaking to me."[8] She was told to make a poultice of slippery elm; she obeyed and placed the poultice on the wound. After being assured that her little boy was out of danger, she began to look for the dead. She wrapped her son Sardius in a sheet and with the help of her eldest son dropped his body down an open well to protect it from mutilation by the mob.

Amanda was determined to stay in the area until her son was well enough to travel. In the days and weeks that followed, Amanda faced further harassment. During this most turbulent time, she asked,

> "Alma, my child, you believe that the Lord made your hip?"
> "Yes, mother," he answered.
> "Well, the Lord can make something there in the place of your hip, don't you believe he can, Alma?" she asked.
> "Do you think that the Lord can, mother?" the boy questioned.
> "Yes, my son. He has shown it all to me in a vision."[9]

Alma survived the ordeal and within weeks was walking. Amanda believed that a flexible cartilage had grown in the place of the missing joint. Alma was never crippled, and later served a mission without the least physical impairment.

On February 1, 1839, Amanda and her four surviving children left the state of Missouri. They eventually settled in Nauvoo, where Amanda married another Warren Smith. She bore him three children before their divorce. Amanda was a member of the Female Relief

Society of Nauvoo, and went with Emma Smith and Eliza R. Snow to see Governor Thomas Carlin of Illinois in behalf of the Relief Society. She received her ordinances in the Nauvoo Temple.

Amanda was among the faithful to journey to the Salt Lake Valley in 1850. Her remaining thirty-six years were filled with service and love of God. One biographer wrote, "Amanda was beloved by all who knew her good works and sterling qualities. She was ever unflinching and firm in her faith in the gospel."[10] She died on June 30, 1886, in Richmond, Utah.

The legacy of Amanda Barnes Smith is one of heroism. Generations of Latter-day Saints marvel at her strength, conviction, faith, and unwavering determination. Few face the death of loved ones in such a tragic manner, and even fewer are called on to endure such heartache. For the heroine of Mormonism, a new generation of believers expresses gratitude.

1   *Autobiography of Amanda Barnes Smith* (1809–1850) [typescript], Church History Library; Edward W. Tullidge, *The Women of Mormondom* (New York: Tullidge and Crandall, 1877), 122–123; Nelson B. Lundwall, *Assorted Gems of Priceless Value* (Salt Lake City: Bookcraft, 1947), 93.
2   *Autobiography of Amanda Barnes Smith*, 91.
3   Marlene Bateman Sullivan, *Latter-day Saint Heroes and Heroines: Stories of Courageous Saints Around the World* (Springville, Utah: Cedar Fort, Inc.), 47–54.
4   *Heroines of Mormondom, Second Book of Noble Women's Lives* (Salt Lake City: Juvenile Instructor Office, 1884), 87.
5   *Autobiography of Amanda Barnes Smith*, 92.
6   Ibid., 88.
7   Tullidge, 122–123; Lundwall, 93.
8   *Autobiography of Amanda Barnes Smith*, 91.
9   Tullidge, 128.
10 Andrew Jenson, *LDS Biographical Encyclopedia* (Salt Lake City: Western Epics, 1971), 2:797.

BARBARA BRADSHAW SMITH

Compassion

Courtesy of the Church History Library, The Church
of Jesus Christ of Latter-day Saints.

"This is a new era for women—a time of greater opportunities, of more choices for personal development and service, of more possibilities for expanding the reaches of the mind and the heart," said Barbara Bradshaw Smith[1] at a time when passage of the Equal Rights Amendment (ERA) seemed eminent and many LDS women were questioning their role as women in the Church. Barbara, Relief Society general president, assured a worldwide Church that the most important role for a woman was to be an honorable daughter, wife, and mother.

Daughter of Don Delos Bradshaw and Dorothy Mills, Barbara Bradshaw was born January 26, 1922, in Salt Lake City. Her father was a barber who worked long hours to provide for his family of six children, and her mother stretched the dollars that were brought into the home. The sacrifices her parents made to support their family were not lost on Barbara, who recalls fondly their sacrifices as well as the joys of growing to maturity in their home:

> For Thanksgiving, we would have a great big table that went
> across [the Bradshaw's] dining room and clear down through

their living room. . . . After the meal was over, the men would say, "You've prepared the meal, we'll now do the dishes." They'd all go in and do the dishes, and they had so much fun we wanted to be there with them. But no, it was just for the men. That was their job.[2]

Barbara dated Douglas H. Smith for two and a half years before they married June 16, 1941, in the Salt Lake Temple.[3] They became the parents of seven children—three sons and four daughters.[4] Their daughter Lillian said of her mother, "She taught us to leave every room or place better than we found it. And she does the same thing with people."[5]

Barbara served as a member of the board of trustees of Brigham Young University, the board of education for the Church, and as a member of the Relief Society General Board. She was also an executive officer of the Daughters of the Utah Pioneers, president of two PTAs, and a board member of a local child center.[6]

President Spencer W. Kimball extended the call to Barbara to be the Relief Society general president in October 1974. Barbara reflected on the day she was sustained: "I was spiritually and emotionally strengthened by the words of a hymn that came to me unbidden: 'Fear not, I am with thee, O be not dismayed.'"[7] Barbara served as general president of the Relief Society from 1974 to 1984.[8] During her presidency, she garnered much public attention for speaking out against the ERA. She said of this highly controversial subject:

The blanket approach of the Equal Rights Amendment is, in my opinion, a confused step backward in time, instead of a clear stride forward into the future. It will create endless litigation in the courts in which legal decisions are made which might create circumstances harmful to the solidarity of the family and the optimum protection of children. And because it does not define some differences between men and women, I think it might be very destructive to families. I will always support—as I believe the Relief Society and the Church have always done—those pieces of legislation that improve and protect a woman's right to development of her full potential as a contributing member of society.[9]

When her views on the ERA movement became public, Barbara was asked to appear on the nationally syndicated *Phil Donahue Show*. After her appearance, she had many people approach her and share their opinions of the ERA.

In spite of the media attention for sharing her views on ERA, Barbara was determined to focus her time and energy on teaching women the importance of visiting teaching and compassionate service. Of visiting teaching, she said, "The most important function of visiting teaching is to help each woman understand that her home is sacred. . . . [V]isiting teaching also plays a significant role in helping newly baptized sisters stay close to the Church. And certainly visiting teaching provides a Church service opportunity for many women. Every sister can serve."[10] As for herself, Barbara visited sisters confined in the Santa Rita prison—a mother of nine with insufficient funds in the bank to cover her checks and a woman addicted to harmful drugs. These heartrending visits enlarged her thinking about compassionate service.[11] Barbara's message of compassion and reaching out to help the "one" was timely: during her presidency the Relief Society grew to two million members worldwide, nearly a 1,300 percent increase from 1942.[12]

Barbara's message of compassion was mirrored in her home as she extended love and support to her husband. Douglas recalled, "When I was elder's quorum president, we were trying to get the couples out to the temple. So we started having temple trips followed by waffle parties at the church—and Barbara usually ended up doing most of the organizing and batter-making. My counselors and I would plan one of these get-togethers, and then I'd go home and tell her. I would never have to stop and think if she would support me."[13] When Douglas served in the First and Second Quorums of the Seventy and as the Asia Area president—which meant living in Hong Kong for three years—Barbara was at his side.[14] Barbara continued to give service to her community and the LDS Church long after that mission. She died on September 13, 2010, at her home in Salt Lake City.

Barbara's willingness to speak out against the ERA helped protect the definition of family. Both women and men sought direction in her teachings. Her example of love and compassionate service encouraged women to be more considerate of their families and others. Through this, Barbara helped many women understand their roles as women and find the happiness that comes from being a daughter, wife, and mother.

1   Barbara B. Smith, "A Conversation with the Relief Society General Presidency," *Ensign*, March 1982, 24.
2   Interview with Barbara Smith by Charlotte Carol Searle, July 23, 2010, Salt Lake City; transcript in author's possession.
3   Barbara B. Smith, *The Light of Christmas* (Salt Lake City: Bookcraft, 1985), 15.
4   Barbara B. Smith, *Behold Your Little Ones* (Salt Lake City: Bookcraft, 1999), 152.
5   JoAnn Jolley, "Barbara Smith: A Call to Service, A Time to Rejoice," *Ensign*, March 1981, 18.
6   Barbara B. Smith, *Roots and Wings* (Provo, Utah: n.p., 1978).
7   Barbara B. Smith, "Relief Society Today," *Ensign*, March 1980, 23.
8   Smith, Behold Your Little Ones, 146.
9   Barbara B. Smith, "A Conversation with Sister Barbara B. Smith, Relief Society General President," *Ensign*, March 1976, 12.
10   Smith, "A Conversation with the Relief Society General Presidency," *Ensign*, March 1982, 26.
11   Barbara B. Smith, *Fourth Annual Harman Lecture*, L. Tom Perry Special Collections, Harold B. Lee Library, Brigham Young University, Provo, Utah.
12   Smith, "A Conversation with the Relief Society General Presidency," *Ensign*, March 1982, 24.
13   Jolley, 18.
14   Smith, *Behold Your Little Ones*, 152.

EMMA HALE SMITH

Affection

Courtesy of the Church History Library, The Church
of Jesus Christ of Latter-day Saints.

Emma Hale Smith is arguably the most famous LDS woman of the nineteenth century, yet she did not leave a journal, autobiography, and but few letters. Gratefully, contemporaries wrote of her life—none more so than her husband, Joseph Smith.

To the Prophet Joseph, she was "My beloved Emma—she that was my wife, even the wife of my youth, and the choice of my heart . . . undaunted, firm, and unwavering—unchangeable, affectionate Emma!"[1] His journal entries tell of his attentive care of her: "Emma began to be sick with fever; consequently I kept in the house with her all day. . . . Emma is no better. I was with her all day. . . . Emma was a little better. I was with her all day."[2]

His journal entries are replete with notations of their time together: "In the afternoon rode to Brother John Benbows, on horseback, accompanied by Emma and others"[3]; "Rode to the big mound on the La Harpe road, accompanied by Emma"[4]; and "Spent the forenoon chiefly in conversation with Emma on various subjects, and in reading history with her—both felt in good spirits and very cheerful."[5]

His letters reveal his abiding love for Emma: "I would gladly go from here to you barefoot and bareheaded, and half naked, to see you and think it great pleasure."[6] It is not surprising that Joseph pled in behalf of Emma and their children: "Have mercy, O Lord, upon [my] wife and children, that they may be exalted in thy presence, and preserved by thy fostering hand."[7]

Emma was the first to know that Joseph received the gold plates from the angel Moroni, and they were kept under the bed in her small home in Harmony, Pennsylvania. They "often lay on the table without any attempt at concealment, wrapped in a small linen table cloth, which I had given him to fold them in. I once felt of the plates, as they thus lay on the table, tracing their outline and shape." To Emma, the plates "seemed to be pliable like thick paper, and would rustle with a metallic sound when the edges were moved by the thumb, as one does sometimes thumb the edges of a book."[8]

She was the only woman to serve as a scribe for the Book of Mormon translation. Joseph wrote, "I have again commenced translating, and Emma writes for me." Emma recalled that as Joseph was translating he "could not pronounce the word Sariah." He asked, "Emma, did Jerusalem have walls surround it?" "When I informed him that it had," said Emma, Joseph replied, "O, I thought I was deceived."[9]

Of her role as scribe, Emma said, "My belief is that the Book of Mormon is of divine authenticity—I have not the slightest doubt of it. I am satisfied that no man could have dictated the writing of the manuscript unless he was inspired; for, when acting as his scribe, your father [this was said to Joseph Smith III] would dictate to me hour after hour; and when returning after meals, or after interruptions, he could at once begin where he had left off, without either seeing the manuscript or having any portion of it read to him. This was a usual thing for him to do. It would have been improbable that a learned man could do this; and, for one so ignorant and unlearned as he was it was simply impossible."[10]

Her testimony of the Book of Mormon and the prophetic calling of her husband led to her baptism on June 28, 1830, by Oliver Cowdery. Less than a month after she entered baptismal waters, Joseph received an important revelation for Emma in which she was told, "Behold, thy sins are forgiven thee, and thou art an elect lady, whom I have called."[11] The revelation was personal for Emma, yet latter-day prophets have used it as counsel for all women.

She compiled a pocket-sized hymnbook titled *A Collection of Sacred Hymns for the Church of the Latter-day Saints,* which contained ninety hymns. The songs of praise in the small book speak volumes of her love for the Lord and the Restoration of the gospel.

Emma became the mother of eleven children, raising five to adulthood. With two babies in her arms and two children at her skirts, Emma walked across the frozen Mississippi River carrying Joseph Smith's papers, including the new translation of the Bible. "No one but God, knows the reflections of my mind and the feelings of my heart when I left our house and home, and almost all of everything that we possessed excepting our little children," wrote Emma to Joseph, "and took my journey out of the State of Missouri, leaving you shut up in that lonesome prison [in Liberty]."[12]

Emma graciously welcomed both the poor and the acclaimed into her home and was the president of the Female Relief Society of Nauvoo. Under her guidance, women searched out those in need and ministered to them. Through their service heavy burdens were lifted, sorrows too severe to be carried alone were shared, and necessities needed to sustain life were freely proffered.

Emma participated in temple ordinance work, acting as proxy for extended family members. She wrote letters in defense of Joseph Smith to the governor of Illinois, even traveling to Quincy to meet with him on this important matter. She cared for Lucy Mack Smith for five years as Lucy suffered from crippling arthritis. Mother Smith said of Emma, "I have never seen a woman in my life, who would endure every species of fatigue and hardship, from month to month, and from year to year, with that unflinching courage, zeal, and patience, which she has ever done."[13]

Emma maintained and preserved properties in Nauvoo that were significant to the life of Joseph Smith and the Latter-day Saints. In her seventy-fourth year, in speaking of Joseph's prophetic calling, she said she believed he was everything he professed to be.[14]

Due to kind remembrances of loved ones, especially Joseph Smith, there is much known and much to celebrate about the life of Emma Smith, including the promise in her patriarchal blessing: "Thou shalt be saved in the kingdom of God even so, Amen."[15]

1   Joseph Smith, Jr., *History of the Church of Jesus Christ of Latter-day Saints,* 7 vols. (Salt Lake City: Deseret Book, 1932–1951), 5:107.
2   Ibid., 5:166–167.
3   Ibid., 5:21.
4   Ibid., 5:25.
5   Ibid., 5:92.
6   Joseph Smith to Emma Smith, April 4, 1839, as quoted in Dean C. Jessee, *The Personal Writings of Joseph Smith* (Salt Lake City: Deseret Book, 1984), 425–427.
7   D&C 109:69.
8   "Last Testimony of Sister Emma," *Saints' Herald* 26, no. 19 (October 1, 1879), 290, col. 1.
9   Emma Smith to Edmund C. Briggs, "A Visit to Nauvoo in 1856," *Journal of History* 9 (January 1916), 454.
10 "Last Testimony of Sister Emma," 290, col. 1.
11 D&C 25:3.
12 Emma Smith to Joseph Smith, March 7, 1839, as cited Jessee, 388–389.
13 Lucy Mack Smith, *History of Joseph Smith by His Mother,* ed. Preston Nibley (Salt Lake City: Bookcraft, 1954), 190–191.
14 "Last Testimony of Sister Emma," 290, col. 1.
15 Patriarchal Blessing given to Emma Smith by Joseph Smith Sr., December 9, 1834, Kirtland, Ohio, as transcribed by Oliver Cowdery, Patriarchal Blessing Book, 2:7., Church History Library, Salt Lake City.

JESSIE EVANS SMITH

Sense of Humor

Courtesy of the Church History Library, The Church
of Jesus Christ of Latter-day Saints.

At the age of fifteen, Jessie Evans—with her rich contralto voice—was invited to join the Mormon Tabernacle Choir. As she matured to adulthood, she was invited to join the Metropolitan Opera in New York City. But when she prayed and fasted about the Metropolitan offer, she was drawn to promises in her patriarchal blessing that assured her the Lord would advance her career as a vocalist within Church circles. She turned down the offer and sang with the Mormon Tabernacle Choir for more than fifty years, a record that has not been surpassed.[1] At age thirty-five she married Joseph Fielding Smith, an Apostle and future president of The Church of Jesus Christ of Latter-day Saints. During their thirty-three years of marriage, Jessie's willingness to sing as she accompanied her husband throughout the world brought joy to thousands and created for her an endearing legacy.

Born December 29, 1902, Jessie Evans met Joseph Fielding Smith at the funeral of his second wife, Ethel Reynolds Smith. Ethel had loved listening to the voice of Jessie Evans and specifically requested that she sing at her funeral.[2] A request to sing at funerals was not unusual for Jessie. During one month she was asked to sing at twenty-eight funerals![3] After the funeral of Ethel Smith, Joseph Fielding Smith sent Jessie flowers from the funeral with a note expressing his gratitude for her beautiful rendition that, he penned, touched many. Jessie responded with a note of her own expressing a willingness to be of further help to the family during their difficult time. From this, a brief correspondence ensued.[4]

Joseph believed that he was being led to Jessie and that the Lord intended him to marry her. After only a few meetings that Joseph formally called "interviews" and even fewer exchanged letters, Jessie consented to marry him. She was then introduced to his children, who referred to her as "Aunt Jessie" at her suggestion. "I'm not going to try to replace your mother. I'm here to love and help you," she told the children. "Call me 'Aunt Jessie.'"[5] Jessie helped raise the three youngest children of Joseph and Ethel, who revered her as their second mother.

One of the favorite pastimes of Joseph and Jessie was singing together at home and in public. When Jessie was asked to sing in meetings where Joseph spoke, she often invited him to join her near the piano. Joseph fondly referred to these duets as "do-it's," implying that "or else" would follow if he did not consent. Joseph loved to hear Jessie sing and remarked that she had "the most lovely voice—to me—that I ever listened to, whose music and song have charmed thousands, but more especially me."[6] When they traveled to foreign countries and exotic islands in behalf of the Church, Jessie learned at least one song to share in each native language.

Many believed it was more than her singing that contributed to the long life of Joseph Fielding Smith—they claimed it was also her humor. Although Joseph was known for his stern countenance in public settings, photographs taken with Jessie reveal him laughing. When she drove the car, Joseph would say, "Look out, Woman driver!" She, in turn, hung a plaque in their home that read, "Opinions expressed by the husband in this household are not necessarily those of the management."[7] Joking aside, Jessie believed that "the deepest tenderness a woman can show her husband is to help him do his duty."

She admitted there were times of hardship and sorrow in their lives, but for them happiness was a choice to be made every day. In the middle of a Church meeting, Joseph leaned over and said to her, "I can't think of one reason . . . why I shouldn't love you."[8]

After Joseph Fielding Smith became president of The Church of Jesus Christ of Latter-day Saints, Jessie's health declined. She died on August 2, 1971. At her funeral a letter from U.S. President Richard M. Nixon was read. President Nixon said of Jessie, "There is no measure to the joy and gladness Sister Smith brought to the lives of those who knew her. Blessed with a beautiful voice and a magnetic personality, she radiated warmth wherever she went."[9]

1   "Jessie Evans Smith 1902–1971," *Ensign,* September 1971, 23.

2   Joseph Fielding Smith, Jr. and John J. Stewart, *The Life of Joseph Fielding Smith: Tenth President of The Church of Jesus Christ of Latter-day Saints* (Salt Lake City: Deseret Book, 1972), 252.

3   Joseph F. McConkie, *True and Faithful: The Life Story of Joseph Fielding Smith* (Salt Lake City: Bookcraft, Inc., 1971), 51.

4   Smith and Stewart, 252–254.

5   Elaine Cannon, "The Legacy of Sister Jessie Evans Smith," *New Era,* September 1971, 19.

6   Francis M. Gibbons, *Joseph Fielding Smith: Gospel Scholar, Prophet of God* (Salt Lake City: Deseret Book, 1992), 279.

7   Smith and Stewart, 261.

8   Cannon, 19.

9   Richard M. Nixon, as quoted in Cannon, 23.

LUCY MACK SMITH

Conviction

"My mother is one of the noblest and best of all women," wrote Joseph Smith. "May God grant to prolong her days."[1] The Lord heard Joseph's plea and extended the life of his mother—and during her long life, Lucy Mack Smith was ever true to her conviction that her son Joseph was a prophet of God and that the Book of Mormon was the word of God.

The steady and predictable path she lived was marked by an unusual assertive tone—first noted when Mr. Murkley, a Methodist exhorter, visited her. As he sat beside her sick bed, Lucy recalled, "I dreaded to have him speak to me, for said I to myself, 'I am not prepared to die, for I do not know the ways of Christ.'" She then determined to know Christ and made a covenant "with God that if he would let me live, I would endeavor to get that religion that would enable me to serve him right, whether it was in the Bible or wherever it might be found, even if it was to be obtained from heaven by prayer and faith."[2] After being healed of her affliction, she was true to the covenant made with God that night. Through the years, she was also true to her mother's admonition: "I beseech you to continue faithful in the service of God to the end of your days."[3]

Lucy was faithful in the cause of Christ. For example, when a delegation from the community of Palmyra visited her home and said, "Mrs. Smith, we hear you have a gold bible, and we came to see if you would be so kind as to show it to us?" Lucy replied, "No gentlemen, we have no gold bible, but we have a translation of some gold plates, which have been brought forth to bring to the world the plainness of the gospel and to give to the children of men a history of the people that used to inhabit this continent." She then proceeded to inform the delegation of the contents of the Book of Mormon. When Deacon Beckwith of the Western Presbyterian Church advised Lucy to never speak of the plates, Lucy replied, "Deacon Beckwith, even if you should stick my body full of faggots and burn me at the stake, I would declare, as long as God should give me breath, that Joseph has that record, and that I know it to be true."[4]

Lucy demonstrated her boldness in the gospel on many occasions. When she saw fellow Saints waiting to board a boat at Buffalo bound for the Fairport Harbor in Ohio, she asked them "if they had told the people that they were Mormons." They replied, "No, by no means—and don't you do it for the world, for if you do, you will not get a boat nor a house, and here you must stay or go back." Lucy told them that she "would let the people know exactly who I was and what I professed. If you are ashamed of Christ, you will not be prospered as much as I shall."[5]

Within a few moments, a man asked Lucy, "Is the Book of Mormon true?" Without hesitation, she replied, "That book was brought forth by the power of God and translated by the gift of the Holy Ghost; and if I could make my voice sound as loud as the trumpet of Michael the Archangel I would declare the truth from land to land, and from sea to sea, and the echo should reach to every isle, until every member of the family of Adam should be left without excuse. For I do testify that God has revealed himself to man again in these last days."[6]

When she was introduced to Reverend Ruggles, a Protestant minister in Pontiac, Michigan, the reverend said, "And you are the mother of that poor, foolish, silly boy Joe Smith, who pretended to translate the book of Mormon." Lucy assured Reverend Ruggles, "I am, sir, the mother of Joseph Smith; but why do you apply to him such epithets as those?" Ruggles answered, "Because he imagines he is going to break down all other churches with that simple 'Mormon' book." Mother Smith asked the reverend if he had read the Book of Mormon. "No," he said. Lucy encouraged him to read the book, for it "was written for the salvation of your soul by the gift and power of the Holy Ghost." The reverend said, "Pooh, nonsense—I am not afraid of any member of my church being led astray by such stuff; they have too much intelligence." Lucy predicted, "Now, Mr. Ruggles, mark my words—as true as God lives, before three years we will have more than one-third of your church; and sir, whether you believe it or not, we will take the very deacon, too."[7] Within three years, one-third of the reverend's congregation joined the Church, including the deacon.

Her assertiveness led Lucy in October 1838 to push her way through a crowd at Far West to the covered wagon where her sons, Joseph and Hyrum, were being held captive by the Missouri militia, pleading to hear their voices one last time. Upon seeing the slain bodies of these same sons, she sank back, crying, "My God, my God, why hast thou forsaken this family?"[8] She later asked Wilford Woodruff to give her a priesthood blessing, in which she was told, "Let thy heart be comforted in the midst of thy sorrows for thou shalt be held forever in honorable remembrance in the congregation of the righteous."[9]

It seems fitting that Lucy's portrait, painted by English artist Sutcliffe Maudsley, portrays her holding a Book of Mormon—for she was, after all, a foremost defender of that sacred writ.

1   Joseph Smith, *History of the Church,* 5:126.
2   Scot Facer Proctor and Maurine Jensen Proctor, eds., *The Revised and Enhanced History of Joseph Smith by His Mother* (Salt Lake City: Bookcraft, 1996), 48.
3   Lucy Mack Smith, *History of Joseph Smith by his Mother* (Salt Lake City: Bookcraft, Inc., 1954), 62.
4   Proctor and Proctor, 212.
5   Proctor and Proctor, 264.
6   Smith, *History of Joseph Smith by His Mother,* 204.
7   Ibid., 216.
8   Lucy Mack Smith, Joseph Smith, *The Prophet and His Progenitors for Many Generations* (Liverpool: S. W. Richards, 1853), 279.
9   Matthias F. Cowley, Wilford Woodruff (Salt Lake City: Bookcraft, 1964), 228.

MARY FIELDING SMITH

Testimony

The life of Mary Fielding Smith exemplified the scriptural verse, "I know that my redeemer liveth, and that he shall stand at the latter day upon the earth."[1] Although she faced hardships and toil, her uncompromising adherence to principles—her determination to put her trust in God—is worthy of imitation.

Daughter of John Fielding and Rachel Ibbotson, Mary was born July 21, 1801, in Honidon, Bedfordshire, England. She migrated to Toronto, Canada, in 1834 to be with her brother Joseph and her sister Mercy, who had emigrated from England two years earlier. The three Fielding siblings were baptized in May 1836 by Parley P. Pratt, and in the spring of 1837 moved to Kirtland, Ohio. Mary supported herself by teaching school and privately tutoring students; it was there that she married widower Hyrum Smith on December 24, 1837, at the age of thirty-six. Hyrum was thirty-seven.

Mary was up to the task of caring for Hyrum's five children with his first wife, Jerusha, but difficulties beset her on all sides. For example, on November 13, 1838—just before the birth of her first child, Joseph F. Smith—religious persecution reared. Hyrum was imprisoned in

Missouri with his brother Joseph and other Church leaders simply for being Mormons. Of his imprisonment and the added responsibilities that fell to her in Hyrum's absence, Mary wrote to her brother Joseph Fielding:

> So great have been my afflictions, etc., that I know not where to begin; but I can say, hitherto has the Lord preserved me, and I am still among the living to praise him as I do today. I have, to be sure, been called to drink of the bitter cup; but you know my beloved brother, this makes the sweet sweeter.
>
> I suppose no one felt the painful effects of their confinement more than myself. . . . I do not feel in the least discouraged. . . . The more I see of the dealing of our Heavenly Father with us as a people, the more I am constrained to rejoice that I was ever made acquainted with the everlasting covenant.[2]

Hyrum escaped the confines of the Missouri jail and joined Mary and his children in Quincy, Illinois. From there, he and his family moved to what would be known as Nauvoo. In Nauvoo, Mary gave birth to Martha Ann in 1841. Happy days followed, but ended too soon: Hyrum died a religious martyr in Carthage Jail on June 27, 1844. After his death, Mary and a few of the leading ladies of Nauvoo paid a visit to Robert D. Foster, a known apostate and suspected member of the mob at Carthage: "[Mary] told him they would not bear his taunts and insults any longer. They ordered him to leave the city forthwith."[3] In fear, Robert fled from Nauvoo.

Although Mary was encouraged by the Smith family to remain in Nauvoo, she packed her belongings and her children and headed west. When Captain Cornelius P. Lott suggested that she wait to better prepare before traversing the plains, Mary told him that she would arrive in the Salt Lake Valley before him.[4] She did beat Captain Lott to the valley, but not before encountering many difficulties.

One incident occurred while she was camped near the Missouri River bottoms. Her best yoke of oxen had wandered off in the night. The next morning, young Joseph F. and his uncle Joseph Fielding unsuccessfully searched for the oxen in the tall grass and nearby woods but returned to camp "fatigued, disheartened and almost exhausted." Joseph recalled that as he approached camp, he saw his mother kneeling in prayer and heard her pleading with the Lord to recover the lost team. She then started walking toward the riverbank. Suddenly she called for young Joseph and her brother to come and see. "And like John who outran the other disciple to the sepulchre, I outran my uncle and came first to the spot where my mother stood," recalled Joseph F. "There I saw our oxen fastened to a clump of willows growing in the bottom of a deep gulch . . . perfectly concealed from view." Joseph F. concluded, "And we were soon on our way home rejoicing."[5]

The family arrived safely in the valley and settled in Salt Lake City on a small farm. Joseph F. recalled that one spring Mary instructed her boys to get a load of the best potatoes—which were scarce that season—so she could take them to the tithing office. Joseph F. was a little boy at the time and drove the team. He remembers, "When we drove up to the steps of the tithing office, ready to unload the potatoes, one of the clerks came out and said to my mother: 'Widow Smith, it's a shame that you should have to pay tithing.'" Mary turned to clerk William Thompson and said, "William, you ought to be ashamed of yourself. Would you deny me a blessing?" She insisted that he accept her tithing. "Though she was a widow," said Joseph F., "you may turn to the records of the Church from the beginning unto the day of her death, and you will find that she never received a farthing from the Church to help her support herself and her family."[6]

On September 21, 1852, Mary died of pneumonia in Salt Lake City at age fifty-one. Although traits of leadership and her uncompromising adherence to principles are apparent in her posterity, it is the words she wrote to her sister that best portray what she valued in life: "The Lord knows what our situations are, and He will support us and give us grace and strength for the day, if we continue to put our trust in Him and devote ourselves unreservedly to His service."[7]

1   Job 19:25.
2   Don C. Corbett, *Mary Fielding Smith, Daughter of Britain* (Salt Lake City: Deseret Book, 1966), 99–100.
3   "History of Joseph Smith," *Millennial Star* 24 (December 6, 1862):775.
4   See "Cornelius P. Lott," in Leonard J. Arrington and Davis Bitton, *Saints without Halos: The Human Side of Mormon History* (Salt Lake City: Signature Books, 1982).
5   Joseph Fielding Smith, *Life of Joseph F. Smith: Sixth President of The Church of Jesus Christ of Latter-day Saints* (Salt Lake City: Deseret News Press, 1938), 131–133.
6   Joseph F. Smith and John A. Widtsoe, *Gospel Doctrine: Selections from the Sermons and Writings of Joseph F. Smith* (Salt Lake City: Deseret News, 1919), 287.
7   "Letter of Mary Fielding Smith to Mercy Rachel Fielding Thompson," *Young Woman's Journal* 1 (October 1890):377.

MARY ELLEN SMOOT

Sisterhood

Courtesy of the Church History Library, The Church
of Jesus Christ of Latter-day Saints.

"God made us sisters, love made us friends" is a saying that holds
much meaning to Mary Ellen Smoot. Her five sisters—her dearest
friends—taught her that "developing love and compassion for everyone
is one of the important challenges we have in this life."[1] Today millions
of sisters around the world are blessed by her compassion and love.

The fifth daughter of Melvin and LaVora Wood, Mary Ellen was
born August 19, 1933. During her growing-up years, her father was
bishop of the Clearfield First Ward, and Church was not just a Sunday
devotional. "Our father would not leave [the home] until we were all
called to kneel in prayer each morning and have breakfast together,"
she recalled. If not going to Church, her father was going next door
to the Smith Canning Factory, where he was field manager and later
plant manager. Her mother had responsibility for hiring women and
overseeing their work. As for Mary Ellen and her sisters, when each was
old enough, "We all had responsible positions at the Canning Factory."[2]

But it was school that captivated the interest of Mary Ellen. In ninth
grade, she was elected studentbody vice-president, and in high school
she was named homecoming queen and senior class vice-president. She

also attracted the attention of Stan Smoot, studentbody president of Davis High School.

Just as these events were shaping the direction of her life, she was asked to be the organist of her ward Primary, but it was an inconvenient calling. "If I played for Primary I had to leave school and catch an early bus home in time to start the prelude music," she said. "I doubted my ability as well as the time commitment." Like so many decisions that would follow, Mary Ellen chose service.[3] She reached out in love and compassion to the children and put aside worldly honors.

Romance was put on hold when Stan received a mission call to the Hawaiian Islands. With him out of the picture for a few years, Mary Ellen entered Utah State University in 1951, where she was elected secretary of the freshman class. It appeared that her life would again be a social whirl, but as Stan's mission drew to a close, Mary Ellen wanted to meet him in Hawaii. Her father said, "There is only one way we could manage this trip. It costs a lot of money to fly to Hawaii. However, if you really want to go, and if you want us to go with you, we need you to come home at the end of this quarter and manage the migrant workers in harvesting the strawberries."[4] Mary Ellen left the university to supervise the workers.

After a few months of working at the cannery, she and her parents made that trip. The Hawaiian vacation led to an engagement with Stan and subsequent marriage in October 1952. During the first eight years of marriage, Mary Ellen gave birth to six children. She believes that these children fulfilled a promise given her that she "would have joy in my posterity." Of her family, she later wrote, "I am grateful for a wonderful husband, devoted loving children and grandchildren and all those with whom we serve each day."[5]

Mary Ellen reached out to her community, writing *The City in Between,* a history of Centerville, Utah. She also served in the Parent-Teacher Association, on the advisory board of *The Friend,* on a correlation writing committee, and as a columnist for her local newspaper. It surprised few when Mary Ellen was named the Outstanding Citizen of Centerville by the Centerville-Farmington Rotary Club. Shortly after, she was named president of the Bountiful Community Theater.

In 1983 when Stan was called to be president of the Ohio Columbus Mission, Mary Ellen set aside her civic activity to support her husband in this important assignment. She was also by his side when he was asked to open the Ohio Akron Mission. The same was true in 1993, when they were both called to be directors of Church Hosting. This assignment placed them in a position to meet politicians, ambassadors, and other dignitaries. Frequently, it also placed them in a position to have many meaningful conversations with Church leaders.

It was during a conversation with President Gordon B. Hinckley in April 1997 that Mary Ellen was called to be the general Relief Society president. Although she felt overwhelmed at the call, Mary Ellen wrote, "I do have a firm testimony that whomever the Lord calls he sanctifies."

During her first year as president of the Relief Society, she traveled to twenty-one countries to meet with Relief Society sisters and attended a planning session for the World Congress on Families held in Rome. As occasional self-doubts arose, she reviewed the words of the late President J. Reuben Clark: "The task ahead of us is never as great as the power behind us." When attempting to share these inspiring words with President Hinckley, she inadvertently said, "The task ahead of us is greater than the power behind us." She recalled, "We both had a good laugh."[6]

To Mary Ellen, "Relief Society exists under the direction of the priesthood to help the sisters and their families come to Christ, that's the whole reason we exist." She is convinced that "as we fill our lives with service to others, miracles happen."[7] She believes that Relief Society is a place to prepare women with faith and testimony to cope with life's challenges. "There is nothing more beautiful in this world than a woman aglow with faith and testimony. A woman who has looked within herself and to the Lord for strength to become a happy woman, a woman filled with compassion and love willing to serve and lift others everywhere she goes." [8] This belief continues to define her life.

Mary Ellen enjoys family history work. She writes short histories and newsletters each year for her family. She has spearheaded the writing of a book about her great-grandmother titled *What Happened to Jane* and a nine-hundred-page book on Smoot family history. In addition, Mary Ellen enjoys serving in the Bountiful Temple. She writes, "I believe in service, and I believe in the fulness of the gospel. We can never learn too much, and we can never serve too much."

A circle of sisterhood is what Mary Ellen has attained. She began with sisterhood in her home, and through the years, she expanded her learning and love in an ever-widening sphere of influence. Today, she is helping women in Third-World countries access micro-credit. Wherever the Lord takes her, Mary Ellen hopes to always reach out in love to her sisters and her wonderful posterity.

1   Mary Ellen Smoot, "A Tribute to Beverly." In author's possession.
2   "History of Mary Ellen Smoot." In author's possession.
3   Mary Ellen Smoot, "Influence of a leader." In author's possession.
4   Mary Ellen Smoot, "A Lesson in Industry." In author's possession.
5   "History of Mary Ellen Smoot."
6   Mary Ellen Smoot, "Ten-Minute Talk to New Area Presidencies," August 7, 1998. In author's possession.
7   "Ten-Minute Talk to New Area Presidencies."
8   Mary Ellen Smoot, "A Vision for the Future of Relief Society." In author's possession.

ELIZA ROXCY SNOW

Being a Witness

Courtesy of the Church History Library, The Church
of Jesus Christ of Latter-day Saints.

"While time shall last," wrote Emmeline B. Wells, "Sister Eliza's songs will be sung in Zion, and her memory live in the hearts of the people, and her name be immortalized as Zion's Poetess."[1] Who has not been stirred by the lyrics of "Awake, Ye Saints of God, Awake!" "Though Deepening Trials," "Behold the Great Redeemer Die," "How Great the Wisdom and the Love," or "O My Father"?[2] These familiar poems are representative of the five hundred poems written by Eliza R. Snow that continue to uplift each new generation.

In addition to poetry, Eliza wrote a brief sketch of her life. "I was born in Becket, Berkshire Co., Mass. Jan. 21, 1804," she wrote at age eighty. "I am the second of seven children—four daughters and three sons: all of whom were strictly disciplined to habits of temperance, honesty and industry." Of her parents, she penned, "[They] carefully imprest on the minds of their children, that useful labor is honorable—idleness and waste of time disgraceful and sinful." Fortunate for Eliza, her parents did not consider reading to be a waste of time. "I was partial to poetical works, and when very young frequently made attempts at imitation of the different styles of favorite authors," recalled Eliza. "In school I often bothered my teachers by writing my lessons in rhyme."[3] By age ten, she was winning prizes for her literary skills.

In 1825 Eliza published her first poem. Within four years, eleven of her poems were printed in the weekly newspaper *Western Courier,* and twenty in the *Ohio Star.* Being shy and perhaps lacking confidence, she signed her poetry with "assumed signatures," or, as she penned, "wishing to be useful as a writer, and unknown as an author."

Timidity still marked her ways in autumn of 1829 when she first learned of Joseph Smith and his sacred record: "A Prophet of God—the voice of God revealing to man as in former dispensations, was what my soul had hungered for, but could it possibly be true—I considered it a hoax—too good to be true."[4] But upon meeting Joseph Smith in the winter of 1831, doubts fled. She considered the Mormon faith, and on April 5, 1835, entered baptismal waters. By December 1835, she "bade a final adieu to the home of my youth, to share the fortunes of the people of God" in Kirtland.[5]

Her stay in Kirtland was short-lived, as violent persecution forced Mormons from town. She and her loved ones migrated to Missouri, settling in "a double log house" at Adam-ondi-Ahman.[6] When persecution reared in Missouri, Eliza once again moved on. "It was December [1838] and very cold when we left our home, and after assisting in the morning arrangements for the journey, in order to warm my aching feet, I started on foot and walked until the teams came up. When about two miles out I met one of the so-called Militia, who accosted me with 'Well, I think this will cure you of your faith.' Looking him squarely in the eye, I replied, 'No Sir, it will take more than this to cure me of my faith.' His countenance dropped and he responded, 'I must confess you are a better soldier than I am.'" She editorialized, "I passed on, thinking that, unless he was above the average of his fellows in that section, I was not complemented by his confessions."[7]

Years of religious persecution and upheaval took their toll on Eliza—especially her poetic urges. It appeared to some that her ability to express herself through poetry had ended. Joseph Smith did not agree. He designated Eliza "Zion's Poetess" and encouraged her to write again. With renewed determination, she took up her pen and wrote of the debauchery of government officials and the sufferings of the Saints. She submitted twenty poems about religious prejudice and persecution to the *Quincy Whig* under the pen of "Mormon girl."[8] In Nauvoo, she filled the LDS newspapers *Times and Seasons,* the *Wasp,* and the *Nauvoo Neighbor* with her inspired poetry.

After the martyrdom of Joseph Smith, her poetic leanings were unpredictable. Recognizing the problem, she wrote, "I have a pen that freely moves/Or does not move at all."[9]

After arriving in Utah, her life was filled with many responsibilities. When the Endowment House was dedicated in May 1855, she was given oversight of the women who participated in holy ordinances. She was later called on to reestablish the Relief Society, the young women's Retrenchment Society, and the children's Primary organization. Eliza penned, "I have traveled from one end of Utah Ter. to the other—into Nevada & Idaho, in the interests of these organizations."[10]

On each visit, she tried to elevate and inspire women to accomplish much good. She enjoyed saying to women, "Were we the stupid, degraded, heart-broken beings that we have been represented, silence might better become us; but, as women of God . . . we not only speak because we have the right, but justice and humanity demand that we should."[11]

Church leader George Q. Cannon said of Eliza, "Much of the intellectual movement among our sisters is due to the example and influence of Sister Eliza R. Snow."[12] In June 1880, she officially became the general president of the Relief Society.

Eliza died on December 5, 1887. The Assembly Hall was draped in white for her funeral. A choir sang "O My Father," written just six years before her death:

On the "iron rod" I have laid my hold;
If I keep the faith, and like Paul of old
Shall "have fought the good fight," and Christ the Lord
Has a crown in store with a full reward
Of the holy Priesthood in fulness rife,
With the gifts and the powers of an endless life,
And a glorious mansion for me on high:
Bury me quietly when I die.[13]

Through poetry, Eliza conveyed her witness of the sacred events in the history of the Church and of her abiding testimony of the doctrine of the Restoration. For her poetic rhymes, Eliza will always be remembered as "Zion's Poetess."

1   E. B. W., "Pen Sketch of an Illustrious Woman," *Woman's Exponent* 10 (November 1, 1881):82.

2   *Hymns of The Church of Jesus Christ of Latter-day Saints* (Salt Lake City: The Church of Jesus Christ of Latter-day Saints, 1985), nos. 17, 122, 191, 195, 292.

3   Eliza R. Snow Smith, "Sketch of My Life," as quoted in *Eliza R. Snow, an Immortal: Selected Writings of Eliza R. Snow* (Salt Lake City: Nicholas G. Morgan Sr. Foundation, 1957), 1–2.

4   Smith, as quoted in *Eliza R. Snow, an Immortal*, 3, 5–6.

5   Ibid., 7.

6   Eliza R. Snow, *Biography and Family Record of Lorenzo Snow* (Salt Lake City: Deseret News, 1884), 28.

7   Smith, as quoted in *Eliza R. Snow, an Immortal*, 9–10.

8   Smith, "Sketch of My Life," p. 1, as quoted in *Eliza R. Snow, an Immortal*, 11.

9   "To—," in Eliza R. Snow, 1842-1882 Journal, as cited in Jill Mulvay Derr and Karen Lynn Davidson, *Eliza R. Snow: The Complete Poetry* (Provo, Utah: Brigham Young University Press and University of Utah Press, 2009).

10   Maureen Ursenbach Beecher, *The Personal Writings of Eliza Roxcy Snow* (Salt Lake City: University of Utah Press, 1995. Reprint, Logan: Utah State University Press, 2000), p. 37; as cited in Jill Mulvay Derr, *Mrs. Smith Goes to Washington: Eliza R. Snow's Visit to Southern Utah* (St. George: Dixie State College, 2004).

11   "Great Indignation Meeting," *Deseret Evening News*, January 14, 1870, 2.

12   Editor, "Anniversary of Sister Eliza R. Snow Smith's Birthday," *Juvenile Instructor* 19 (February 1, 1884): 39.

13   "The Life and Labors of Eliza R. Snow Smith; with a Full Account of Her Funeral Services" (Salt Lake City: Juvenile Instructor Office, 1888), 35.

BEVERLEY TAYLOR SORENSON

Generosity

With her generous philanthropic contributions, Beverley Taylor Sorenson has benefited tens of thousands of young children in the state of Utah—donating liberally for arts instruction through a foundation she established, Art Works for Kids. "Recently I was asked what motivated me to put forth so much effort and money into developing art education in Utah's elementary schools," Beverley said. "My answer was because of my love for little children."[1]

Daughter of Frank and Bess Taylor, Beverley was born into a family that valued the arts. As she grew to maturity in the Great Depression, where poverty was seen on every side, her home in her Sugarhouse neighborhood was filled with music. An upright Steinway was the focal point of her family life. "We had a piano in our home and mom saw to it that we all practiced," Beverley said.[2] "In those days all performances were live."[3] Not having the means to hire a private music teacher, Beverley's older sisters taught her how to play the piano and to sing in harmony.

By age thirteen, Beverley was performing with her older sisters. Although she never viewed herself as musically gifted, she was proficient enough to earn 50 cents an hour accompanying dancers at the Jean Renae Ballet School during her junior and senior high school years. She graduated from Salt Lake City's East High in 1941 and then enrolled in the University of Utah. To support herself, Beverley sorted mail after college classes. In 1945 she graduated from the University of Utah with a teaching certificate in elementary education.

Wanting an adventure, Beverley moved to New York City to teach kindergarten in a Brooklyn Quaker school. In that city she furthered her musical talents by studying with a concert pianist—and in the Big Apple she met James LeVoy Sorenson, a native of Rexburg, Idaho. James had completed a mission for The Church of Jesus Christ of Latter-day Saints in New England and was serving his country in the Maritime service. After just three dates, he asked Beverley to be his bride. They were married in the Logan Utah LDS Temple on July 23, 1946. Soon after their marriage, they moved to Utah to spend what would become sixty-one years together. James passed away in January 2008 after a short battle with cancer.

Beverley and James are the parents of eight children. Beverley is currently the grandmother to forty-seven grandchildren and is the great-grandmother to forty-four, with more on the way. As one might expect, Beverley has always encouraged her children, grandchildren, and great-grandchildren to improve their God-given musical talents. As for James, he founded numerous companies and business enterprises. He invented numerous medical devices that are now commonplace in hospitals, including a disposable surgical mask, disposable venous catheter, and a computerized heart monitor. Today there is hardly a surgical center in the world that does not use one or more of his inventions.

James also founded LeVoy's, a very successful modest lingerie business. While LeVoy's was gaining momentum among shoppers, Beverley worked to help build Excelcis, a cosmetic line of skin and hair products. James was equally successful in real estate and became one of the largest landowners in Utah. Through the years, this successful

medical inventor, businessman, and real estate developer turned his attention to philanthropic causes.[4]

It is little wonder that Beverley also sought ways to give back to society. Her philanthropic interests have centered on arts for children. In 1995, during a visit to Lincoln Elementary School in Salt Lake City, she saw the impact of a "quality visual arts program" on at-risk children.[5] She saw firsthand that the arts can bridge gaps created by cultural and economic differences. During her visit, she learned that students participating in the arts significantly increased their ability to learn in other subjects and at the same time their behavioral problems decreased. The experience at Lincoln Elementary School, coupled with a concern for a grandson struggling at the time in school, led her to launch the Art Works for Kids foundation.

Beverley believes that today's youth "[have] lost critical opportunities for personal and academic development because of the absence of art education [in the public schools]," and she "decries the erosion of the arts from elementary education."[6] It is her goal to bring arts education to every elementary school in Utah. It is her belief that "all children [should] receive the best possible education, an education that includes the arts."[7] To her this means that music, dance, drama, and the visual arts deserve a place in elementary education. She expressed these views to the Utah State Legislature and persuaded the Utah Legislature to fund $15 million to hire art specialists to work with elementary teachers over a four-year period, beginning in 2007. A prominent Utah State Senator who helped sponsor the legislation said of Beverley, "She won you over with sweet love."[8]

To ensure that her vision of children immersed in the arts is never lost in the state of Utah, Beverley, along with another family foundation, has donated millions of dollars to teacher arts education at various Utah colleges and universities, including the University of Utah, Southern Utah University, Brigham Young University, and Utah State University. "We're helping to teach the teachers and find the best of the best," says Beverley. "You have artists who are wonderful, but aren't trained teachers, and you have teachers who are wonderful, but don't know the arts. Now you have the top universities, the deans, and the Utah school districts all working together."[9]

Beverley plans to continue her support of the arts in Utah's elementary schools. Through her contributions of both time and money, she has become one of Utah's most generous—and most strategic—art patrons. Her donations have inspired an increased emphasis on the arts within Utah's elementary education curriculum. It has not always been easy for her to persuade state leaders to share her vision for children. But Beverley says, "Together we have faced many obstacles and seen many triumphs. Through it all one thing has continued to inspire us: doing what is right for our children."[11] Of her contributions to the arts, University of Utah President Michael Young said, "She ennobles [children] and raises their awareness of the world."[12]

1   "About Beverley Taylor Sorenson," College of Education and Human Development, Southern Utah University.
2   "About Beverley Taylor Sorenson."
3   Brian Maffly and Julie Checkoway, "Beverley Taylor Sorenson's Legacy," *Salt Lake Tribune*, November 6, 2008.
4   See "James Sorenson, Medical Devise Pioneer, Is Dead at 86," *The New York Times*, January 22, 2008; Max Knudsen, "Billionaire Sorensen: He's a lot like You," *Deseret News*, August 29, 1999.
5   See "Philanthropist Tries to Raise Awareness of Art," Provo *Daily Herald*, October 4, 2009.
6   Maffly and Checkoway.
7   "About Beverley Taylor Sorenson."
8   Maffly and Checkoway.
9   Ibid.
10   Ibid.
11   "About Beverley Taylor Sorenson."
12   Maffly and Checkoway.

BELLE SMITH SPAFFORD

Leadership

Courtesy of the Church History Library, The Church
of Jesus Christ of Latter-day Saints.

In 1974 Belle Spafford told an interviewer, "Membership in the Church is a tremendous privilege. Membership in Relief Society is a special privilege. There's nothing like [Relief Society] for a woman to develop herself, to serve humanity, to find self-expression, to structure her own life wisely and well."[1] No one realized these truths more than Belle, who served for twenty-nine years as the Relief Society general president. In her faithful service, Belle not only helped others realize the great blessings offered by Relief Society, but demonstrated her leadership skill as she helped thousands become converted to the organization's purpose, "Charity Never Faileth."

Seventh child of John Gibson Smith and Hester Sims, Belle was born October 8, 1895. Belle's father died seven months before her birth; her mother's leadership in the home and her refusal to allow the children to feel fatherless had a great impact on Belle. Her mother often said to her children, "You have a father. He's not with us, but he is taking care of us, I'm sure. And you have a Heavenly Father, and you have the father of the ward who is the bishop."[2] From her mother's example, Belle learned early that women have the capability to lead and to do it well, particularly when they are guided by inspired priesthood holders.

Despite difficult economic circumstances, the importance of education was emphasized in her home. Belle completed a two-year degree at the University of Utah, and then taught school in Salt Lake City and Provo for several years.[3] In 1921 Belle married Willis Earl Spafford, and they became the parents of two children.

While a young mother, Belle was called to be second counselor in her ward Relief Society. She was "shocked" by the call because she had told the bishop of her desire to teach children or youth. At the time she believed that Relief Society was an organization for her mother and that she did not have the right experience for her new calling. Her bishop reminded Belle that the calling was from God and refused to grant Belle's requests to be released—one when her children became ill and one when she was injured in a car accident. Both times her bishop said, "I still don't get the feeling that you should be released from Relief Society."[4] Years later, Belle felt great gratitude to her bishop for the opportunity to serve in Relief Society, for it helped prepare her for greater responsibilities ahead.

In 1935 Belle was called to be a member of the Relief Society General Board. Two years later, she was not only serving in a general capacity, but still had her ward Relief Society calling and also served as counselor in her stake Relief Society. In the same year, she was invited by editors of *The Relief Society Magazine* to join their staff; she accepted, and within a short time, President Heber J. Grant requested that Belle become editor of the magazine. With no previous experience, Belle worried about her adequacy until being reassured by President Grant that she could fulfill the responsibility. Belle edited the magazine from 1937 to 1945. During that interim she saw a tremendous growth in the number of magazine subscribers.[5]

Belle's experiences in ward, stake, and general Relief Society positions and her interactions with the "leading women of the Church"

while editing the *Relief Society Magazine,* prepared her well to be the second counselor to Amy Brown Lyman in the Relief Society general presidency in 1942. Three years later, Belle was called to be the Relief Society general president.

She expected to serve as president for "only five years."[6] Much to her surprise, Belle served for the next twenty-nine years, serving under six presidents of the LDS Church. Under their guidance and Belle's capable leadership, Relief Society grew and improved in the areas of visiting teaching, compassionate service, social service, and Sunday instruction. Belle oversaw the construction of the Relief Society Building in Salt Lake City that now houses the general boards of the Relief Society, Young Women, and Primary. But Belle's greatest influence came from her desire to fulfill the society's motto, "Charity Never Faileth." Belle involved LDS women in extensive compassionate service projects as she "expanded and professionalized the delivery of social services by the Relief Society in cooperation with the Church welfare program."[7]

Like all great leaders, Belle realized the importance of "reaching the one." She encouraged her sisters to fulfill their obligations to visit teach by saying, "While the actual visit to the home may seem a simple and uneventful call, countless times it has been the means whereby a miracle takes place in the life of a sister."[8] Belle demonstrated in a clear manner a love for each sister in her society. After her death in February 1982, countless women told her grieving family that "Belle was their best friend." One friend wrote, "[Love] made her a great leader because she could talk to anyone, she could approach anyone and be accepted. She had that quality about her."[9]

Over her years of service as Relief Society general president, Belle became a great and much-beloved leader. She lived by her conviction that "compassionate service is an expression of testimony." She promoted love and understanding among Relief Society members by giving fully of her talents. After her release as Relief Society general president, Belle said, "The Church offers us opportunities that often make us go beyond ourselves."

Though Belle had initially doubted that Relief Society was meant for her, she found an inner strength to go beyond herself and develop the skills of service, compassion, and self-expression that are the hallmarks of Relief Society. By her example, Belle taught women that membership in Relief Society "is not only a privilege but an obligation," for Relief Society can help any woman become her best self.[10]

1   Belle S. Spafford, "Reaching Every Facet of a Woman's Life: A Conversation with Belle S. Spafford, Relief Society General President," *Ensign,* June 1974, 14.

2   Janet Peterson and Connie Lewis, "Making A Difference for Women: Belle S. Spafford," *Ensign,* March 2006, 45.

3   Gayle Morby Chandler, "Belle S. Spafford: Leader of Women," Master's Thesis (Provo, Utah: Brigham Young University, 1983), 10.

4   Boyd K. Packer, "Relief Society Conference Emphasizes Spirit of Compassion," *Ensign,* January 1974, 133.

5   Chandler, 15–16.

6   Chandler, 17.

7   Peterson and Lewis, 48.

8   Belle S. Spafford, *A Woman's Reach* (Salt Lake City: Deseret Book, 1974), 60.

9   Peterson and Lewis, 50.

10   Spafford, "Reaching Every Facet of a Woman's Life," 16.

ANITA STANSFIELD

Self-Esteem

Because she was much younger than her siblings, Anita Stansfield learned to play alone as a child. Her playmates were imaginary, and her fun unbounded.[1] Little did she know that the vivid imagination honed in childhood would one day help her become the reigning queen of LDS romantic fiction. Known for shattering the stereotypical romance novel, Anita masterfully weaves "great storytelling with intense psychological depth as she focuses on the emotional struggles of the human experience." From heartwarming to heartstopping fiction, readers find her characters and their stories not easily forgotten.[2]

The road from childhood imagination to romantic novelist has been bumpy for Anita, and few of those familiar with her many accomplishments would guess that she has struggled to overcome feelings of low self-esteem. She was born in 1961 to Arnold and Dawn Nita Barney, good people who loved each other and Anita. However, both parents were raised in dysfunctional families and suffered from poor self-esteem, which they unintentionally passed to their daughter.

Anita believes that the majority of her personal struggles come from feelings of inadequacy. "Satan knows just when to throw the punches during the emotional cycles that women are prone to," she says. "A little whisper goes a long way when we look at the flaws of our lives through a magnifying glass and everyone else's through a telescope turned backward."[3]

Anita started writing at the age of sixteen, making a conscious decision that she would someday be a published novelist. At the age of nineteen, she married Vince John Stansfield, and they became the parents of five children. Anita describes motherhood as being either "completely challenging" or "joy beyond description."[4] She feels the same way about writing. In 1994 she published her first novel—*First Love and Forever.* More than fifty novels have followed. By mixing motherhood and writing, Anita has learned to "expect interruptions and deal with them." Her motto is "Practice. Practice. Practice."[5]

Anita "relies on inspiration to bring all the elements together and lend authenticity and balance to her work." In so doing, she quips, "I have to give credit where it's due or I could get struck by lightning. . . . Over the years, line upon line, my Heavenly Father has taught me the true source of my gift, and that what I do is absolutely from Him." She adds, "A person can be extremely gifted and never go anywhere with it. I believe that my persistence and tenacity are the reasons for my success. The talent is a gift. My choice to work hard, sacrifice, face the opposition, and keep going is exactly that: a choice. I have many people express envy for my gift (usually facetiously) but my secret thought is that they would never want to pay the price of persistence that got me to where I am today."

When readers tell Anita that the characters in her books seem real, she considers it a great compliment. But a far better compliment is when she learns that lives have been changed and testimonies strengthened because of reading her novels.[6]

After writing romance novels for more than twenty years, her perception of romance has changed from when she was a teenager. She now believes that real romance is "about mutual love, respect, and admiration between two people." Writing romance novels has also

changed her views of her husband, Vince, who is "a mountain man whose interests seem far from her desire to be a stay-at-home writer." She said that one day it hit her, "This guy's just like those rugged heroes in historical novels." She admits that his willingness to help with the children so she can write "makes me feel loved."[7]

Anita has become the first LDS romance novelist to sell a million copies of her books, and her efforts have garnered impressive awards—including the Independent LDS Booksellers' Best Fiction Award; the League of Utah Writers' Golden Quill Award; and Covenant Communications' 1997 special award for Pioneering New Ground in LDS Fiction. In 2007 she won the Lifetime Achievement Award from the Whitney Academy.

In spite of these accolades and others, Anita believes that her greatest achievement has been starting adulthood as "a relatively dysfunctional person who was pretty clueless about life" and becoming "emotionally healthy." She has worked very hard to overcome childhood issues and create a functional family.

Lyrics from the song "Wunderkind" by Alanis Morissette on the *Narnia* soundtrack hang on a wall in her home. She explains, "Because I've always struggled to feel good about myself, and to recognize that the strangeness that comes with my gift is a good thing, this song speaks feelings I've never been able to put into words." Her favorite phrase from the song is, "I am a magnet for all kinds of deeper wonderment."[8] Those who know Anita agree that she is a magnet for the wonderment that has come into her life as a prize-winning novelist and for overcoming childhood issues that threatened to mar her adulthood.

1   Anita Stansfield, "Questionnaire," August 29, 2010. Transcript in author's possession.
2   Anita Stansfield, www.anitastansfield.com [accessed 24 July, 2010].
3   Anita Stansfield, *Reflections* (American Fork: Covenant Communications, 2002), 56.
4   Stansfield, *Reflections,* 7.
5   Christopher Kimball Bigelow, Conversations with Mormon Authors (New York: Mormon Arts and Letters, 2007), 193.
6   Stansfield, "Questionnaire," 1–2.
7   "LDS Romance Novelist Explores Power of Love," Provo *Daily Herald,* February 1, 1998, C4.
8   Anita Stansfield, "Questionnaire."

LIZ LEMON SWINDLE
Inspiration

"I am continually amazed at how willingly we pass by life's rare moments of inspiration as we struggle to make it through another day," says portrait artist Liz Lemon Swindle. "In my life I have found that my greatest moments of spiritual growth come when I have hit the spiritual wall. It seems that hitting this wall is the way the Lord has of stopping me long enough to realize what I have been missing." At one of those pivotal moments, Liz realized that she had shown too little artistic interest in Joseph Smith and the restoration of the gospel of Jesus Christ. She said, "I was unknowingly turning away from the quiet glimpses of eternity, always on my way to somewhere else."[1] In the 1990s she changed her art focus and turned her artistic talents to portraying Joseph Smith as the Prophet of the Restoration and Jesus Christ, the Son of God.

Daughter of Elmer Matthews and Marie Wight, Liz Matthews was born January 13, 1953, in rural Utah. Her art career, which spans more than fifty years, began when her father placed her first drawings on the refrigerator and encouraged Liz to do more. She did, and the world is now more beautiful as a result of her artistic renderings. She studied fine arts at Utah State University before working for several years as a set designer and painter for Osmond Studio Television Productions.

Wanting a more flexible career than set design, she took up oil painting. In the 1980s she studied with the renowned wildlife artist Nancy Glazier. Not long after, Liz established her own reputation as a wildlife artist. Her paintings were displayed in major galleries in the western and central United States.

Although fame was hers in this genre, Liz wearied of painting feathers on ducks and fur on elk. Hoping that portraying children would provide a needed change to her art, she painted little girls cuddling dolls and rowdy boys on a campout, and made her mark as a pictorial storyteller. Admirers often remarked that her paintings resembled those of Norman Rockwell.[2] Although she begged to differ, after winning the Founders Favorite Award at the National Arts for Parks competition in October 1988, her confidence grew. With confidence came a determination to be a portrait artist.

"Uplifting, elevating music drives my art," says Liz. "It is a superb violinist who captures my imagination and creativity. A violin and bow in the hands of a capable musician like Jenny Oaks [Baker] is hard to beat for inspiration." Liz continues, "When I listen to a consummate musician play uplifting and inspiring music, my paintings come alive. It is as if they have no borders or boundaries. It is then that all is well in my world, and I can paint for hours."[3] By so doing, her talent matured and Liz became recognized as a portrait artist.

It was not until the 1990s that she reached the decision to paint what was closest to her heart—faith. With actors and cameras to document reenactments of major events in the life of Joseph Smith, Liz set a pictorial stage to ensure a greater sense of realism in her paintings. By studying photographic prints of historic reenactments, Liz has created an unusually authentic representation of Joseph Smith in her lifelike works of art and has become one of the premier painters of Joseph Smith. *Joseph Smith: Impressions of a Prophet* is her unique vision of Joseph, from his early childhood through the last moments of his life. Through hours of painting the life of the Prophet, her testimony of Joseph Smith has grown. She says, "I know that Joseph Smith is indeed the Lord's prophet called to restore His gospel to the earth."[4]

Upon completing her artistic impressions of Joseph Smith, Liz embarked on the ambitious "Son of Man, God with Us" project that now features more than fifty paintings depicting the life and ministry of Jesus Christ—heralded as her signature pieces. Her admirers boast that her talent for portraying the sacred is unique and refreshingly new. Although the Bible stories are familiar—a blind man seeing, the lame walking, and the leprous becoming clean—Liz depicts with stunning realism a time when the sick and afflicted were restored to health and glorified God. "The Savior that I knew when I began painting Him is not the one I know today," she confesses, "and I do not believe it will be the one I know in the future."

The Catholic Archbishop Augustine DiNoia, believing that Liz has captured in her paintings the real essence of Christianity, ordered ten thousand copies of her paintings of Christ for prayer cards for his worshippers. And the City of New York purchased one of Liz's paintings to display at a newly opened women's shelter. City fathers see true charity in her art. It is not a stretch to say that her Christian art is recognized throughout the world. Pope Benedict XVI now has one of Liz's paintings in Rome; she received a beautiful blessing from the Holy Father thanking her for her touching gift of art. Her portraits are also displayed in gallery exhibitions, LDS visitors' centers, and homes throughout the United States and abroad.

"I get to bear my witness of Jesus Christ every day," says Liz. "I just get to do it with a paint brush."[5] For her singular blessing of testimony through art, she expresses gratitude to a loving Heavenly Father for "sticking by me when the going looked hopeless, and for the patience to teach me when I didn't want to be taught."[6]

WOMEN *of* CHARACTER

1 Susan Easton Black, *Joseph Smith: Impressions of a Prophet* [Artwork by Liz Lemon Swindle] (Salt Lake City: Deseret Book, 1998), ii.

2 Susan Easton Black, *Every Superman Needs a Dad* [Illustrated by Liz Lemon Swindle] (Salt Lake City: Millennial Press, 2002), vii.

3 Interview with Liz Lemon Swindle, August 2009; transcription in author's possession.

4 Black, *Joseph Smith: Impressions of a Prophet,* ii.

5 Interview with Liz Lemon Swindle.

6 Black, *Joseph Smith: Impressions of a Prophet,* i.

LEONORA
CANNON TAYLOR
Following the Spirit

A willingness to be led by the Spirit of the Lord defines the life of Leonora Cannon Taylor. Whether speaking of her childhood, conversion to the gospel of Jesus Christ, marriage, or motherhood, Leonora was directed by the Lord to greater righteousness. She was the wife of an eyewitness to the martyrdom of Joseph and Hyrum Smith, and her husband, John Taylor, served as president of the Church from 1877 to 1887.

The eldest daughter of Captain George Cannon and Leonora Callister, Leonora was born October 6, 1796, on the Isle of Man. When she was thirteen, her father died a violent death at sea, which led to a reversal in the family fortune. To help make ends meet, Leonora was hired out in her youth to serve as a companion to a lady of rank in London.[1] There Leonora became a Methodist and turned her life over to the Lord to "direct her in all her movements."

After attending the lady of rank until well into her twenties, Leonora returned to the Isle of Man where she befriended the daughter of a Mr. Mason, a private secretary to Lord Aylmer, newly appointed governor of Canada. When Mr. Mason agreed to accompany Lord

Aylmer to Canada, his daughter insisted that her friend Leonora come along as her companion. At first Leonora declined the offer—but after praying she read in Genesis 12, "Get thee out of thy country, and from thy kindred and from thy father's house, into a land that I will shew thee," and believed the scriptural passage was an answer to prayer.[2]

While living in Toronto, Leonora attended a Bible class held under the direction of English immigrant John Taylor. His story of coming to America struck a chord with her. As a boy in England, John had seen "in vision, an angel in the heavens, holding a trumpet in his mouth, sounding a message to the nations." John interpreted the vision to mean that one day he would preach the gospel in America. Recognizing the hand of the Lord in each others' lives, John and Leonora were naturally drawn together. When John proposed marriage, however, Leonora declined his proposal—John was twenty-five and Leonora was thirty-seven. It was an inspired dream that caused Leonora to change her mind and accept his proposal. In the dream, she saw "herself associated with him [John] in his life-work, [and] she became convinced that he would be her husband."[3] When John proposed a second time, she accepted; they were married January 28, 1833, in Canada.

Three years later, obedience to the promptings of the Spirit led them to accept the restored gospel of Jesus Christ. In 1836 Parley P. Pratt heard Heber C. Kimball prophesy that he would find in upper Canada "a people prepared for the fulness of the gospel." When Parley arrived in the Toronto area, Leonora and John kindly gave him a room in their home but were unwilling to listen to his message. That evening he overheard Leonora telling her neighbor Mrs. Walton of her sadness at his departure. "He may be a man of God," she said. Mrs. Walton exclaimed, "Well, I now understand the feelings and spirit which brought me to your house at this time."[4] Mrs. Walton offered Parley her house as a place to hold study groups. She even helped him find a congregation.

The Taylors attended Parley's study lessons. John took copious notes on Parley's lectures for three weeks and compared them with scriptural passages in the Bible. After much study and prayer, John and Leonora concluded that Parley spoke the truth and both were baptized on May 9, 1836.

Hoping to gather with the Saints of God, John and Leonora and their two young children traveled by sleigh to Kirtland, Ohio. Instead of receiving a warm welcome, they were confronted with religious intolerance. The Taylors arrived in Far West, Missouri, in the fall of 1838. Near the time of their arrival Missouri Governor Lilburn W. Boggs issued an extermination order against the Latter-day Saints, and the Taylors had to flee from militia harassment. Through these hardships and others, Leonora believed that the Lord sustained her family and the Saints of God.[5]

That same sense of care sustained Leonora as she and her family settled in log barracks in Montrose, Iowa. John did not remain long with his family in the barracks—he had been ordained an Apostle and was called to be a missionary to the British Isles. As his departure for England drew near, Leonora became very sick with a fever, but John continued to make plans for leaving the states. However, before commencing his journey, he dedicated his wife and family to the care of the Lord and blessed them in His name. While acutely aware of what they had already and might still suffer, the thought of taking the word of God to his native land overcame all other feelings.[6]

Leonora recovered, and John's mission to the British Isles proved a blessing to Leonora's extended family and others; among his first converts were Leonora's brother, George Cannon, and his wife, Ann Quayle.[7]

John's missionary assignments kept him away from home for nine of the next eighteen years.[8] During his long absences, Leonora looked to the Lord to direct her paths as she led her children in righteousness. When John was in the home, Leonora was his constant support as he

labored to overcome afflictions so that he might continue to strengthen the Church and the kingdom of God. Leonora died on December 9, 1868, revered by many as a dedicated Latter-day Saint.

Her thoughts, recorded on the back page of her diary, reflect a life led by the Spirit of God: "The Lord often led me by a way that I knew not and in a path that I naturally did not wish to go, every sweet had its bitter, the way seemed to me narrower every day without his almighty power to me I cannot walk in it to whom shall I go or look for succor but unto thee my Father and only Friend."[9]

1   B. H. Roberts, *Life of John Taylor* (Salt Lake City: Bookcraft, 1963), 471–472.
2   Ibid.
3   Ibid., 473–474.
4   Richard L. Jensen, "The John Taylor Family," *Ensign,* February 1980, 51; Parley P. Pratt, *Autobiography of Parley P. Pratt,* 130–136.
5   Lambert, "Leonora Cannon Taylor," *The Young Women's Journal,* 19, 345–350.
6   Ibid.
7   Jensen, 53.
8   Jensen, 52.
9   Roberts, 474.

MINERVA TEICHERT

Spirituality

"I do not make calls or play bridge," said Minerva Teichert. "That is the 'spare' time in which I glory."[1] The glory of her "spare" time was found in a paint brush and palette; no day was a good day until she picked up her brush and "a long piece of wood dabbed with oil paints" and spent a few moments in an artistic endeavor.[2] Minerva never painted for amusement; to her, life and its subjects must never be taken lightly in an artistic rendition. She believed the trek of the Mormon pioneers was heroic and the storyline of the Book of Mormon was true. These were her subjects, and in these she found glory.

Minerva was born August 28, 1888, in North Ogden, but spent her childhood in Idaho. She had little formal education, but that enhanced her imagination. "My parents were dreamers," she recalled. "Oh, the fairyland we lived in."[3] With her first set of watercolors, she illustrated that fairyland.

At age fourteen, Minerva went to San Francisco to work as a "nursemaid" for a wealthy family and to enroll in the Hopkins Art School. By age nineteen, she was studying at the Art Institute of Chicago under the tutelage of artist John Vanderpoel.[4] In 1912 she finished her work at the institute, convinced that her future lay in painting murals on public buildings and churches.

Although Minerva considered marriage, she left Idaho in April 1915 to attend the Art Students' League in New York City. To earn money, she sketched cadavers for medical schools and performed rope tricks and Indian dances for appreciative audiences. (Her artistic trademark—a headband—was a reminder of her employment as a dancer in New York.) She once asked her gifted teacher, American realist Robert Henri, why he was so critical of her work when he hardly noticed the work of other students. He answered, "Miss Idaho, can it be possible you do not understand; they're not worth it, they will drop out, but you—ah, there is no end."[5]

With art instruction taking her from coast to coast, Minerva was now poised to make her contribution as a major American artist. Professor Henri asked her if any artist had painted the "great Mormon story." She answered, "Not to suit me." Henri exclaimed, "Good Heavens, girl, what a chance. You do it. You're the one. . . . That's your birthright. You feel it. You'll do it well." With that seemingly simple interaction, Minerva said, "I felt that I had been commissioned."[6] She thought of establishing a great art school in Salt Lake City and of painting the ceiling of the Salt Lake Tabernacle, much as Michelangelo had painted the ceiling of the Sistine Chapel, but her dreams of art faded all too soon.

She returned home and married Herman Teichert. "I thot [sic] of all the men I had met in my search for getting gold, back on the Idaho desert, herding his cattle and branding his calves was a man more nearly meant for me than anyone else in the world," she wrote.[7] In the early years of their marriage, money was too scarce for her to advance her talent. Yet she always painted or sketched on something— scraps of wood and even brown paper. She painted a self-portrait on her chopping board.

When Minerva contracted influenza during her husband's absence in World War I, "I was sinking so fast when I thot *[sic]* of prayer. I thot [sic] of my years of study and so I had done nothing with my art education," she said. "Suddenly I was keenly sensitive. I promised the Lord if I'd finish my work and he'd give me some more, I'd gladly do it. With this covenant in my heart I began to live."[8]

Not long after her husband returned from the war, they made their home in Cokeville, Wyoming. For more than forty years (1927–1970), her living room was her studio. Although it proved too small for large murals, she said, "I must paint."[9] She liked to fold her canvas and paint one section and then turn it over and paint the other section. To see her murals in perspective, she looked through the large end of a pair of binoculars. In near artistic isolation, she was able to develop her own style. Artist Ted Wassmer said of her work, "In her painting, the suggestion is greater than the completed statement. I think that is why her painting is so alive and has such a spiritual quality."[10]

Minerva is particularly noted for her artistic renderings of the Book of Mormon. When asked why she painted forty-two scenes from the Book of Mormon, Minerva replied, "I believe in it."[11] In most of these paintings, she included the color red. "I want a touch of red in my heaven," she explained.[12] When family members and close friends suggested that she paint more beautiful subjects in the Book of Mormon, she said, "There is too much sage brush in my blood."[13] She filled her palette with colors of the desert and blues and greys to show the distant mountains.

Devastated when LDS Church leaders showed little or no interest in her work, she gave some of her paintings to Brigham Young University to pay the college tuition of relatives. She was equally disappointed when the murals she had created for the LDS Tabernacle in Montpelier, Idaho, were taken down to make room for a heating system. Fortunately, her murals in the World Room of the Manti Temple remain.

Minerva died in 1976 in Provo at age eighty-seven. "Eternity seems very real to me," Minerva said. "I want . . . to be able to paint after I

leave here. . . . One life time is far too short but may be a schooling for the next."[14]

1   Minerva Teichert to Professor B. F. Larsen, undated, Museum of Art at Brigham Young University Files, as quoted in Laurie Teichert Eastwood, *Letters of Minerva Teichert* (Provo, Utah: BYU Studies, 1998), x.

2   Jan Underwood Pinborough, "Minerva Kohlhepp Teichert: With a Bold Brush," *Ensign,* April 1989, 34. (See John W. Welch and Doris R. Dant, *The Book of Mormon Paintings of Minerva Teichert* [Salt Lake City: Bookcraft, 1997]; Marion Eastwood Wardle, "Minerva Teichert's Murals: The Motivation for Her Large-Scale Production," Master's Thesis, Brigham Young University, 1988.)

3   "Miss Kohlhepp's Own Story," Pocatello, Idaho, 1917, as quoted in Pinborough, "Minerva Kohlhepp Teichert," 36.

4   Pinborough, 36–37.

5   Ibid., 37.

6   Ibid., 38.

7   Ibid., 40.

8   Ibid., 38.

9   Ibid., 38.

10   Ibid., 41.

11   Ibid., 40.

12   Ibid.

13   Ibid., 36.

14   Pinborough, 40.

EMMA LOU THAYNE

Imagination

Courtesy of the Church History Library, The Church
of Jesus Christ of Latter-day Saints.

Emma Lou Thayne, recognized as a gifted poet, writer, teacher, speaker, and sportswoman, has found fulfillment in her career, but also in caring about people, both in her home and away from it. Her belief is that both make for a life that is interesting and full of purpose. "Only as my fulfilled self can I maintain a pitcher full enough to pour from for others."[1]

Daughter of Homer C. (Pug) and Grace Richards Warner, Emma Lou was born October 22, 1924, in Salt Lake City and grew up with her parents and three rambunctious brothers, Homer, Rick, and Gill, to delight and inspire her. Their home was an interesting mix of the athletic and the aesthetic. Her father, a member of the general board of the YMMIA (Young Men's Mutual Improvement Association), started the Churchwide M-Men basketball tournaments. He taught the young men, as well as his family, that in in all endeavors they should "try hard, play fair, and have fun." Her aesthetic mother, who spent almost all of her time at home, wrote poetry and painted. Emma Lou remembers poems all over the house and verses tucked into lunchboxes.[2]

Of her home, Emma Lou has said, "Our family's approach . . . was simply, Live your life to its fullest. Live it and love it and enjoy it. And enjoy people. Let them in and relish what each has to offer."[3] Emma Lou has taken this approach, allowing time to create and savor relationships with all kinds of people. She also notes that she learned on her own to love her family "with all my heart, but not with all my time."[4] She has loved nothing more than mothering her five daughters but has also sought more space in her life to respond to people and to the impetus of her talent.

Emma Lou's gift for writing began when she was in elementary school. In fourth grade her teacher doubted she had written an assigned poem; she said it was too good.[5] Her flair for writing lasted all through school and into college. From the University of Utah she received a bachelor's degree in English, and thirty years later a master's degree in creative writing. She taught English on every level, from junior high to high school and at the University of Utah for thirty years as a part-time instructor in everything from freshman English to creative writing and poetry. She also was the coach of the university's first women's tennis team—which, she says with as smile, "did a lot more laughing than winning."[6]

Emma Lou served on the YWMIA General Board, writing manuals and putting on June conference. For that conference she wrote the words to a much-sung and much-recorded hymn, "Where Can I Turn for Peace?" written at a time when her oldest daughter was struggling with manic depression and bulimia.[7] Her writing runs the gamut of life's experiences from the personal and mundane to the global and universal—from dealing with "the dichotomies, frustrations, pleasures and harmonies tangled in the dailiness" of motherhood to arguing for peace and celebrating the eminence of God and triumph of the human spirit (in *The Place of Knowing*).[8] Always she has taught as she now teaches in an Osher class at the University of Utah that "We Are Our Stories": the death of a grandbaby or the excitement of a mission for a daughter, a car accident that relegated her skiing days to a growing list of used-to-do's, or a trip to Russia bearing her translated "peace poems" that, to her surprise, became a passport into the hearts and stories of the poetry-loving Russian people.[9]

Her innumerable articles as well as fourteen published books and chapter books, often including both her poetry and prose, have explored the joys and challenges of motherhood and tell of her being overwhelmed with loving "too many and too much."[10]

In *As for Me and My House,* one of her most well-loved books, Emma Lou describes a typical day. She tells of talking with four of her grown daughters, of cutting a son-in-law's hair, of listening to a old friend, of writing a talk "right out of sleep," all while getting on with the necessary busyness of keeping a house. She learned in her thirties when her five daughters were all under ten, "If I do it obliquely, housework can be background to whatever I choose to let matter most . . . for what is really occupying me—people and ideas." At the end of the day she says that, for sure, "It's the people, not the jobs, that stay."[11]

Passionately involved in civic life, church, and the community, she was for seventeen years the only woman among the general authorities on the board of directors for the Salt Lake City newspaper, the *Deseret News.* Emma Lou has traveled the globe and included her gleanings from cultures and people in books such as *Once in Israel* or *How Much for the Earth?* She has traveled the country speaking to women's groups as well as to countless groups at home, from her grandchildren's school classes to various church and community groups. Every talk urges listeners to live life to its fullest. For her commitment to service and to the community, Emma Lou was awarded an honorary doctorate of humane letters from the University of Utah and also from the Salt Lake Community College, where the Thayne Center for Service and Learning was named in her honor. She cheers for "the amazing work students do to better our community and help people in need." [12]

Those who know Emma Lou Thayne the best say that her most unique quality is her "capacity to give undivided attention to others.

While some might complain about a traffic-congested ride from the airport, Emma Lou makes friends with the taxi driver. She is tuned in to people, to words, and to the divine."[13] Emma Lou recalls that her mother's teaching, "'You're no better than anyone, but you're just as good' meant that 'We got to be friends with people that weren't a bit like us.'[14] What could be more fun and more worthwhile?"[15]

Emma Lou's belief that people come first—and the inspiring way she has put this belief into action—have influenced women and families throughout the world for good.

1   Emma Lou Thayne, *As for Me and My House* (Salt Lake City: Bookcraft, 1989), 27.
2   James N. Kimball and Kent Miles, *Mormon Women: Portraits & Conversations* (Salt Lake City: Handcart Books, 2009), 213–214.
3   Ibid., 216.
4   Thayne, 45.
5   Nettie Pendley, "A Woman of Gentle Strength," *Continuum Magazine* 12, no. 3 (Winter 2002).
6   "Emma Lou Warner Thayne," *Who's Who in Mormon Literature,* http://mldb.byu.edu/Who/B-THAYNE.HTM; Personal interview, December 3, 2010, notes in possession of author.
7   R. Scott Lloyd, "Life Celebration Emerges in Stories," *Deseret News,* July 3, 2010, 11.
8   "Emma Lou Thayne," Mormon Literature and the Creative Arts, http://mormonlit.lib.byu.edu/lit_author.
9   Thayne, *As for Me and My House,* passim; Pendley.
10 Personal interview.
11 Thayne, *As for Me and My House,* 9, 16.
12 Pendley; Personal interview.
13 Pendley.
14 Lloyd, 11.
15 Personal interview.

JANIE THOMPSON
Nurturing Talent

"For those who have seen a Janie Thompson show," writes her biographer, "her name suggests lights and music and non-stop action that leave audiences clapping for more." But for the Brigham Young University stage crew and student performers, the name Janie Thompson suggests "a stern taskmaster who could love the best out of them. She expected them to succeed, and they did."[1]

Daughter of J. Henry Thompson and Lora Harmon, Janie was born August 20, 1921, the oldest of seven children. "We were a family of modest means, but rich in blessings that really count," she recalls. "We love to sing together, pray together, serve together, and just be together."[2] As for her singing ability, Janie says, "My siblings sang better than me . . . I was the black sheep of the family. I stuck with pop music."[3]

Her mother was known as the Carbon County Nightingale—"a bundle of talent who could sing a crystal clear F above high C and her feet could put choreographers to shame." She loved to sing and dance until a train accident "left her legs unable to do what her heart wanted." Janie said, "I was Mom's legs. Mom could think up steps, but couldn't do them. So I would be her legs and show the kids how to dance."[4]

Janie began performing in her living room. Her first floor show was with cowpokes in Malta, Idaho, at age fourteen. She laughs, "I had them thinking they were Fred Astaire and Ginger Rogers."[5]

In 1939, after graduating from Raft River High School in Malta, she enrolled at Brigham Young University. She worked her way through college playing piano for dance classes. On campus she wrote and arranged music, directed programs, and put on productions. But it was her association with the Army Cadet Marching Band that launched her career. She was asked to join the band as the lead female singer: "I almost didn't go through with it. My first song was 'The Man I Love.' The best-looking guy on campus came up after and said I sounded like Ella Fitzgerald. From then on you couldn't shut me up."[6]

After graduating with a bachelor's degree in music, Janie entered a singing competition in the San Francisco Bay area. She performed well enough to be awarded a job as a Civilian Actress Technician, which meant that she would be entertaining the Army of Occupation with her musical talents. She became a "girl-vocalist" with the 314th Army Special Service Band and was part of the weekly broadcast from the Weisbaden Opera House in Germany,[7] where she sang with a young soldier named Tony Bennett. Bennett recalled, "Janie was loaded with energy and excitement, and she really thrilled the crowds when she launched into a boogie-woogie number and accompanied herself on the piano."[8]

In 1947 Janie left Europe and joined the popular jazz pianist and band leader Ike Carpenter. Although she had developed a name for herself in the music industry, in 1950 she left Carpenter to accept a mission call to the British Isles. For eighteen months she labored in Wales, where her musical talents were always in demand.

When Janie returned to the States, she made plans to once again join the Ike Carpenter Band. But a phone call from W. Cleon Skousen in behalf of BYU President Ernest L. Wilkinson changed her plans. Skousen wanted to know if Janie would leave a budding career to direct the BYU Student Program Bureau. "Away flew my dream of continuing my career as a big-band singer," she said. Janie knew in her heart that BYU was where she was meant to be.[9] She later wrote, "I cried all the way to Provo."[10]

In 1952 Janie led a small group of student performers on campus. By the next year, the small group had become a large assembly of talented students. She founded and directed Young Ambassadors and the Lamanite Generation (now Living Legends). She also served on the YWMIA General Board. "Running Program Bureau and serving on the YWMIA General Board was equivalent to two busy full-time jobs. I found myself going night and day with very little sleep," she said. "Even to President Wilkinson it was evident I couldn't keep up this schedule indefinitely."[11]

For Janie, the solution to her hectic schedule was to leave BYU and settle in New York City, where she taught music on Long Island and trained children in Manhattan to sing. She received offers to write musical commercials for a New York advertising agency and much more until 1959. In that year, President Wilkinson called her back to BYU. "My conscience strongly let me know I should return," she said.[12]

By 1960 Janie was taking BYU performing groups throughout the United States and overseas. "Nearly every tour resulted in reports that people had been baptized or re-activated into the church because they had been touched in their hearts by what they saw and felt," she said. "Something that touched my heart deeply was that the Lord saw fit to use our little shows to get His servants into communist countries such as Russia, and China, and others." Her most delightful experience was working with the Lamanite Generation for thirteen years (1971–1984).[13]

Literally thousands of students are grateful to Janie for her work at BYU. Though she officially retired in 1984, Janie continued to direct and produce stage productions on campus and for Church events. Musical moments have never been far away in her retirement. A visit to her home is always "punctuated with snatches of song and hearty

laughter." One biographer said of her, "One minute she'll be seated behind her desk, and the next she'll be at the piano belting out a tune."[14] In her late eighties she still describes her life as "a blessing and privilege to be able to use our talents and everything the Lord has given us to help 'build his Kingdom' on earth."[15]

1   Jayne B. Malan, "Janie Thompson," *Ensign,* March 1986, 32.
2   Life Sketch of Jane (Janie) Thompson. L. Tom Perry Special Collections, Harold B. Lee Library, Brigham Young University, Provo, Utah, mss sc 2967.
3   Genelle Pugmire, "'Energizer' Janie Keeps Going," *Deseret News,* May 3, 2006.
4   Ibid.
5   Ibid.
6   Ibid.
7   Life Sketch of Jane (Janie) Thompson.
8   Charlene Winters, "Janie Thompson to Headline at Homecoming '99," *BYU Magazine.*
9   Life Sketch of Jane (Janie) Thompson.
10   Pugmire.
11   Life Sketch of Jane (Janie) Thompson.
12   Ibid.
13   Ibid.
14   Malan, 32.
15   Life Sketch of Jane (Janie) Thompson.

LAUREL THATCHER ULRICH

Ambition

When Laurel Thatcher Ulrich graduated from the University of Utah in 1960 with a bachelor's degree in English, writing a Pulitzer Prize–winning history could not have been further from her mind. Laurel, who married Gael Ulrich in 1958, said she had always assumed that she would just "get married and have children." Laurel placed her family plans before a career, and had not given serious thought to life after college aside from being a wife and mother—stating her goal was primarily "to finish school, and [she] didn't really think much beyond that."[1]

Things changed after the Ulriches moved to Massachusetts for Gael's continuing education; Laurel discovered that she had deep ambitions that were not incongruent with married life. With hard work and a great desire, Laurel channeled her ambition to successfully achieve both her family and academic goals.

Daughter of John Kenneth Thatcher and Alice Siddoway, Laurel Thatcher was born July 11, 1938, in the small town of Sugar City, Idaho. When Laurel was a sophomore at the University of Utah, *Seventeen* magazine accepted an article she had written about Christmas in her hometown in Idaho. To her surprise, the editors deleted several parts of the article and made fanciful additions to "Sugar City Magic," published in *Seventeen* in December 1957. At this time there were few models for women writers. It would take the women's movement to help restore Laurel's voice in her own writing.

In 1965, Laurel's bishop asked the Relief Society sisters in his ward to write a guidebook for newcomers to Boston. Laurel and the other sisters dedicated themselves to the successful project, which garnered recognition in the *Boston Globe.* Laurel's work on *A Beginner's Boston* helped her realize that even as a full-time mother she "could do a lot with small amounts of time," which meant she "could handle taking a class or two" toward a second degree.[2] After five years of coursework in a one-year master's program, Laurel finished her master's degree in 1971 and moved with her family to New Hampshire, where Gael was hired as a chemical engineering professor at a state university.

Laurel launched into a doctoral program in history at the University of New Hampshire. At first, she would get up at 5 A.M. and work on her dissertation until it was time to get her five children ready for school at 7 A.M. She describes that it was "murder to come down and get their lunches ready and get them out the door" because she could never recover her desire to write until the next morning.[3] Wanting to help, Gael offered to make breakfast each morning and get the children off to school. This meant Laurel could focus uninterrupted on writing her dissertation from 5 A.M. until 11:30 A.M. and then spend her afternoons with the children when they returned from school.

Laurel confesses she was not the "stereotypically good mom" who wrote names on lunch boxes with magic markers. As the years passed, her children "made their own lunches and did their own laundry as soon as they could." Gael and Laurel felt such an approach to family life would help their children become capable adults. Looking back, Laurel does not regret dividing up chores, for her children can now "do anything."[4]

Sharing responsibilities had benefits for the entire Ulrich family: the five children learned a degree of independence, Gael played a larger role in his children's lives, and Laurel was able to dedicate a few additional hours each day to her academic pursuits. The length of time it took her to attain her master's and doctorate degrees suggests that she was intent on maintaining a careful balance between family and education. Refusing to neglect either, Laurel learned to manage her time effectively to achieve her ambitions.

After receiving her doctorate degree in 1980, Laurel published her first book, *Good Wives,* that was based on her dissertation. She then began studying Martha Ballard, who was an eighteenth-century midwife and healer. Before her PhD program she had little experience writing history; after her doctoral degree she found enjoyment in writing about "the silent work of ordinary people"—a category in which Laurel placed herself.[5] Her book, *A Midwife's Tale: The Life of Martha Ballard Based on Her Diary, 1785–1812,* was published in 1991. In a 2006 newspaper article, the editor stated that *A Midwife's Tale* "staked out new territory, focusing on seemingly inconsequential events in the life of a common woman—the kind of things other scholars had typically overlooked."[6]

While the majority of historians tend to focus on larger historical themes and events, Laurel's approach to history demonstrated "the interconnection between public events and private experiences."[7] Laurel, who identifies herself as a feminist and a Mormon, feels that her personal history has influenced her writing.[8] She was educated in the 1950s, when very few women were thinking about careers; raised her children in the 1960s and 1970s, when the women's movement was in full swing; and profited immensely from opportunities that emerged for educated women in the 1980s and 1990s. Laurel's life is one that is grounded within broad social change. After the success of her second book, Laurel claimed that "Martha Ballard's life had something to do with my own life experience, but perhaps a lot more to do with the collective experience of a generation of Americans coping with dramatic changes in their own lives."[9]

Little did Laurel realize just how much change she would undergo in the years following the publication of Martha's story. Laurel not only won the Pulitzer Prize in history for her biography, but also won awards from the American Historical Association, one for the best book on United States history. In 1995 Laurel was invited to become a professor of history and women's studies at Harvard University.

Laurel describes achieving her ambitions in academia as having her best dream come true. However, she says it is wasn't about "winning awards, but realizing that people are reading my work, and liking what they read."[10]

1   James N. Kimball and Kent Miles, *Mormon Women: Portraits and Conversations* (Salt Lake City: Handcart Books, 2009), 91–93.

2   Ibid., 92–94.

3   Ibid., 97.

4   Ibid., 98.

5   Jan Lewis, "Book Review: The Age of Homespun," *The Journal of American History* 89 (March 2003), 1495.

6   Robin Wilson, "A Well-Behaved Scholar Makes History," *The Chronicle of Higher Education,* March 24, 2006.

7   Ken Gewertz, "Two University Professors Appointed," *The Harvard Gazette,* February 2, 2006.

8   See Laurel Thatcher Ulrich and Emma Lou Thayne, *All God's Critters Got a Place in the Choir* (Aspen Books, 1995).

9   Laurel Thatcher Ulrich, "A Pail of Cream," *The Journal of American History* 89 (2002), 47.

10   Karen J. Winkler, "A Prize-Winning Historian in Spite of Herself," *The Chronicle of Higher Education,* June 26, 1991, A3.

COLLEEN KAY HUTCHINS VANDEWEGHE

Joy

Courtesy of the Church History Library, The Church
of Jesus Christ of Latter-day Saints.

Whether posing for a beauty contest or just walking down the street, Colleen Kay Hutchins Vandeweghe turned heads. "[She] once stopped a University of Pennsylvania basketball game when she came in late and walked down the sidelines."[1] As Miss America, she attributed her poise to being a member of The Church of Jesus Christ of Latter-day Saints: "I consider that any poise I may have, any ability to meet people easily and speak on my feet are probably directly traceable to those many appearances, watched and applauded by parents and friends in our different wards, in which I so proudly participated." To her it was more than beauty that won the title of Miss America: "I have been told many times that my philosophy of life and expression of my belief in God made me stand out before that great crowd of fifty thousand people, and probably decided the contest in my favor."[2]

Daughter of Hugh Allen Hutchins and Maple Perry, Colleen was born May 23, 1926, in Salt Lake City. She was raised in Arcadia, California, in a modest house with a loving family where she enjoyed participating in sports and hobbies with her family. She especially enjoyed being with her father, an LDS convert and motorcycle

enthusiast considered one of the "best amateur hill climbers and cow trailers in the area."[3] In her family Colleen learned the importance of prayer, Sabbath day observance, obeying the Word of Wisdom, and faithfully paying an honest tithe.

In Church she found joy in developing her talents. "From my earliest years, I have had the opportunity to speak before groups, to appear in plays, pageants, dances, speaking contests, and all sorts of Church activities," recalled Colleen. "This experience has been of inestimable worth in preparing me for my present job as Miss America."[4]

Beauty pageants were easily won by the tall beauty. In 1942 she was chosen "Sweetheart" of her ward ball. In 1947, while a sophomore at Brigham Young University, she was crowned homecoming queen by LDS Church President George Albert Smith. When she transferred to the University of Utah to participate in the university's drama program, she was crowned Miss University of Utah. In 1950 she was chosen Miss Armed Forces of Salt Lake City. In 1951 she was crowned Miss Utah and in 1952, Miss America—the first Miss Utah to win the Miss America pageant. Colleen was the oldest (twenty-five) and tallest (5'10") to win the crown. "I don't know how it happened," she told reporters. "I thought I was too darned tall."[5]

During her first nine months as Miss America, Colleen made "nine trips across the continent and visited South America. Almost every minute of her waking hours was filled with a bustle of activity with travel (mostly by plane to save time), fashion shows, radio and television programs, appearances at sports events and participation in pageants, parades, fairs and festivals." She garnered so much national publicity that the director of the Miss America Pageant announced that Colleen was "the busiest and most popular of all Miss Americas."[6] This was in part due to television sweeping the nation—and being "Miss" anything seemed important to television viewers. Colleen is viewed as the "first Latter-day Saint media superstar."[7]

When her crown passed to another, Colleen settled in New York City and acted on Broadway for a couple of years.[8] It was in the Big Apple that she met and married Ernest Vandeweghe, a player with the New York Knicks for six seasons. They became the parents of four children—Heather, Tauna, Kiki, and Bruk. Her daughter Heather said that her mother taught her "that it's not the trophies that you come home with that's important; it's how you love." Nevertheless, her children won their share of trophies. In 1976 her daughter Tauna was a member of the U.S. Olympic swim team and in 1984, a member of the U.S. Olympic volleyball team, winning a silver medal. In 1994 her son Bruk won a medal at the Goodwill Games. Her son Kiki had an NBA career and became the general manager of the New Jersey Nets. Her daughter Tauna claims that "the only reason why we were successful was because of [mother]. She pushed us in a way that I can't figure out how she did it. I never felt pushed like I had to do it. She would tell us that God gave us gifts, and the only way we weren't faithful to God was by not using our gifts. She wanted us to make sure we did the best we could with them." Her daughter Heather added, "[Mother] was incredibly devoted to her children and her husband. She would do anything for us."[9]

Colleen remained an active member of the LDS Church throughout her life. She was in a lot of pain with intestinal issues for about seventeen years. During this time, she lived with her husband, Ernie, in Indian Wells, California. Three days before her death, Ernie was baptized a member of the LDS Church. Colleen died on March 24, 2010, at her home in Newport Beach, California, at age eighty-three.[10]

Colleen is remembered for the way she conducted herself as Miss America—conduct that "reflected honor upon herself, her family, and the Church." Colleen said, "I have never had any embarrassment whatever in sustaining my convictions. People in the various cities and countries I've visited have been very much interested in my religion."[11]

1   Sara Lenz, "Former Miss America, BYU Homecoming Queen Colleen Kay Hutchins Dies," *Deseret News,* March 25, 2010, B5.

2   Doyle L. Green, "Colleen Hutchins—Miss America—1952," *Improvement Era,* June 1952, 464.

3   Ibid., 397.

4   Ibid., 464.

5   Sarah Lenz, "Ex-Miss America Left a Legacy of Family and Her Faith in God," *Mormon Times,* April 6, 2010; Green, 464.

6   Green, 396.

7   Lenz, "Ex-Miss America Left a Legacy of Family and Her Faith in God."

8   "Former Miss America Colleen Kay Hutchins Dead at 83," *New York Daily News,* March 24, 2010.

9   Lenz, "Ex-Miss America Left a Legacy of Family and Her Faith in God."

10   "Former Miss America Colleen Kay Hutchins Dead at 83"; Lenz, "Ex-Miss America Left a Legacy of Family and Her Faith in God."

11   Green, 396.

LILIA WAHAPAA

Longevity

Photo credit BYU—Hawaii, the Byron Jones Collection.

Since the first representatives of The Church of Jesus Christ of Latter-day Saints arrived in the Hawaiian Islands in 1850, missionaries laboring on the Island of Kauai have known of and loved the memory of Sister Lilia Wahapaa. In Hawaiian *Lilia* means "work the hands" and *Wahapaa* means "mouth closed." Lilia lived up to both names as she quietly worked to further the kingdom of God in the Hawaiian Islands for nearly a hundred years. On the small garden isle of Kauai she was an example of faith and a mainstay of perseverance to the Hawaiian Saints and missionaries alike. To them she endured in faith to the end, an end that was long in coming: she was born twenty-six years before Abraham Lincoln was elected president and lived through the administrations of twenty-five United States presidents.[1]

Lilia was born December 27, 1835, in a grass hut near the fork of the Waimea and Makaweli rivers on the Island of Kauai. She was one of the earliest converts to the LDS Church in Kauai when in 1853 Elder Kaulaulau of Maui was assigned to Kauai by Elder George Q. Cannon and baptized Lilia near her home in a deep pool at the junction of the two rivers.[2]

In 1870 Lilia and her family moved to Laie, Oahu, where she met and married Makuakane. Makuakane died early, but not before he and Lilia became the parents of a baby daughter. Shortly after his death, Lilia returned to Waimea Valley, where she married Kaneihalau Papa. Together with her second husband, Lilia and her family resided at Haikoa, Kauai, on land given to them by a Hawaiian king. Eight children were born to Lilia at Haikoa.

Lilia's home was four miles along crooked paths and swing bridges from an LDS chapel where she attended Church services. Among her own people, Lilia was revered as a healer. Among the missionaries, she was "Mother Wahapaa," for she quietly looked after their needs. She often bore her testimony in the Hawaiian language, inspiring her people to greater righteousness.[3] Lilia outlived her second husband and married a third, Keoua. She survived her third husband and eight of her nine children.

In 1893 when Lilia was fifty-eight years old, she was called to be president of her ward Relief Society. She faithfully served as president for the next thirty-three years. In 1926 she was released due to advanced age; she was ninety-one.

Fifteen years later, when the Japanese bombed Pearl Harbor on December 7, 1941, Lilia was visiting her grandson, George Kauhi, on Oahu. The outbreak of war disrupted her plans to return home to Haikoa in Kauai. As the weeks passed she grew lonesome for her home and her ward members. "I want to go home," she simply said. Amid the commotion caused by the attack on Pearl Harbor, arrangements were made to fly her home—her first airplane ride. She was 106.

After arriving home, Lilia walked the four-mile distance to her chapel in Waimea every Sunday until her death.[4] Her shoulders were bent, but white-haired Lilia was determined to walk. She was still alert and able to take an active interest in Church services at this time. Although she was deaf, she could read her fine-print Bible without the aid of glasses. She had an amazing memory and loved to recall the time many years earlier when the gospel of Jesus Christ was first preached in the Islands.[5]

Lilia is a wonderful example of a Latter-day Saint woman who endured to the end. On November 12, 1944, Lilia Wahapaa Kaneihalau said "Aloha to her family and peacefully wrapped her Kihei about her and went to sleep, not weary of life—for she loved life," but weary in body. "She had graced this land of her birth with her queenly presence and vibrant leadership for more than a century."[6] At her funeral Lilia was eulogized as being an enthusiastic spiritual battery that would not quit. This remark aptly described Lilia, for she devoted her life to serving the Lord and his children in a "dedicated manner of humility."[7]

1   Castle Murphy, "The Passing of Wahapaa," in Linda Gonsalves, *The History of the Church of Jesus Christ of Latter-day Saints on Kaua'i* (Kauai, Hawaii: Kauai Hawaii Stake Relief Society Ad-Hoc Committee, 1997).

2   Leon Huntsman, "The Evidence of Things Not Seen," *Kauai Komments* (March 1940, 25, in Gonsalves.

3   Virginia Bennett Hill, "Wahapaa, 106, To Get Her First Plane Ride," in Gonsalves; and Huntsman, 25.

4   "A Life that Spans the Mormon Era," *The Hawaiian Mission in Review,* 34.

5   Hill.

6   Ibid.

7   Old Hawaiian saying told to Leilani Fuller Grange by Caroline Sorensen, wife of Elder Roscoe Sorenson, who served a mission in Kauai with Clyde Norman Fuller, in Gonsalves, 2, 4.

OLENE S. WALKER

Hard Work

Courtesy of the Church History Library, The Church
of Jesus Christ of Latter-day Saints.

In 2003, Olene S. Walker was installed as the first female governor of Utah—and at age seventy-two, this mother of seven and grandmother of twenty-five was the oldest governor in the United States. "I don't know when you start feeling old," Olene said. "But I'm certainly not there yet."[1] In her administration of government affairs, she proved her vitality on a daily basis. One columnist wrote, "The recently promoted lieutenant governor exudes a grits-and-cornbread charm that explains why legislative colleagues called her 'Aunt Bea.'" Utah Senator Genevieve Atwood said that Olene "is very easy to underestimate. Part of it is that she is often pushing other people into the spotlight."[2]

Daughter of T. O. and Nina Smith, Olene was born November 15, 1930, in Ogden, Utah. Her father was superintendent of Ogden City Schools, and her mother was a homemaker and teacher. Olene grew to maturity on the family farm near Ogden, where people were "quite poor, but nobody ever thought they were." On the farm, she learned the value of hard work: "My father called farming his golf game and we all played."[3]

Olene attended Weber College on a debate scholarship her freshman year before attending Brigham Young University for three years, where she served as vice-president of the studentbody her senior year. She graduated with honors in 1953 with double degrees in political science–history and secondary education. She then pursued a master's degree at Stanford University, graduating in political theory in 1954. Her plans to continue her education in Italy were changed when she married Myron Walker.

During the first eleven years of their married life, Olene became the mother of seven children and moved thirteen times, including a two-year stop in Boston for Myron to graduate from Harvard Business School. They eventually settled in Utah when they bought a potato chip business—Country Crisp. Olene was a stay-at-home mom for many years. She describes herself as "just a typical mom.[4] . . . I was a PTA president at every school because when you have seven children, that's what you do."[5]

Olene wanted to pursue her career, so she started to work when her youngest child was in preschool. She always negotiated part-time work so she could attend her children's activities. She felt that "there are seasons in life."[6] She worked in the Salt Lake School District with at-risk students and founded the Salt Lake Education Foundation, where she worked as director. In 1989, she became director of the Utah Division of Community Development. She did her work for her PhD at the University of Utah by studying and writing after her children were in bed.

Olene then launched a political career as a moderate Republican. From 1980 to 1989 Olene served in the Utah House of Representatives, including a term as assistant majority whip and majority whip. Her best-known legislation established the "Rainy Day Fund," which helped stabilize the budget. She was elected to serve as the first female lieutenant governor of Utah, a position she held for ten and a half years. During that time, she worked to establish the Work Force Services Department, chaired the health policy commission, and was over elections. She was elected president of the National Secretaries of State and later chair of the National Association of Lieutenant Governors.[7]

She chaired the Commission on Criminal and Juvenile Justice, the Utah State Housing Coordinating Committee (in fact, the State Housing Fund is named after her), the Governor's Commission on Child Care, and much more. By any standard, Olene was influential in making Utah a great place to live.

Olene was appointed the fifteenth governor of Utah and sworn into office on November 8, 2003, when Utah Governor Michael O. Leavitt stepped down to head the United States Environmental Protection Agency. "I felt a great weight on my shoulders, being the first female governor. I didn't want to just be a caretaker," she said. "I wanted to make my presence felt."[8]

To her colleagues on Utah's Capitol Hill, Olene did just that. Her administration was "full of surprises."[9] She worked very well with all Congressional members. She dined with President George W. Bush and swapped one-liners with Arnold Schwarzenegger. She clashed with conservative Republicans and fought against storing nuclear waste in Utah. But key to her administration was better education of children. She said, "Good education demands not only adequate public funding, but personal investment of time."[10] But the conservative state legislators were not supportive of her veto of a voucher bill and threatened to hold a meeting to override her veto.

On May 8, 2004, the Utah Republican Party delegates chose to not put Olene Walker's name on the ballot for the primary election—an unconscionable decision, since Olene had an 87 percent approval rating at the time she left office.[11] Convention delegates defended their choice by claiming that many of the delegates were pledged to other candidates. She left office in January 2005, after serving as governor for only seventeen months.

After leaving office, Olene and her husband, Myron, served as Public Affairs missionaries for the Church in New York City from June

2005 through December 2006. Their primary charge was to make friends and build bridges with United Nations ambassadors. She is currently battling pulmonary fibrosis, a disease of the lungs.

"I think I have been given a lot of opportunity both in the Church and outside of the Church to develop leadership," she said.[12] "Through my years of involvement in the private sector, in the public sector and with my family, I have found that money, fame and power do not bring happiness. In the long run it is how we live our lives on a daily basis, how we treat other individuals, the routine decisions that establish who we are and what our reputation is."[13]

1   Lucinda Dillon Kinkead, "Walker 'Oldest' Governor—only on Paper," *Deseret News*, November 12, 2003.
2   Mark Sappenfield, "Utah's First Woman Governor Rules with Grit and Charm," *The Christian Science Monitor*, April 28, 2004.
3   Sarah Jane Weaver, "'Let's Get Started' says New Governor," *LDS Church News*, November 22, 2003.
4   Ibid.
5   Sappenfield.
6   Weaver.
7   "Walker elected Chief of Lieutenant Governors," *Deseret News*, June 22, 1998.
8   Arthur Raymond, "Walker Notes Kindred Feeling with Herbert," *Deseret News*, August 11, 2009.
9   Sappenfield.
10 Mark Thiessen, "Walker Sworn in as Utah's First female Governor," *Deseret News*, November 5, 2003.
11 "Walker to Serve an LDS Mission," *Deseret News*, May 11, 2005.
12 Weaver.
13 "Romney Institute Honors Walker," *Deseret News*, April 20, 2005.

JENNIFER WELCH-BABIDGE

Composure

In opera houses and theaters all over the world, Jennifer Welch-Babidge delights audiences with her voice. Her stunning portrayals of Lucia in *Lucia di Amore,* Constanze in *The Abduction from the Seraglio,* Marzelina in *Fidelio,* and The Doll in *Tales of Hoffman* leave opera houses applauding for more.[1] Yet along the way Jennifer has turned down many opportunities to perform with the best to be with her family. The excitement of the spotlight and the applause of the crowds pale when it comes to the joy Jennifer finds in her marriage and with her children. Directors and producers struggle to understand her priorities, but to her, family comes first.

Daughter of Jerry and Shirley Welch, Jennifer was born April 2, 1972, in Aulander, North Carolina. Her enthusiasm for singing began as a child; although she enjoyed singing for church events and in school choirs, nothing came close to the excitement she felt performing solos in front of captive audiences. At age seventeen she auditioned for acceptance to the prestigious North Carolina School of the Arts and was immediately accepted[2]; there she earned a high school diploma, her bachelor's degree, and a master's degree. It was there that Jennifer heard her first opera and became fascinated with this art form.

In 1997, Jennifer felt ready to share her talents with the world. After winning several musical competitions, including the Metropolitan Opera Competition, she was invited to join the Lindemann Young Artist Program, a three-year paid apprenticeship in New York City.[3] That same year she also joined the Wolf Trap Opera Company and performed as a guest soloist with the National Symphony. In 1998, a year after she was accepted into the Lindemann program, Jennifer also joined the Church. She loved the feeling of family that the members provided for her, especially while living in a busy city like New York City. She reflected:

> Once I joined the Church, there was really a core base of people that had the same beliefs that I had and there was a great sense of fellowship, and that was just a real blessing for me. I felt like I was able to find a group of people who were like family, that we were able to spend time together.

Jennifer always knew there was more to life than just singing. "I felt like singing was just an extension of who I was and not all of who I was."[4]

At the age of twenty-six, Jennifer debuted with the Metropolitan Opera. Her successful career with the Metropolitan Opera began with her performance as a flower girl in *Le Nozze di Figaro* alongside Renee Fleming, Bryn Terfel, and Cecilia Bartoli in the 1998–1999 season.[5]

In 2000 she married vocalist Darrell Babidge, a graduate of the Royal Northern College of Music in England and Brigham Young University. Initially she resisted the thought of marrying a singer; she now says, "It's nice to have somebody who knows what you're going through and things like that, but it's never been the main focal point of our relationship."[6]

A year after their marriage, Darrell received a professional degree in vocal performance from the Manhattan School of Music.[7] From the beginning of their marriage, the Babidges have juggled two musical careers, and have strengthened their marriage by performing together. From the Metropolitan Opera to Carnegie Hall, Jennifer and Darrell have sung to standing-room-only crowds.[8] They have also appeared as guest artists with the Mormon Tabernacle Choir and in Brigham Young University's production of *The Book of Gold,* portraying Joseph and Emma Smith.[9] In addition, Jennifer and Darrell were featured soloists in the LDS productions of *Long Walk Home* (as seen on KBYU) and *An Evening with Joseph and Emma.*[10]

Jennifer's faith that "there's a Higher Power involved" in her talent helps her balance a singing career while rearing children. Before the birth of her first son, John Chandler, Jennifer was "in 23 different beds in the first trimester and I had really bad morning sickness. I actually did a recording where I had a bucket right on stage!" When she was six months pregnant with her second child, Joseph, she was commended by a New York Times opera critic for singing "with authority, agility, and bright-toned beauty" in Lucia di Lammermor. James Robinson, director of the production, embraced Jennifer's pregnancy and incorporated it into the storyline.[11]

While Jennifer has been able to garner many prestigious opportunities in her career, she has stated that "[her] kids are [her] best accomplishments" and that "being a mother enhances [her] artistically." Having children has also helped her strengthen her testimony:

> I think that what they say is true—it is amazing how much you love your children and you're willing to do for your children. More than anything, and how you want the best for them and you want them to be happy. It is a glimpse into how much our Heavenly Father and our Heavenly Mother must feel towards us, and how much they love us. I have a great testimony of this.[12]

Jennifer has managed these family responsibilities while creating an enviable career. She has been a guest artist with the San Francisco Opera, Opera Company of Philadelphia, Opera Theatre of Saint Louis, and the Munich Philharmonic. Symphony orchestras from one end of the country to the other compete for her participation as a guest soloist in their productions.[13] She has received the prestigious ARIA Award and the Richard Tucker Career Grant.[14]

For Jennifer, marriage and family come first. She sees some musical potential in all four of her children, but says she won't push any to pursue a career in music. She does believe that their family will always sing: "I think we're always going to sing. . . . Whatever capacity Heavenly Father wants that to go in, and to whatever extent, then that's what I want to do."[15]

1   "Jennifer Welch-Babidge," ARIA Biography, http://www.fanfaire.com/aria/welch.html [accessed October 27, 2010].
2   Melissa Kotter, Interview with Jennifer Welch-Babidge, October 14, 2010, Cedar Hills, Utah, transcription in possession of author; Yoga, "Jennifer Welch-Babidge," *OperaMom Newsletter,* 2004, http://operamom.com/featured_artist_babidge.html [accessed October 27, 2010].
3   "Jennifer Welch-Babidge," *OperaMom Newsletter.*
4   Kotter.
5   Yoga, "Jennifer Welch-Babidge," OperaMom Newsletter.
6   Kotter.
7   "Darrell & Jennifer Babidge," *Nauvoo Entertainment Biography,* BYU Fine Arts Entertainment, http://www.josephandemma.com/index.php?option-com_content&task=blogcategory&id=16&Itemid=50 [accessed 27 October 2010].
8   "Darrell & Jennifer Babidge."
9   Brian Rust, "'Book of Gold' to Premier at BYU's de Jong Concert Hall Nov. 4," BYU News Release, October 24, 2005; "Darrell & Jennifer Babidge."
10 Kotter.
11 Yoga, "Jennifer Welch-Babidge," *OperaMom Newsletter;* Anthony Tommasini, "City Opera Review; Lucia in That Condition, Who Would Have Killed Whom?," *The New York Times,* September 15, 2003.
12 Kotter.
13 "Jennifer Welch-Babidge," ARIA Biography.
14 Ibid.
15 Kotter.

EMMELINE B. WELLS

Being Positive

Biographer Elaine L. Jack said of Emmeline B. Wells, "I am drawn to her because of her ability to maintain a positive and progressive outlook when things were not easy or smooth or fair."[1] That observation could refer to Emmeline's loss of three husbands and three children or to her failed attempts to raise the consciousness of a nation to women's issues. Emmeline did not curse God in her extremities, nor did she retreat from seeking women's rights. She wrote confidently that the Lord was the one who understood her frustrations and sorrows:

> And so some lives go on in tragedies, each part
> To be sustained by human effort grand;
> Though 'neath the outward seeming lies the broken heart,
> That only One above can understand.[2]

As a child, Emmeline enjoyed educational opportunities, including schooling at the private New Salem Academy. At age fifteen, she was well versed enough in the rudiments of academia to be hired as a teacher in Massachusetts. At the same time, she entered into baptismal waters even though "threats were made by the town authorities, and ministers, judges and others came to the water's edge to forbid the baptism."[3] Fifteen-year-old Emmeline married sixteen-year-old James Harvey Harris on July 29, 1843.

The couple journeyed to Nauvoo in hopes of uniting with the Saints and of meeting the Prophet Joseph Smith. She said of first meeting Joseph, "He took my hand, I was simply electrified,—thrilled through and through to the tips of my fingers, and every part of my body, as if some magic elixir had given me new life and vitality. . . .The one thought that stilled my soul was, I have seen the Prophet of God, he has taken me by the hand."[4] Unfortunately, her husband did not share her views. He left Nauvoo and never returned. Although he wrote letters to Emmeline, she never saw him again.

She remained in Nauvoo and endured the vicissitudes that led to the martyrdom. In August 1844, she was in attendance at the meeting in which Brigham Young appeared to look much like Joseph Smith: "I could see very well, and every one of them thought it was really the Prophet Joseph risen from the dead. But after Brigham Young had spoken a few words, the tumult subsided, and the people really knew that it was not the Prophet Joseph but the President of the quorum of the Twelve Apostles. It was the most wonderful manifestation, I think, that I have ever known or seen."[5]

In 1845 Emmeline became a plural wife to Presiding Bishop Newel K. Whitney, to whom she bore two children. At the time of the forced exodus from Nauvoo, she journeyed with the extended Whitney family to the Territory of Iowa. In Iowa, she began writing in a diary, the first of her forty-seven journals. Her entry of February 27, 1846, reads, "There was a snowstorm without, yet all was peace and harmony within."[6] Such an entry was typical of her writings. Just before Newel died in 1850, he told Emmeline that she would be a "tremendous influence in the building of the kingdom in the west."[7]

In October 1852 Emmeline married Daniel H. Wells, with whom she bore three daughters. While her children were young, Emmeline devoted herself to their care, but then turned her attention to writing. She wrote for the *Woman's Exponent* under the pen name of "Blanch Beechwood."[8] On May 1, 1875, she was appointed the assistant editor of the *Exponent.* In July 1877, she was installed as the senior editor. Of this assignment, Brigham Young said, "I give you a mission to write brief sketches of the lives of the leading LDS women of Zion, and publish them."[9] She did as directed. Along with writing and leading the *Exponent* for more than a quarter of a century (1877–1914) and writing a book of stories, she published a book of her poetry in 1896; among her best-known poems is "Our Mountain Home So Dear."[10] Of her intellect, it was said, "Her marvelous memory is an encyclopedia of facts upon any subject in which she is interested."[11]

Emmeline traveled extensively with Eliza R. Snow and other leading women in the interest of the Relief Society and helped organize the Young Ladies and Primary associations. For nearly thirty years, she represented Utah women in the National Woman's Suffrage Association. When Utah women were franchised in February 1870, she was among the "first to wield the ballot,"[12] and she chaired the Utah Woman's Republican League. For twenty-two years, she served as general secretary of the Relief Society. As to how she accomplished so much, her answer was, "Work is [my] most congenial atmosphere, [my] very breath of life."[13]

On October 3, 1910, President Joseph F. Smith called eighty-two-year-old Emmeline to be the fifth general president of the Relief Society.[14] She accepted the call and penned, "I feel deeply the great responsibility resting upon me in being called to fill this public office; but hope to be guided and sustained by the Holy Spirit in this calling and duty that I may keep humble and be qualified to do all things that are required of me."[15] She led the society for eleven years.

Emmeline died April 25, 1921. Flags were flown at half-mast at prominent Church structures throughout Salt Lake City in remembrance of her many contributions. On the hundredth anniversary of her birth, women of Utah placed a marble bust of Emmeline in the capitol building in Salt Lake City. The inscription on the memorial reads, "A Fine Soul Who Served Us."[16]

In 1874 as Emmeline looked back on her many adventures in life, she realized that her personal tragedies would have left most downcast. Her frustrated efforts in behalf of Utah women would have left some discouraged. Yet throughout her life, Emmeline maintained a sense of optimism. Why? Perhaps her eulogy in the *Deseret News* explains it best: "[She] had her full share of bitter sorrows but these only served to test and refine the pure gold in her nature."[17]

1   Elaine L. Jack, "Believing in the Light after Darkness: Emmeline B. Wells," *Heroines of the Restoration,* Barbara B. Smith and Blythe Darlyn Thatcher, eds. (Salt Lake City: Bookcraft, 1997), 165.
2   Emmeline B. Wells, "Faith and Fidelity," *Musings and Memories,* 2d ed. (Salt Lake City: Deseret News, 1915), 221.
3   Orson F. Whitney, *History of Utah,* 4 vols. (Salt Lake City: George Q. Cannon & Sons Company, 1904), 4:587.
4   *Young Woman's Journal,* December 1905, 554–555.
5   Preston Nibley, *Faith-Promoting Stories* (Independence, Missouri: Zion's Printing and Publishing Co.), 137B138, 150. (See also Leon R. Hartshorn, comp., *Remarkable Stories from the Lives of Latter-day Saint Women* [Salt Lake City: Deseret Book, 1973–1975], 173.)
6   Emmeline B. Wells, diary, February 27, 1846, Church History Library.
7   Augusta Joyce Crocheron, ed., *Representative Women of Deseret: A Book of Biographical Sketches* (Salt Lake City: J. C. Graham and Co., 1884), 65.
8   Whitney, 4:588.
9   "The Jubilee Celebration, The Need of Press Representation," *Woman's Exponent* 20, March 15, 1892, 132. (See also Carol Cornwall Madsen, "Telling the Untold Story: Emmeline B. Wells as Historian," in *Telling The Story of Mormon History,* William G. Hartley, ed. [Provo, Utah: Brigham Young University, Joseph Fielding Smith Institute, 2002], 17–22.)
10 *Hymns of The Church of Jesus Christ of Latter-day Saints* (Salt Lake City: The Church of Jesus Christ of Latter-day Saints, 1985), #33.
11 Whitney, 4:590.
12 Ibid., 4:588.
13 Ibid., 4:590.
14 Annie Wells Cannon, "Mothers in Israel," *Relief Society Magazine* 3, no. 2 (February 1916):63.
15 Emmeline B. Wells, diary, April 1, 1875.
16 Jack, 165.
17 "Emmeline B. Wells," *Deseret News,* April 25, 1921.

MARY WHITMER

Reliability

Open Window © Julie Rogers.

"If the statements of persons who have always been considered reliable and truthful can be taken as authority, there is, besides the eleven witnesses of the Book of Mormon, still another one, who testifies to having seen the plates," wrote Church Historian Andrew Jenson. "This person is a woman, and if her statement is reliable she is the only woman on earth who has ever enjoyed the privilege of seeing the holy treasure."[1] Her name was Mary Musselman Whitmer, better known to Latter-day Saints as "Mother Whitmer."

Born August 27, 1778, Mary married Peter Whitmer in 1810. She and Peter reared seven children; an eighth, a daughter, died in her first year. The Whitmer family moved to western New York and settled on a hundred-acre farm in Fayette Township.

In Fayette, Peter was known as "a hard-working, God-fearing man, a strict Presbyterian [who] brought his children up with rigid sectarian discipline"[2] who attended the German Reformed Church. His pastor said that Peter was "a quiet unpretending, and apparently honest, candid, and simple-minded man." In 1829 when he warned Peter of what he perceived as "errors and delusions" that surrounded Joseph

Smith, Peter repeated in German the words, "Jesus Christ, yesterday, to-day, and forever."[3]

Instead of accepting his pastor's warning, Peter encouraged his son David to "bring up the man [Joseph Smith] with his scribe," Oliver Cowdery, to their home in Fayette, convinced that "there must be some overruling power in this thing."[4] While Joseph Smith and his scribe were staying with the Whitmers, Mary claimed to see the gold plates. Years later David Whitmer repeated her claim to Orson Pratt and Joseph F. Smith.[5] When Edward Stevenson and Andrew Jenson visited Richmond, Missouri, in 1888, her grandson, John C. Whitmer, testified that he heard his grandmother tell of seeing the plates. The following are the words John C. Whitmer said to Edward Stevenson and Andrew Jenson:

I have heard my grandmother (Mary Musselman Whitmer) say on several occasions that she was shown the plates of the Book of Mormon by a holy angel, whom she always called Brother Nephi. (She undoubtedly refers to Moroni, the angel who had the plates in charge.) . . . . One evening, when (after having done her usual day's work in the house) she went to the barn to milk the cows, she met a stranger carrying something on his back that looked like a knapsack. At first she was a little afraid of him, but when he spoke to her in a kind, friendly tone and he began to explain to her the nature of the work [translation] which was going on in her house, she was filled with inexpressible joy and satisfaction. He then untied his knapsack and showed her a bundle of plates, which in size and appearance corresponded with the description subsequently given by the witnesses to the Book of Mormon. This strange person turned the leaves of the book of plates over, leaf after leaf, and also showed her the engravings upon them; after which he told her to be patient and faithful in bearing her burden a little longer, promising that if she would do so, she should be blessed; and her reward would be sure, if she proved faithful to the end. The personage then suddenly vanished with the plates and where he went, she could not tell. From that moment my grandmother was enabled to perform her household duties with comparative ease, and she felt no more inclination to murmur because her lot was hard.[6]

Her grandson concluded, "I knew my grandmother to be a good, noble and truthful woman, and I have not the least doubt of her statement in regard to seeing the plates being strictly true. She was a strong believer in the Book of Mormon until the day of her death."[7] If his remembrance is correct, Mary's experience precedes the account of the Eleven Witnesses of the Book of Mormon.

Mary is also remembered as the mother of five of the Eleven Witnesses of the Book of Mormon—David, Christian, Jacob, Peter Jr., and John. She was also the mother-in-law of two additional witnesses of the Book of Mormon—Oliver Cowdery, who married her daughter Elizabeth, and Hiram Page, who married her daughter Catherine. By blood or marriage, then, Mary Whitmer was related to seven of the Eleven Witnesses of the Book of Mormon.

Recognizing this fact, biographer Richard Lloyd Anderson penned, "Joseph Smith's family had carried the first burden in inquiry and persecution in the gospel's restoration, but the Whitmers were the family that nourished the Church."[8] Examples abound: The Church was organized on April 6, 1830, in the Whitmer home. Church conferences were held there in 1830 and 1831, and about half of the New York revelations contained in the Doctrine and Covenants—twenty—were received in the Whitmer home.

Receptive to the teachings of the Restoration, Mary was baptized April 18, 1830, in Seneca Lake by Oliver Cowdery. The following year, she and her family moved to Kirtland, Ohio, and in 1832 to Jackson

County, Missouri, to be with the Saints of God. They were numbered among the Saints in Clay and Caldwell counties in the state of Missouri. However, in 1838 in Far West, Caldwell County, the Whitmer family broke away from the leadership of Joseph Smith.

Even though Mary separated from the main body of the Church, she never altered her testimony of the Book of Mormon. She carried to her grave her conviction that she was a witness of the Book of Mormon plates. She died in Richmond, Missouri, in January 1856, and her remains rest in the old Richmond burial ground.

1   Andrew Jenson, "Still Another Witness," *The Historical Record* (Salt Lake City: Andrew Jenson, 1888), 7: 621.
2   *Chicago Tribune,* December 17, 1885, as cited in Richard Lloyd Anderson, "The Whitmers: A Family that Nourished the Church," *Ensign,* August 1979, 35.
3   Diedrich Willers to Ellen E. Dickinson, January 19, 1882, in Ellen E. Dickinson, *New Light on Mormonism* (New York: Dunk & Wagnalls, 1885), 249–252, as cited in Anderson, 36.
4   Lucy Mack Smith, *Revised and Enhanced History of Joseph Smith by His Mother,* Scot Facer Proctor and Maurine Jensen Proctor, eds. (Salt Lake City: Bookcraft, 1996), 190–191.
5   "Report of Elders Orson Pratt and Joseph F. Smith," *Deseret News,* November 16, 1878; *Journal History,* September 17, 1878, 5.
6   "Sketch of David Whitmer and Peter Whitmer," *Historical Record,* 7:621, as cited in Andrew Jenson, *Latter-day Saint Biographical Encyclopedia* (Salt Lake City: Andrew Jenson History Company, 1901), 1:283.
7   Ibid.
8   Anderson, 35.

ELIZABETH ANN WHITNEY

Spiritual Gifts

Elizabeth Ann Whitney joined the Campbellites—also known as the Disciples of Christ—with the hope that she would learn from church leaders "how to obtain the spirit and the gifts bestowed upon the ancient saints."[1] Instead of learning or receiving the ancient gifts, she was given vague answers to her questions. Still hoping to press forward in her quest for sacred gifts, she claimed that at about midnight one evening as she prayed with her husband, Newel K. Whitney, "The Spirit rested upon us and a cloud overshadowed the house. It was as though we were out of doors. The house passed away from our vision. . . . A solemn awe pervaded us. We saw the cloud and felt the Spirit of the Lord. Then we heard a voice out of the cloud saying 'Prepare to receive the word of the Lord, for it is coming.'"

The word of the Lord came to the Whitneys with missionaries called to take the gospel to Native Americans; they were baptized in November 1830. When Joseph Smith arrived in Kirtland about February 1, 1831, Elizabeth wrote, "I remarked to my husband that this was the fulfillment of the vision we had seen of a cloud, as of glory, resting upon our house."[2] From that time forward, Elizabeth enjoyed gifts of the spirit—most prominent being the gift to sing in tongues.

Daughter of Gibson Smith and Polly Bradley, Elizabeth Ann Smith was born December 26, 1800, in Derby, New Haven, Connecticut. When she was about eighteen, Elizabeth was sent to live with a maiden aunt, Sarah Smith, in northeastern Ohio. There she met Newel K. Whitney; they were married October 20, 1822, in Kirtland, Ohio. Elizabeth and Newel became the parents of eleven children—seven sons and four daughters.

In spite of what would appear to be a crowded situation in the Whitney home, the Prophet Joseph Smith and his wife were welcomed guests of the Whitneys in Kirtland. Of his stay in their home, Joseph wrote of receiving "every kindness and attention which could be expected, and especially from Sister Whitney."[3] He referred to Elizabeth as "The Sweet Songstress of Zion." The reason for such a reference was that Elizabeth received the gift of tongues in song. The Prophet promised Elizabeth "that if she kept the faith, the gift would never leave her." [4]

It appears that Elizabeth enjoyed the gift of tongues all her days. One example was her singing in tongues (the pure language) in the Kirtland Temple. After listening to her song, Parley P. Pratt felt impressed to interpret her lyrics. He said that her hymn was "descriptive of the different dispensations from Adam to the present age."[5]

Elizabeth was very happy with her unique gift, her growing family, and her husband's increasing success in the merchandising business. With their monetary success came a growing sense of their need to be generous with the less fortunate. One example of their generosity was hosting a three-day feast in January 1836 for the poor in the Kirtland vicinity. The Prophet wrote of attending the feast: "Attended a sumptuous feast at Bishop Newel K. Whitney's. This feast was after the order of the Son of God—the lame, the halt, and the blind were invited, according to the instructions of the Savior."[6]

It was not until the collapse of the Kirtland Safety Society Banking Company and the religious persecution that followed that the Whitneys were reduced in wealth. Even so, the Whitneys praised God and made plans to journey in 1838 to Missouri to unite with Latter-day Saints gathered there. Upon learning that the Saints were being driven from Missouri, the Whitneys moved on to Illinois. They were with the Saints in Quincy in 1839, and later in Commerce (Nauvoo).

On March 17, 1842, Elizabeth was one of twenty women in attendance at the Nauvoo founding meeting of what would become a worldwide Relief Society. At this first meeting, Elizabeth nominated Emma Smith to be president of the Female Relief Society of Nauvoo. After being elected president, Emma chose Elizabeth to be her counselor. At the time Elizabeth was forty-one and the mother of seven children, aged one to nineteen. As she recalled that first meeting, Elizabeth said that "the Prophet foretold great things concerning the future of this organization, many of which I have lived to see fulfilled."[7] As a counselor to Emma Smith, Elizabeth encouraged society members to relieve the poor and "cast in our mites to assist the brethren in building the Lord's House."[8] Her work in the early days of the Relief Society remains laudable.

In 1846 Elizabeth and Newel joined Church members fleeing from Nauvoo to the Territory of Iowa. They crossed the Mississippi River on the ice to escape religious intolerance. In Iowa, Elizabeth suffered terribly from inclement weather and privations. Yet without a murmur she journeyed across Iowa to reach Winter Quarters, where her youngest son was born. She then journeyed to the Salt Lake Valley in the Heber C. Kimball Company, arriving in fall 1848.

Two years after her arrival in the valley, her husband, Newel, died in September 1850. Although distraught and left with nine children to rear, Elizabeth did not retreat from the task. She served as both mother and father to her children as they grew to adulthood. Although encumbered with heavy family responsibilities, Elizabeth took the time to strengthen Latter-day Saint women by sharing with them her "most implicit faith in a divine power, in infinite truth emanating from God the Father."[9] Due to her nurturing manner, Elizabeth became known affectionately as "Mother Whitney." But to Eliza R. Snow, she was much more. In spite of her age, Eliza selected Elizabeth as her counselor in the Relief Society general presidency. At the same time, she also served as a temple ordinance worker. Elizabeth died in February 1882 in Salt Lake City from general debility.

Of her many contributions to the Church, none is more re-membered than her gift of tongues. The last time Elizabeth was heard to sing in tongues was on her eighty-first birthday at the home of Emmeline B. Wells, who had arranged a party in her honor.[10]

1   Edward W. Tullidge, *The Women of Mormondom* (New York: Tullidge and Crandall, 1877), 41.

2   Andrew Jenson, *Latter-day Saint Biographical Encyclopedia* (Salt Lake City: Andrew Jenson History Company, 1901), 1:224.

3   Joseph Smith, *History of the Church,* 1:145–146.

4   Elizabeth Ann Whitney, "A Leaf from an Autobiography," *Woman's Exponent* 7 (August 15, 1878):91.

5   Jenson, 3:563–564.

6   Smith, 2:362.

7   Elizabeth Ann Whitney, "A Leaf from an Autobiography," *Woman's Exponent* 7 (November 15, 1878):91.

8   Relief Society Minutes, June 16, 1843, as cited in Jill Mulvay Derr, Janath Russell Cannon, and Maureen Ursenbach Beecher, *Women of the Covenant: The Story of Relief Society* (Salt Lake City: Deseret Book, 1992), 51.

9   Whitney, "A Leaf from an Autobiography," *Woman's Exponent* 7 (August 1, 1878):33.

10   Jenson, 3:563–564.

LEAH WIDTSOE

Establishing a Home

Courtesy of the Church History Library, The Church
of Jesus Christ of Latter-day Saints.

Leah Widtsoe was in a key position to influence home economics at Brigham Young University and Utah State University—and it was not long until her influence spread from the university classroom to the nation and then to Europe. Leah lectured and wrote about the importance of a proper diet in maintaining health, kitchen planning, and home management. She conducted her own extension service a decade before the Smith-Lever Act in 1914 ushered in the Agriculture and Home Extension work across the nation.[1] In 1960 she received an honorary doctorate of humanities from BYU for her work in improving family life in the home.

Daughter of Dr. Alma B. Dunford and Susa Amelia Young, Leah Eudora Dunford was born February 28, 1874.[2] Her parents were legally separated when she was young; custody of Leah was given to her father, and custody of the couple's son, Bailey, was given to his mother, Susa. Her mother did not help in the rearing of Leah, and her father became an alcoholic. Leah referred to her "home life as a nightmare."[3] She wrote, "During my lonely childhood I promised myself that if the Lord would ever grant me my great desire and let me be a mother in the flesh to some of His spirits that I would give my all to make for them a happy home where they should be loved and understood which at times is better than love."[4]

With her resolve to make the world better for her future children, Leah enrolled in the University of Utah. In 1893 she attended a summer session at Cambridge, where she met John A. Widtsoe. The two were inseparable that summer. Over the next five years Leah and John corresponded frequently and visited occasionally.[5] In the meanwhile, Leah pursued her studies in chemistry, physics, and bacteriology at Pratt Institute in Brooklyn, New York, then the largest and most efficient school of home economics in the country. She received a teacher's certificate in 1896 from the University of Utah and was honored as the valedictorian of her class.[6]

After completing her studies at the institute, Leah accepted an appointment as head of the Department of Domestic Science at BYU,[7] where she emphasized the importance of establishing a proper home environment for future generations. At the same time, she made plans to establish her own home. On June 1, 1898, Leah and John were married in the Salt Lake Temple.[8]

John helped Leah establish the type of home she had been denied in childhood and encouraged her to continue her professional interests while fulfilling her roles as wife and mother. But such encouragement was ridiculed by her peers, and Leah discovered that she was ahead of her time in ideas about women and their role in the home. For example, she hired college students to help clean her home so she could teach, and some of her peers felt "they had to do all their housework . . . [and] Leah should set an example and do all her housework, too." Leah maintained that she had other objectives at home and that her energy could be put to better use than scrubbing and cleaning.[9] For her, energy was better spent helping women find solutions to the drudgery of housework, teaching women how to establish a family-friendly policy in the school system, and discussing with women crucial health and wellness issues facing their children.

In 1900 Leah and her family moved to Logan, Utah, where John accepted an appointment as a professor of chemistry and director of the Experimental Station of the Utah Agricultural College. In 1907 he became president of the Utah Agricultural College. During their years in Logan, Leah organized and conducted the first Agricultural College Women's Institute in Utah with an agenda to improve the life of women in the areas of home economics, nutrition, and health.[10] While visiting in the homes of farmers' wives, she observed that more was being done for the animals on the farm than for the farmers' wives. "We can spend money galore on the perfecting of machines that will help in the breeding of better chickens or hogs, but not one penny of a nation's money can be used for improving the conditions of its women in their home life," she quipped.[11]

Although Leah was not allowed to vote in national elections due to her gender, she formulated ideas for legislation to help women in their homes and wrote letters about the needs of women to prominent government officials like U.S. Senator Reed Smoot. Largely due to her efforts, Senate Bill S7006—prepared by Senator Smoot in 1911—provided an endowment of $10,000 to each state and territory for research and experiments bearing directly on home economics, including domestic science and domestic art. The bill also provided for the printing and dissemination of research results.[12] Other outgrowths of Leah's legislative efforts included bills to teach family science and consumer education to young adults and provide vocational guidance to students in the public schools.

Leah maintained her proactive stance on women, home economics, and health long after her husband was called to the Quorum of the Twelve Apostles. She believed that she had a message about home life to give, and whether in a chapel, university classroom, or private dwelling, Leah was the champion of a proper home environment for children. Even into her eighties, Leah continued to be a great advocate of family science. At age ninety-one, a few months before her death on

June 7, 1965, in Salt Lake City, she gave a two-hour lecture on one of her favorite subjects, health in the family.[13]

Leah Widtsoe was all about establishing a proper home life for future generations. To her this meant gaining more knowledge about nutrition to improve the health of families and passing that knowledge to all who would listen. It also meant sharing with women tips for improving labor in the home. Leah was ever true to her childhood promise that they would make "a happy home."[14]

1   John A. Widtsoe, *In a Sunlit Land* (Salt Lake City: Deseret News Press, 1952), 116.

2   S. Hollis, "Oral history interview with Mrs. John A. (Leah Eudora) Widtsoe," n.p., February 11, 1965, L. Tom Perry Special Collections, Harold B. Lee Library, Brigham Young University, Provo, Utah.

3   Leah D. Widtsoe to Anna and Marcel Widtsoe, July 10, 1916, Honolulu, Hawaii; Utah State Historical Society Collection, Mss. B-92, Box 8, Fd. 8.

4   Leah D. Widtsoe to her daughter Eudora, October 26, 1929; Utah Historical Society Collection, Mss. B-95, Box 2, Fd. 5.

5   Leah Widtsoe to her daughter Eudora, October 26, 1929.

6   "Death Takes Widow, 91, LDS Writer," *Salt Lake Tribune,* June 9, 1965.

7   Anonymous, "Daughters of Zion," *The Puritan,* December, 1897, 2:111–112.

8   Widtsoe, *In a Sunlit Land,* 53.

9   Virginia F. Cutler, *A Twenty-one-Gun Salute for Leah Dunford Widtsoe* (Logan, Utah: College of Family Life, Utah State University, 1976), 22.

10   "Sketch of Leah Eudora Dunford Widtsoe," n. p.; Utah Historical Society Collection, Mss. B-92, Box 8, Fd. 4.

11   Leah D. Widtsoe to Senator Reed Smoot, September 20, 1911; Reed Smoot Collection, Mss. 1187, Box 109, Fd. 2., L. Tom Perry Special Collections.

12   To provide for an increased annual appropriation for agricultural experiment stations to be used in research in home economics, and regulating the expenditure thereof, S280, 63d Congress, First Session, 1913.

13   Cutler, 12.

14   Leah Widtsoe to her daughter Eudora, October 26, 1929.

BARBARA WINDER

Cheerfulness

Courtesy of the Church History Library, The Church
of Jesus Christ of Latter-day Saints.

When Barbara Winder received a letter informing her that she smiled too much, she said, "I thought that must be a really unhappy person! I do try to be cheerful, so I was complimented by that person's observation."[1] Her cheerfulness and ability to remain optimistic in difficult times affected for good the lives of sisters throughout the world during her presidency of the Relief Society.

Daughter of Willard Verl and Marguerite Woodhead, Barbara was born May 9, 1931, in Midvale, Utah. She grew up in the rural area of East Millcreek in the Salt Lake Valley; her mother worked as a waitress to help support the family, and her father often worked out of town.[2] Barbara and her siblings earned money picking strawberries and raspberries from their family garden to sell to neighbors.

Financial challenges were not the only ones in her childhood home; there were spiritual challenges as well. Inactive in the Church, Barbara's parents supported her activity, but seldom took her to meetings.[3] She spent lots of time at the neighbors' home because she "enjoyed the spirit there and the gospel discussions."[4]

Barbara worked part-time as a secretary to pay for her schooling at the University of Utah, where she majored in home economics. During her sophomore year she met Richard Winder, who had just returned from a mission in Czechoslovakia; two and a half weeks after their first date, Richard and Barbara were engaged. They were married on January 10, 1951, in the Salt Lake Temple.[5]

Barbara and Richard raised their four children on Winder Lane, a rural road on the Winder dairy farm in Granger, Utah. Up and down the lane there were families related to Richard. "We raised our children together," Barbara recalled. "Cousins were more like brothers and sisters to our children than cousins. They were free to go into anyone's home and were always welcomed."[6] Barbara was fortunate to be a stay-at-home mother, a role that she cherished. She found on most days that she could accomplish some task or project around the house, but she reflected:

> I remember one day when my children were young. They had been ill, and I hadn't been able to accomplish any of the routine things I would have liked. The house was not at all orderly, and I was not feeling at all lovely. When my husband came home that night, I told him, "I feel like a failure today; I've been caring for the children and haven't done what I wanted to get done." He said, "Tell me the things that you have done today." I enumerated the things that I had done, and then my husband said, "I want you to think about those things, not about the things that you haven't done."[7]

Realizing her husband's good advice, Barbara changed her outlook on life. The optimism and happiness that came into her life was needed for the trials ahead. When her four-month-old son had an operation, she was able to have an optimistic attitude and be "of good cheer," especially when another mother in the hospital waiting room comforted her. The mother "took me down the hall to meet her twelve-year-old daughter, who was suffering from leukemia," Barbara said. "I found [the daughter] to be like her mother, peacefully and cheerfully accepting this fatal illness. The girl was busy knitting dishcloths for her nurses. Her brightness helped me put my own concerns temporarily aside."[8]

Barbara's cheerfulness proved a blessing to her family and friends. Her daughter, Susan Winder Tanner, remembers that on her first day of kindergarten, Barbara spotted a crying child. She said to Susan, "Oh, look at that little girl. Go make her happy." Susan said, "After that, I didn't worry about being nervous myself. I've often thought how right that was, and how typical of Mother."[9]

In 1982 Richard was called to preside over the California San Diego Mission, and Barbara served as the "mission mother." Barbara loved working closely with her husband. She remembered one evening when she was expected to host fifty missionaries for dinner and prepare a talk with precious little time to accomplish either. She heard a voice say, "Sister Winder, this is not your time; this is the Lord's time." Of this experience, she said, "I knew the Lord would bless me. No matter how I felt physically, no matter what had to be done, I knew He would be with me."[10]

In 1984 Richard's mission presidency ended when Barbara was called by President Gordon B. Hinckley to be the eleventh general president of the Relief Society. During her presidency she emphasized that the Relief Society program was a means of accomplishing the mission of the Church—Come unto Christ. She was also a leading advocate of visiting teaching.[11] "It is vital that each sister have visiting teachers—to convey a sense that she is needed, that someone loves and thinks about her," said Barbara. "But equally important is the way the visiting teacher is able to grow in charity. By assigning our women to do visiting teaching, we give them the opportunity to develop the pure love of Christ, which can be the greatest blessing of their lives."[12]

When Barbara was released in 1990, Richard was called to be president of the Czechoslovakia Mission, a mission that reopened after the fall of the Iron Curtain. Barbara was concerned because she didn't have a background in the Czech language. "How I longed to just be able to have a conversation with the sisters. . . . I didn't have the ability to do that," she said.[13] Yet during that mission she saw to it that Church materials were translated into the Czech language.

In 2002 when the reconstructed Nauvoo Temple was first opened, Richard was called to serve as temple president, and Barbara was called as the temple matron. Service in the Nauvoo Temple proved to be a glorious time for both of them. In her characteristic manner, Barbara was optimistic and cheerful with all who entered the temple. Her example and happy countenance continue to bless many.

1   Charlotte Carol Searle, Interview with Barbara Winder, July 29, 2010, South Jordan, Utah; transcription in author's possession.

2   Jan Underwood Pinborough, "Barbara Woodhead Winder: A Gift of Loving," *Ensign*, October 1985, 28.

3   Ibid., 30.

4   Janet Peterson and LaRene Gaunt, *Elect Ladies: Presidents of the Relief Society* (Salt Lake City: Deseret Book, 1990), 186.

5   Pinborough, 30.

6   Gerry Avant, "A Woman with Purpose," *LDS Church News*, May 6, 1984, 14;

7   Barbara W. Winder, "Enriching and Protecting the Home: A Conversation with Barbara W. Winder, Relief Society General President," *Ensign*, March 1986, 19–20.

8   Barbara W. Winder, "Finding Joy in Life," *Ensign*, November 1987, 96.

9   Pinborough, 29.

10   Ibid., 31.

11   Ibid., 30.

12   Barbara Winder, "Striving Together: A Conversation with the Relief Society General Presidency," *Ensign*, March 1985, 12.

13   Searle.

ZINA DIANTHA HUNTINGTON YOUNG

Charity

Courtesy of the Church History Library, The Church
of Jesus Christ of Latter-day Saints.

During Zina Diantha Huntington Young's final years, she expressed the hope that her influence and that of other LDS women would not be lost on future generations. "As the mantle of time is fast draping its fold around many of us," she said, "many in the future may have reason to praise God for the noble women of this generation."[1] Zina was one of the most noble woman in her generation, during which she served the women of the LDS Church in the Relief Society general presidency for more than thirty-two years.

The eighth child of William Huntington and Zina Baker, Zina was born January 31, 1821, in Watertown, New York. During her childhood she learned the domestic art of homemaking—weaving, soap making, candle dripping, and spinning.

While in her mid teens, she and her family became very concerned for their immortal souls and prayed to find greater religious truths. In answer to their prayers, Hyrum Smith and David Whitmer visited her family and shared the gospel of the Restoration. Zina and her family prayed intently to know the truthfulness of their words; several family members received a confirming answer, including Zina.[2] Zina said of her conversion, "One day on my return from school, I saw the Book of Mormon, that strange, new book, lying on the window sill of our sitting-room. I went up to the window, picked it up, and the sweet influence of the Holy Spirit accompanied it to such an extent that I pressed it to my bosom in a rapture of delight, murmuring as I did so, 'This is the truth, truth, truth!'"[3]

By October 1836 Zina and her family had sold their property in New York and gathered with the Saints in Kirtland, Ohio. Her family remained devoted to Mormonism in spite of religious persecution, moving from Kirtland to Far West, Missouri, and then to Illinois, hoping to escape religious intolerance.

In Commerce (Nauvoo), Illinois, Zina—extremely ill from the effects of living in a marshy swampland—despaired of her life. Learning of her distress, the Prophet Joseph Smith sent his daughter Julia to care for her. Zina recovered and became close friends with the Smith family. She said of the Prophet Joseph that when he was "filled with the spirit of revelation or inspiration to talk to the saints his countenance would look clear and bright."[4]

Zina married Henry Bailey Jacobs on March 7, 1841 she became the mother of two sons and one daughter. Zina later married Brigham Young.[5]

Zina joined the Mormon exodus from Nauvoo, and while crossing the plains to reach the Salt Lake Valley, she provided comfort to many women on the trek. Emmeline B. Wells said that "she so distinguished herself among the sick and the sorrowing, that she . . . gained with many the appellation of 'Zina, the comforter.'"[6] Hoping to increase her ability to help the sick, in 1848 she attended classes in herbal medicine, home nursing, and midwifery. In 1872 she helped establish Deseret Hospital in Salt Lake City, serving as vice-president of the hospital board. She also organized a nursing school, taught in a school of obstetrics, and promoted home industry and self-sufficiency as president of the Deseret Silk Association.[7]

Zina's greatest accomplishment, however, was her service in the Relief Society general presidency. She served as first counselor to Eliza R. Snow when, with Zina by her side, Eliza organized Relief Society units in the pioneer stakes of Zion. Of this twosome, it was said, "Sister Snow was keenly intellectual, and she led by force of that intelligence. Sister Zina was all love and sympathy, and drew people after her by reason of that tenderness."[8]

Eliza and Zina were also instrumental in the development of the Young Ladies' Retrenchment Association and the Primary Association for children. After Eliza died in 1887, Zina was called to be the matron of the Salt Lake Temple and the Relief Society general president. During her thirteen years as president, she established a close association between the Relief Society, the National Council of Women, and the International Council of Women. Zina died on August 28, 1901.[9]

Zina's compassion and love was felt by those who knew her best. Friends referred to her as "the heart of the women's work in Utah," and associates and strangers called her "Aunt Zina." Susa Young Gates wrote of Zina, "There have been many noble women, some great women and a multitude of good women associated, past and present, with the Latter-Day work. But of them all none was so lovely, so lovable, and so passionately beloved as was 'Aunt Zina.'"[10]

---

1   Mary Firmage Woodward, "Zina D. H. Young," in Daniel H. Ludlow, ed., *Encyclopedia of Mormonism* (New York: Macmillan Publishing Company, 1992), 4:1613.
2   Woodward, 4:1612.
3   Zina D. H. Young, "How I Gained My Testimony of the Truth," *The Young Woman's Journal*, April 1893, 318.
4   Young, "Autobiographical Sketch," 4; Mary Brown Firmage, "Great-Grandmother Zina: A More Personal Portrait," *Ensign*, March 1984, 37.
5   Woodward, 4: 1612.
6   "Zina D. H. Young, A Distinguished Woman," *Woman's Exponent*, November 15, 1881, Vol. 10, No. 12, 91.
7   Woodward, 4:1612.
8   Susa Young Gates, *History of the Young Ladies' Mutual Improvement Association* (Salt Lake City: Deseret News, 1911), 21.
9   Woodward, 4:1612–1613.
10 Gates, 21.

ABOUT *the* AUTHORS

SUSAN EASTON BLACK

Dr. Susan Easton Black joined the faculty of Brigham Young University in 1978, where she is currently a professor of Church history and doctrine. She is also past associate dean of General Education and Honors and director of Church History in the Religious Studies Center.

The recipient of numerous academic awards, she received the Karl G. Maeser Distinguished Faculty Lecturer Award in 2000, the highest award given a professor on the BYU Provo campus. Dr. Black has authored, edited, and compiled more than 100 books and 250 articles.

MARY JANE WOODGER

Dr. Mary Jane Woodger is a professor of Church history and doctrine at Brigham Young University. After obtaining a master of education degree at Utah State University, she received from BYU a doctor of education degree in educational leadership, with a minor in Church history and doctrine. She was honored by Kappa Omicron Nu with the Award of Excellence for her dissertation research on the educational ideals of President David O. McKay.

She is the author of several books and has also authored numerous articles on doctrinal, historical, and educational subjects that have appeared in various academic journals and religious publications. Recently, Dr. Woodger received the Best Article of the Year Award from the Utah Historical Society, as well as the Brigham Young University Faculty Women's Association Teaching Award.